Irrationality and the philosophy of psychoanalysis is concerned with the problems of self-understanding engendered by the experience of irrationality. In a reconstruction of the theories of Freud and Klein, Sebastian Gardner asks: what causes irrationality? what must the mind be like for it to be irrational? to what extent does irrationality involve self-awareness? and what is the point of irrationality? He argues that psychoanalytic theory provides the most satisfactory answers to these questions, and that this amounts to an argument for its truth. Rejecting the widespread view of psychoanalytic theory as dependent on a picture of persons as divided, and of the unconscious as a 'second mind', he describes the unconscious as a source of inherently irrational desires seeking expression through wish-fulfilment and phantasy.

Psychoanalytic explanation is shown to be a coherent extension of everyday forms of psychological explanation, and scepticism about psychoanalysis is met by exhibiting this continuity: psychoanalytic theory requires neither hermeneutic reconstruction, nor the scientifically oriented criticism which analytic philosophers have tended to accord it.

IRRATIONALITY AND THE PHILOSOPHY OF PSYCHOANALYSIS

IRRATIONALITY AND THE PHILOSOPHY OF PSYCHOANALYSIS

SEBASTIAN GARDNER

Department of Philosophy, Birkbeck College, University of London

CAMBRIDGE
UNIVERSITY PRESS

Published by the Press Syndicate of the University of Cambridge
The Pitt Building, Trumpington Street, Cambridge CB2 1RP
40 West 20th Street, New York, NY 10011–4211, USA
10 Stamford Road, Oakleigh, Victoria 3166, Australia

© Cambridge University Press 1993

First published 1993

Printed in Great Britain at the University Press, Cambridge

A catalogue record for this book is available from the British Library

Library of Congress cataloguing in publication data
Gardner, Sebastian.
Irrationality and the philosophy of psychoanalysis / Sebastian Gardner.
p.   cm.
Includes bibliographical references and index.
ISBN 0–521–41090–8
1. Psychoanalysis.   2. Reason.   3. Subconsciousness.   4. Freud,
Sigmund, 1856–1939.   5. Klein, Melanie.   1 Title.
BF173.G364   1993
150.19′52–dc20   92-12861 CIP

ISBN 0 521 41090 8 hardback

UP

To Luke, Dad and Jim

Why, then, enquire
Who has divided the world, what entrepreneur?
No man. The self, the chrysalis of all men

Became divided in the leisure of blue day
And more, in branchings after day. One part
Held fast tenaciously in common earth
      Wallace Stevens, 'An ordinary evening in New Haven'

Que deviendra donc l'homme? Sera-t-il égal à Dieu ou aux bêtes? Quelle effroyable distance! Que serons-nous donc? Qui ne voit par tout cela que l'homme est égaré, qu'il est tombé de sa place, qu'il la cherche avec inquietude, qu'il ne la peut plus retrouver?

Cette duplicité de l'homme est si visible, qu'il y en a qui ont pensé que nous avions deux âmes. Un sujet simple leur paraissait incapable de telles et si soudaines variétés d'une présomption démesurée à un horrible abattement de cœur.

 Il est dangereux de trop faire voir à l'homme combien il est égal aux bêtes, sans lui montrer sa grandeur. Il est encore dangereux de lui trop faire voir sa grandeur sans sa bassesse. Il est encore plus dangereux de lui laisser ignorer l'un et l'autre. Mais il est très avantageux de lui representer l'un et l'autre.

 Il ne faut pas que l'homme croie qu'il est égal aux bêtes, ni aux anges, ni qu'il ignore l'un et l'autre, mais qu'il sache l'un et l'autre.

Pascal, Pensées

Contents

Acknowledgements

My thanks go in the first instance to Richard Wollheim and James Hopkins, to both of whom I am indebted for substantial suggestions; had I been able to pursue these as they deserved, this book would have been very much better. I owe a very great debt to James Hopkins for past and continuing help and encouragement. My indebtedness to the writings of Richard Wollheim will be clear throughout the book.

My thanks then go to John Lee, for inspiring my interest in both philosophy and psychoanalysis; John Forrester; Shaun Whiteside, for help with language, and a great deal else; Eric James; Grahame Lock; Marie-Suzanne Kalogeropoulos; Isobel Hunter-Brown; Richard Stockdale; Tom Baldwin; Kathy Wilkes; Galen Strawson; James Doyle; and Derek Bolton. I owe special thanks to Michael Tanner for his constant encouragement. At Birkbeck College I wish to thank Christopher Janaway, for comments on the penultimate draft; Barry Smith; and Maureen Cartwright, for help in preparing the manuscript; and at Cambridge University Press, Judith Ayling, for editorial advice on the form of the book; Catherine Max; and Susan Beer.

My appreciation of help goes most especially to my family, above all to my mother; and to Jim Warren, Monica Whitlock, and Jude Ibison. Jim Warren, an artist, was killed in a tragic accident two years ago; his company can not be replaced, and I wish to thank him here for all of his help with the book.

I would like to acknowledge the following sources for permission to reproduce copyright material: Leo Tolstoy, *Anna Karenina*, trans. Rosemary Edmonds (Harmondsworth: Penguin Classics, 1975), copyright © Rosemary Edmonds, 1954, p. 143; Fyodor Dostoyevsky, *Notes from underground*, trans. Jessie Coulson (Harmondsworth:

xiii

Penguin Classics, 1972), copyright © Jessie Coulson, 1972, p. 31; Fyodor Dostoyevsky, *The devils*, trans. David Magarshack (Harmondsworth: Penguin Classics, 1973), copyright © David Magarshack, 1953, 1971, p. 58; E. M. Forster, *The longest journey*, King's College, Cambridge and The Society of Authors as the literary representative of the E. M. Forster Estate; Richard Wollheim, *Freud* (Fontana, an imprint of HarperCollins Publishers Limited, 1991); Agatha Christie, *Hercule Poirot's Christmas* (Agatha Christie Mallowan, 1939); Marcel Proust, *Remembrance of things past*, trans. C. Scott Moncrieff and Terence Kilmartin (Chatto & Windus and Editions Gallimard); Wallace Stevens, *The collected poems of Wallace Stevens* (Faber and Faber Limited), and *Opus posthumous*, ed. Milton J. Bates (Faber and Faber Limited); Prosper Mérimée, *Carmen and other stories*, trans. Nicholas Jotcham (Oxford University Press, 1989); Brian O'Shaughnessy, *The will* (Cambridge University Press, 1980); Peter Clark and Crispin Wright eds., *Mind, psychoanalysis and science* (Basil Blackwell, 1988).

Note on the text

Bibliographical references are given in a shortened form in the notes, and in full in the Bibliography. References to Freud's works are given by date, followed by page number (first to the *Standard edition*; second, where appropriate, to the *Pelican Freud library*); title and volume number are given in Works of Freud cited.

Introduction

0.1 THE PROBLEM

This book is concerned with the problems of self-understanding which are engendered by the experience of irrationality. The recognition that one's thoughts, behaviour and feelings run contrary to reason, and contradict one's identity as a rational being, naturally provokes self-interrogation, along the following lines: What causes irrationality? Is it the result of choice, or the effect of a mechanism? To what extent does irrationality involve self-awareness? Should it be said that the irrational mind is divided? What – if anything – is the purpose of irrationality? Where does responsibility for irrationality and its effects ultimately lie?

These questions are philosophical. The first assumption is that irrationality exists at the level of personal experience, where it is directly recognised; this is the enquiry's 'existential' point of departure. No metaphysical identification of one's Being with Reason, or commitment to a special theory of the nature of the mind, is therefore needed in order to set an investigation into irrationality in progress.

I will argue that psychoanalytic theory provides the most penetrating and satisfying explanation of irrationality. Given that irrationality is real, and requires explanation, this amounts to an argument for the truth of psychoanalytic theory.

0.2 THE SCOPE OF THE ENQUIRY

The topic of irrationality will be recognised by analytic philosophers as circumscribing a set of interconnected problems in the philosophy of mind, which can be defined in two ways, one narrow and one broad.

I

Narrowly: How are instances of irrationality to be explained? Irrationality comprises a variety of psychological phenomena intermediate between error and madness,[1] and the focus of the enquiry will be on forms of irrationality involving *motivated failure of self-knowledge*.[2] On this level, competing kinds of explanation of irrationality will be described and assessed. What is to count as explanation in this field is a question to which attention will be paid. It will not, however, be considered important to distinguish sharply between psychological and philosophical explanation; with regard to psychoanalytic theory, the goal will be to interrelate these as closely as possible. The enquiry will not attempt to provide an exhaustive taxonomy of the forms of irrationality, or to lay out all of the distinctions that are possible and relevant. The 'traditional' categories of irrationality, such as self-deception and akrasia, are employed from the outset.

Broadly, the question is: What must the mind be like, for it to be capable of irrationality? This requires an account of what might be called the *conditions of possibility* of irrationality,[3] a notion which captures part of Freud's concept of metapsychology. The enquiry attempts to determine what, against a background which makes the existence of irrationality prima facie hard to understand, makes it possible, and in so doing underwrites a certain kind of explanation of it, namely psychoanalytic explanation.

Sartre has a prominent place in the enquiry. Sartre provides a philosophical term of contrast for Freud, and his critique of psychoanalytic theory – which highlights its relation to issues of personal identity, rather than its epistemology – represents, in my view, the most serious challenge to psychoanalytic claims which needs to be met. Sartre therefore helps, negatively, to bring psychoanalytic concepts into their own. An important strategy, in which Sartre also assists, will be to delineate contrasts between Freudian, and ordinary or commonsense patterns of psychological explanation and pictures of the mind: although some of our pretheoretical intuitions may seem to oppose the psychoanalytic picture, it will be argued that they must in the end be reconcilable with it, if they are not to lead us off to an 'impossible' picture of the mind (of the sort to which Sartre is committed).

0.3 DEFINING IRRATIONALITY

What exactly is irrationality? One way of defining 'irrational' would be to take it as the contrary of 'rational', and to understand rationality in formal terms, as consisting in the conformity of choice to a determinate set of rules. Then, behaviour would be irrational in so far as it departs from the set of rules which define rationality. Such an approach – which is likely to appeal to those who favour the application of sophisticated analytical techniques to the concept of rationality – might lead to a cataloguing of the kinds of behaviour that deviate from the principles of rational choice, and, as a further task perhaps, a specification of the causes of such deviation; but there is nothing in this approach to guarantee, or even encourage, the notion that the psychological causes of deviation – which will come out as irrational in a derivative sense – will themselves form an interestingly unified class. Nor does it match the way in which ordinary thought forms judgements of irrationality. The background to such judgements is as follows. Ordinarily, as we survey the course of a person's behaviour, we take it that his understanding of what he is doing, and the psychological states manifested in his behaviour, are systematically connected: he has direct knowledge of the causes of his actions. This assumption is of a piece with the primitive assumption that persons have non-inferential knowledge of the contents of their own minds. The seeds of irrationality lie in a discrepancy between action and self-explanation, the recognition of which is bound up with the possibility of interrogation: if the result, actual or hypothesised, of interrogating a person – calling him to account for his actions – reveals inconsistency between how he represents himself, and how his action shows him to be, then he is on the verge, at least, of being irrational.

By contrast with the view that assigns priority to the theory of rational choice, this enquiry takes as a starting-point what will be called *irrational phenomena*. These, on my view, are directly met with in experience, and pre-theoretically assigned to a single class. Irrational phenomena have the following form: a person exhibits irrationality when he does not, or could not – without altering himself in a way that would tend towards the eradication of the phenomenon in question – think about himself in a way that would both make adequate sense of his own thought and/or action, and at the same time avoid exhibiting incompleteness, incoherence, inconsistency, lapse into unintelligibility, or some other defect of a kind to signify, in a suitably broad sense, *self-contradiction*. An irrational subject is thus one who will in some loosely cognitive sense fail the test of self-confrontation: either he will be unable to provide an explanation-cum-justification of himself, or, in the course of attempting to do so, he will betray a failure of self-knowledge.

This definition locates a problem of reflexivity at the heart of irrationality: the same subject who at each instant of wakeful self-consciousness experiences himself ineluctably as rational, contradicts his own rationality. As Brian O'Shaughnessy says, of the self-deceiver: 'This man is a man who, in the name of reason, takes a leap into the dark of unreason! It seems that, on the score of rationality, a kind of antinomy lurks within this act. It can give expression to forces of reason that necessarily it negates as it gives such expression!'[4]

The definition of irrational phenomena is intended to stand poised between being a statement of what irrationality consists in, and a criterial statement of how it is recognised. It is meant to exclude the following: error; madness; failure of competence; mere difficulty in self-knowledge; failure to resolve conflicts of values; the alleged 'cold' forms of irrationality that consist in for example tendencies to mis-infer quantitative properties; and failure to maximise the satisfaction of desire, or optional epistemic desiderata, such as certainty and fineness of discrimination. It is also meant to exclude situations where minds appear opaque due to such factors as cultural divergence or straightforward difference of opinion. Note also that judgements of irrationality are, on the account given here, genuine descriptions, rather than disguised self-ascriptions of the interpreter's; they are not just roundabout ways of saying that one fails to understand another person.

It may seem to be a defect of the definition that the nature of self-contradiction is left open-ended. But this notion, hazy though it is, has firm priority in ordinary thought over any theoretical, formalised understanding of the nature of rationality: we can recognise irrationality even though we are unable to say in any systematic way what rationality itself consists in. Enough is given in the intuitive command of such notions as 'incoherence', 'inconsistency' and so forth for one to proceed to investigate irrationality without having to make any assumptions about the principles of rational choice.[5] The definition makes a basic connection between irrationality and inconsistency of belief, without reducing irrationality to being a function of the latter, and, whilst pushing to the fore the idea of the subject's relation to himself, welds together at the outset first- and third-person perspectives, without giving priority to either.

0.4 THE ARGUMENT

I will summarise here the content of the book's chapters and give an idea of the overall argument.

Part I aims to prepare for the introduction of psychoanalytic material, and to help set up the philosophical framework necessary for examining psychoanalytic concepts. It does this, first, by discussing forms of irrationality recognised in ordinary psychology which, it will transpire later, are to be sharply distinguished from those with which psychoanalysis is concerned; and, second, by arguing against a certain view of the nature of psychoanalytic theory which is tempting but incorrect.

Only two philosophical accounts of psychoanalytic theory are regarded in this enquiry as deserving intensive scrutiny. One is the view of the unconscious as a Second Mind, a subject of instrumental thought and source of strategy; the other, of the unconscious as a repository of inherently irrational desires seeking expression. Both of these regard psychoanalytic explanation as an extension of ordinary psychology, but the extensions they envisage are opposed. Part I argues against the view of the unconscious as a Second Mind; Part II, in favour of the alternative view. There are of course many other philosophical perspectives on psychoanalytic theory – hermeneutic, neurophysiological, Lacanian and so on – but it will be argued that these either altogether misunderstand Freudian theory, or distort it by misidentifying the important issues in the philosophy of psychoanalysis.

Chapter 1 attempts to see how far ordinary psychology may be pushed when faced with the problem of explaining irrationality, and takes self-deception as a prime candidate for explanation in such terms. Self-deception, as well as being intrinsically interesting, provides an important term of contrast for the psychoanalytic irrational phenomena to be considered in Part Two. Akrasia is also discussed, and it is argued that the key to its explanation lies in the mind's potential for passivity. Once again, this is a result that speaks in favour of ordinary psychology's power to make certain forms of irrationality – to be called 'ordinary irrationality' – intelligible.

There is, however, a limit to ordinary psychology in this context: it does not explain why there should ever be irrational rather than rational outcomes to psychological problems. This, the Specific Problem of irrationality, is left over for treatment later. Finally, a contrast is made between the psychological explanation of irrationality – which is what we have in ordinary psychology and psychoanalysis – and the 'metaphysical' strategy exemplified by Sartre's account of bad faith, and found elsewhere in Continental philosophy.

The view that the irrational mind is necessarily divided is then examined, in chapters 2 and 3. This issue is central and difficult, in part because of the way in which partitive claims vacillate between having a conceptual, and a merely empirical, status.

Chapter 2 begins with an exposition of Freud's 1915 discussion of the unconscious, and gives the reasons for thinking that Freud was attracted by the thought that the irrational person is divided, and that he has, in the form of the unconscious, a Second Mind. Such explanation – by mental partition – is the explicit target of Sartre's critique of Freud, which focuses on Freud's concept of the censor mechanism. Sartre's argument is set out and its strengths indicated.

The final sections of chapter 2 distinguish the form of partition involved in such attempts to explain irrationality, from the superficially similar postulation of 'modular' parts of the person in cognitive psychology. Cognitive psychology raises another relevant question: When does psychological theory remain consistent with, and when does it depart from, the ordinary concept or 'manifest image' of the person? Discussion here of this important issue refers to Jerry Fodor and Thomas Nagel, and it is suggested that – given that the relation of cognitive psychology to ordinary psychology is far from perspicuous – there is reason for endorsing a sharp working distinction between personal and sub-personal psychology.

On one view, little importance should be accorded to the description of the individual as either having, or lacking, parts, and the issue seen instead as a matter of degree or theoretical convenience. Chapter 3 opposes this lax view and seeks to up the stakes. In the course of an exegesis of the relevant writings of Donald Davidson and David Pears, a distinction of weak and strong forms of division is drawn. It is agreed that a weak form of mental division is present in irrationality, but claims for the stronger form are rejected. This result is argued for by presenting the stronger form of division (which is set out clearly in Pears' 'sub-systemic' theory) with a dilemma: either it fails to yield what we ordinarily consider proper explanation, or (as alleged by Sartre) it runs into paradox. Much time is devoted to Davidson and Pears, since the clarity of their formulations of the partitive model of explanation of irrationality enables this question to be brought to a definite conclusion, yielding a result with great importance for the philosophy of psychoanalysis.

The chapter closes with a brief suggestion regarding the metaphysical underpinnings of its argument: it is proposed that subsystemic theory's rejection of personal unity is connected to a Humean view of the self, and that ordinary psychology's intolerance of partition reflects its contrary commitment to a view of persons as substantial unities. This explains the importance of the issue of partition for the philosophy of psychoanalysis. At stake in it is the harmony between psychoanalysis and ordinary psychology: if psychoanalytic theory is partitive, its agreement with ordinary thought is questionable. While this would not necessarily make psychoanalytic theory false, it would nevertheless have the unwelcome effect of making its legitimacy harder to establish.

The overall role of Part I is therefore preparatory: the negative result derived from chapter 3 implies that psychoanalytic thought should avoid the model of explanation which attributes the irrational person with two minds, one of which is unconscious.

Explicating psychoanalytic theory is potentially a lengthy and highly detailed task, and Part II only sketches its outlines. Chapter 4 concentrates, as much philosophical commentary on psychoanalysis has done, on Freud's case of the Ratman. The first aim is to demarcate the proper object of psychoanalytic theory, the particular kind of irrational phenomena which it seeks to explain. The basic concepts used by Freud in understanding unconscious motivation are then described, and the theory of repression considered in some detail. A widespread view of the nature of Freud's postulation of unconscious motives – as simply transposing ordinary psychology into an unconscious key – is criticised, and an alternative view of psychoanalytic explanation argued for as being most likely to lead to a satisfactory understanding of Freudian theory: it is to see psychoanalytic theory as neither breaking altogether with ordinary psychology, nor seeking to enforce rigidly its commitment to explanation in terms of reasons for action. This – the approach explored by Richard Wollheim – outlines the broad strategy of reconstruction pursued in the chapters that follow.

Chapter 5 describes wish-fulfilment, the most logically and causally basic process assumed by psychoanalytic explanation, and the correlative concept of symbolism. Wish-fulfilment is argued to provide a perspicuous, unifying ground on which to base more complex psychoanalytic concepts. Later sections attempt to bring out what is distinctive about Freud's concept of symbolism, and comment on the longstanding issue of cause and meaning in the philosophy of psychoanalysis.

The more sophisticated psychoanalytic concepts are introduced in chapter 6. The concept of phantasy is the chief of these. Melanie Klein's theory of development is summarised with a view to giving a sense of the detail and strength of explanation in terms of phantasy. Phantasy is considered from the angles of its causal origins, and its capacity for influencing conscious, propositional thought. Also examined are the manner in which external objects acquire unconscious significance, the role of the Omnipotence Belief, the goals of psychoanalytic therapy, and such key concepts as sublimation and acting-out. By the end of the chapter, the preconditions of Freud's original interpretation of the Ratman in chapter 4 are argued to have been successfully established.

Whereas chapter 4 revolves around concepts of Freud's, such as repression, chapter 6 refers chiefly to Kleinian theory. It is argued that the concept of phantasy is essential to the full explication of psychoanalytic explanation and that, in this sense, Klein's metapsychology is immanent in Freud's.

Part II may be read as if it were tracing the story of an unconscious motive's ascendant influence over the conscious mind: we start with the idea of an insulated power of autonomous self-gratification (wish-fulfilment), and develop it into a permanent mental structure (phantasy) capable of generating the kind of overt irrational phenomena found in the case of the Ratman. In this story, a sharp contrast between unconscious psychoanalytic, and conscious rational mental process is maintained, but this is shown to be fully consistent with the picture of persons (from Part I) as substantial unities. The attempt to describe a single, canonical form of psychoanalytic explanation risks suppressing its variety and detail, but the hope is that this approach will be justified by the clarity and simplicity of the picture that results.

Part III aims to consolidate and expand the claims of Part II. It remains concerned with the narrow topic of the enquiry – the problem of explaining instances of irrationality – but also aims to consider the general philosophical features of the mind involved in psychoanalytic metapsychology. Chapter 7 therefore gives further treatment to some of the concepts introduced in Part II, such as the ego, internal figures and the inner world, and the conception of the unconscious as a dynamic source of influence on propositional mental life. The pertinence of psychoanalysis for the explanation of ordinary irrationality, and the degree to which psychoanalytic explanation respects the ordinary, manifest self-conceptions of persons are discussed. Finally, the chapter considers the implications of psycho-analytic theory for our metaphysical view of persons, including the question of whether psychoanalytic mental states are 'owned' by persons.

Chapter 8 begins by discussing the topic of consciousness, asking whether psychoanalytic theory is able to respect our ordinary intuitions about the centrality of consciousness to the mind. A priori objections to the concept of unconscious mentality are set out and rejected, and Freud's own theories of consciousness briefly discussed. The place of consciousness in psychoanalytic theory is then explored in terms of the role of phenomenology in psychoanalytic explanation, and a sense in which unconscious states may figure in the stream of consciousness defended.

The second half of chapter 8 attempts to deal thoroughly with other important issues. The relations between psychoanalytic ex-planation and two general views of the nature of psychological explanation – the theoretical view, and Davidson's attributionism – are examined, the conclusion being that psychoanalytic explanation should be harnessed to plain realism about ordinary psychology. It is then argued that psychoanalytic theory enables ordinary psychology to deflect the objection that the inexplicability of irrationality, and other incompletenesses, betray an essential inadequacy on its part: in this way psychoanalytic theory 'vindicates' ordinary psychology. The legitimation and epistemological foundations of psychoanalytic theory are saved for last. The strongest argument for psychoanalytic theory, it is claimed, lies in exhibiting its conceptual workings with reference to our demand for an intentional explanation of irration-ality; which is what earlier chapters have sought to provide.

The Appendices contrast Kleinian metapsychology with its chief competitors, respond to some criticisms and indicate its advantages.

0.5 THE CLAIMS

The results of the enquiry can be summarised as follows. Freud's theories are directed primarily at the explanation of irrational phenomena which are distinct in kind from others that we are more familiar with, such as self-deception and akrasia. Psychoanalytic theory is therefore not, pace Sartre and others, a theory of self-deception, and does not stand in competition with ordinary, non-psychoanalytic explanations of ordinary forms of irrationality. Psychoanalytic theory is not fundamentally dependent on the concept or metaphor of a divided person, and nor is irrationality in general to be explained by positing a 'second mind'. Sartre's criticisms indicate another constraint that psychoanalytic theory must observe: unconscious processes must not be assimilated to ordinary, rational mental processes. Psychoanalytic theory attempts to go beyond ordinary psychological explanation in specific directions, and these hinge on its employment of the concepts of wish-fulfilment and phantasy. The combination of claims on which Freudian explanation depends are cogent in terms of assumptions to which ordinary psychology is either already committed, or capable of accommodating. Freud's metapsychology is developed conceptually in the work of Klein, who resolves some difficulties surrounding Freud's earlier metapsychological formulations. A metaphysical view of persons as substantial unities is embedded in commonsense's picture of persons, and psychoanalytic modelling of the mind is consonant with this view. Psychoanalytic propositions are known in roughly the same sorts of ways as the propositions of ordinary psychology are known: scepticism about psychoanalytic explanation can be met by exhibiting its continuity with ordinary psychological explanation. Freud's claims do not therefore require special scientific corroboration. It follows that psychoanalytic theory requires neither the kind of scrutiny based in the philosophy of science which analytic philosophers have for the greater part accorded it; nor the kind of hermeneutic reconstruction undertaken in some Continental philosophy of psychoanalysis.

0.6 FREUD AND KLEIN

The treatment of Freud and Klein in this enquiry is in the nature of a rational reconstruction. The order of exposition is largely indifferent to the actual course of development of psychoanalytic theory, and it makes no claims to contribute to its historical understanding. Also, it has of course been necessary to simplify or ignore a large number of issues. This does not however exempt the account from the obligation to represent Freud and Klein's thought accurately within the terms set by a project of a kind which aims to produce a single, unified picture: its claims may be appropriately impugned wherever they fail to make the best sense of Freud or Klein. It will be clear at what points the concepts described are not properly Freud's or Klein's, but are philosophical concepts brought to bear on their own concepts. The notes indicate the degree to which the discussion derives from specific textual sources. Reconstruction, it should be said, has nothing to do with 'cashing out' psychoanalytic theory conceived as a set of 'metaphors': psychoanalytic theory does not need any such reworking.

It is in the nature of rational reconstructions that, precisely because they aim to make the best sense of a thinker, an ambiguity is created whenever there is more in the original subject than gets preserved in the reconstruction. For this reason, it may be helpful to state here that the exegetical upshot of my account of Freud is to see his writings as giving expression to two philosophical interpretations of the unconscious: Part I focuses on the Second Mind interpretation, Part II on the interpretation in terms of wish and phantasy. The crucial point is that the former is dissolved into, and superseded by the latter.

Freud's and Klein's writings are not quoted extensively in the course of discussing their theories, despite the consequent loss of exegetical leverage, since this practice, too often in writings on psychoanalysis, produces texts cluttered with references which are impossible for anyone without an extensive grasp of the psychoanalytic corpus to digest; it is in any case not suited to a more abstract, philosophical presentation. Detailed references are confined to the notes.

0.7 READING THE BOOK

Finally, some suggestions on reading the book. Part One may be read on its own as an essay on irrationality and personal unity. Readers with more narrowly defined, exclusively psychoanalytic interests could safely pass over all of Part I (perhaps glancing at 2.2) and begin with chapter 4. The reading of Parts II and III could be shortened by the omission of chapters 5 and 7; chapters 4 and 6 contain between them the essentials of the account of psychoanalytic theory. Any reader is, however, likely not to want to omit 8.4 and 8.5, which are crucial for completing the picture of psychoanalytic theory.

Nothing beyond a very rough or second-hand familiarity with Freud and the relevant philosophical issues is assumed. Some of the terminology of current philosophy of mind is used; readers for whom it is not familiar should be able to pick up its sense en route.

PART I

Dividing persons

CHAPTER I

Ordinary irrationality

'M. Poirot, I *can't* believe it!'
'Madame, you *can* and you *do* believe it!'

I.I MAPPING ORDINARY IRRATIONALITY

The main concern of Part I is with the idea of explaining irrationality by positing a divided mind. Before getting on to that, however, it is necessary to set out the topic of irrationality as it figures in ordinary, pre-psychoanalytic thought. This will help to determine whether there is anything in ordinary psychology that invites such a manoeuvre.

There is a further reason for not simply starting the enquiry with a psychoanalytic case history. Psychoanalytic theory should not be made to seem to appear out of nowhere; as if it had evolved autonomously in response to problems of psychopathology whose existence can only ever be witnessed in the seclusion of the clinical hour. Looked at in that hermetic way, psychoanalytic theory is bound to seem forever strange, arbitrary and unpersuasive. A fundamental and central contention of this book is that, on the contrary, psychoanalytic theory lies in a direct line of descent from problems and strategies of explanation encountered and deployed in ordinary psychology[1] – the form of explanation to which our everyday talk of people as believing, remembering, feeling and wanting commits us – and that it is with reference to these that its concepts should be understood and its claims to explanation measured.

It is consequently of prime importance to have a picture of the relation between ordinary psychology and irrational phenomena. The goal of this chapter is to describe the salient forms of irrationality recognised in ordinary psychology, and identify and evaluate the

15

corresponding kinds of explanation that it offers. Its target is the view that irrationality is off limits to ordinary psychology, or that ordinary psychology deals only with rationality.[2]

Wishful thinking, self-deception and akrasia are, plausibly, the main forms of irrationality that commonsense acknowledges. With regard to these, we have no difficulty in saying, in broad terms, what each of them consists in. Wishful thinking is a matter of believing something simply because you desire it to be so. Self-deception consists in getting yourself to believe one thing in order to avoid facing what you know to be the truth. Akrasia consists in failing to do what you know it to be best to do.

The first claim of this chapter is that these forms of ordinary irrationality, the forms of irrationality – those recognised in ordinary psychology – are *propositionally transparent*, by which it is meant that they are *constituted and defined by a particular structure of propositional attitudes*.[3] The second claim – which will need some argument – concerns their explanation. It is that, although the propositional description of ordinary irrationality does not alone suffice to make it fully intelligible, and its explanation in terms of ordinary psychology does eventually run out of force, this is because propositional description requires supplementation, not replacement.

I will begin by demonstrating these two claims in some detail with reference to a particular form of self-deception. Having done that, and extracted some more precise conclusions about ordinary irrationality, I will consider akrasia briefly, in order to show that the same generalisations apply to it as well. Finally I will contrast ordinary psychology with some philosophical interpretations of irrationality, to be found in Continental philosophy, that seek to transform irrationality from a psychological into a metaphysical phenomenon.

1.2 SELF-DECEPTION

Self-deception, as the earlier colloquial gloss brought out, involves the idea of a person suffering a failure of self-knowledge because her motivation interferes with her beliefs. This is however insufficient for self-deception: ordinary psychology recognises a wide variety of conditions where self-knowledge fails because belief is affected by motivation, bordering on self-deception, but distinct from it. How then is self-deception distinguished from these other conditions? Some contrasts will help to answer this question.

(a) Self-deception is not the same as skewed, oscillating, confused, naive or unrealistic belief. When José says of Carmen, 'I wonder whether that girl ever spoke one word of truth in her life; but whenever she spoke, I believed her – I couldn't help it', what he admits to is not self-deception, but a condition of exaggerated credulity. (b) Self-deception is also quite distinct from the common phenomenon of variability in self-knowledge: propositions about oneself may be readily available for self-ascription on one occasion but not on another – just as I may be able to remember a telephone number one day but not the next – but even where such variation is connected to motivation, it does not amount to self-deception. (c) Nor is self-deception just tenacity in believing something in the face of evidence to the contrary: so long as the subject's overview remains truth-directed, this counts as faith, hopefulness or epistemic gambling (Pascal's wager, for example, and the research scientist who stakes his all on a hunch). (d) Nor is self-deception the same as delusion, a category which implies some impairment of the very faculty of belief-formation, a fault at the level of competence rather than performance. (e) Nor is self-deception merely an unusual attitude of self-directed cynicism, irony, hypocrisy or insincerity. Indeed, judgements of self-deception overtake judgements of these kinds: if I am self-deceived with regard to some matter, I can assert it neither sincerely nor insincerely, the will to self-knowledge needed for sincerity to be an issue having been suspended. (f) Nor is self-deception just self-distraction, a category which ranges from instinctively averting one's gaze from the scene of an accident, to something as complex as preventing oneself from getting depressed at the thought of one's bad qualities. In such cases the means employed consist in a redirection of awareness, and the goal is restricted to a change in experience; whereas the goal of self-deception is something closer to a change in belief.

Such contrasts are fairly obvious. A more complex differentiation is the following. (g) Self-deception is more than self-manipulation. There are situations where it is prudent to get oneself tied to the mast (Ulysses' strategy for avoiding the call of the sirens), or to shoot oneself in the foot (the infantryman in the front line). These are acts for which intra-psychic analogues can be found, situations where it makes sense to form an intention to bring about a condition in which one knows one will hold a false belief.[4] These are cases of 'reasonable irrationality', of rational intra-psychic self-manipulation, and they do not represent the same psychological phenomenon as self-deception. Ulysses' intention is bounded in a way that the self-deceiver's is not: he plans to be impaired in limited respects for a specific length of time, solely with a view to achieving some determinate and fully realistic end, after which he means to return to a state of full epistemic capacity. The intention in self-deception lacks analogous parameters: it is not an intention to hold a false belief for a specific length of time, after which to return to a condition of true belief. Consequently, the state which self-deception aims to produce is not simply the instrument of an ultimately truth-respecting intention. The difference can also be expressed in terms of control: whereas Ulysses tied to the mast remains logically in control of himself, the individual in self-deception is not similarly under the aegis or control of herself as a subject of self-deceptive intent: in self-deception, no true practical hold over error is kept.

It would be wrong, therefore, to see self-deception as resulting from a preference for trying to solve an internal or psychological problem over its external or real counterpart. Instead, self-deceivers should be seen as mistakenly taking themselves to have solved their real problem in solving their psychological problem; or, put another way, as failing to make a proper distinction between psychological and real problems. This means that self-deception is not fully rationalised at the level of a meta-intention: self-deception involves a plan in so far as all intention does, but there is confusion between how things are, and how they are believed to be – in the state of affairs that it envisages.[5]

The basic feature of all cases covered by ordinary use of the term 'self-deception', which distinguishes self-deception from wishful thinking and akrasia, is motivated self-misrepresentation. More precisely, all self-deception involves what can be called a *structure of motivated self-misrepresentation*, defined as:

a structure in which a psychological state S prevents the formation of another state S', where (i) S involves a misrepresentation of the subject, (ii) this feature is necessary for S to prevent the formation of S', and (iii) this structure answers to the subject's motivation.

In this definition it is left open how such a structure may operate. So, a number of things fit this bill, including some animal behaviour described by zoologists as 'self-deception'.[6] Now, it is plausible to say that there is *a* use of 'self-deception' which is explicable in terms of the supposition that the structure may operate *through the intention of the subject*. Reviewing the grounds on which self-deception was differentiated from other categories shows as much. Contrasts (a)–(g) imply that self-deception involves an ability to form true belief, combined with an attitude of truth-violation (or at least truth-indifference); that its target is belief; and that its means is an intention, directed at one's own beliefs. All of which means nothing less than that a subject is self-deceived when he *believes one thing in order not to believe another*. So we seem to have:

Self-deception is a structure of motivated self-misrepresentation in which S and S′ are *beliefs* and the process occurs through an *intention* of the subject's.

This identifies what will be called *strong* self-deception. Weak self-deception, by contrast, is any structure of motivated self-misrepresentation that does not involve an intention.

1.3 SELF-DECEPTIVE INTENT AS EXPLANATION

The notion of strong self-deception has been arrived at by thinking about how self-deception differs from other psychological conditions. It matches what we want to say about particular cases. Here are two examples, taken from Tolstoy and E. M. Forster:

At first Anna had avoided the Princess Tverskoy's set as much as she could, because it meant living beyond her means and also because she really preferred the other; but since her visit to Moscow all this was reversed. She avoided her serious-minded friends and went into high society. There she saw Vronsky and experienced a tremulous joy every time she met him. She met him most frequently at Betsy's, who had been a Vronsky herself and was his cousin. Vronsky went whenever there was a chance of meeting Anna and whenever he could speak to her of his love. She gave him no encouragement, but every time they met her heart quickened with the same feeling of animation that had seized her in the train the day she first saw him. She knew that at the sight of him joy lit up her eyes and drew her lips into a smile, and she could not quench the expression of that joy.

At first Anna sincerely believed that she was displeased with him for daring to pursue her; but soon after her return from Moscow, having gone to a party where she expected to meet him but to which he did not come, she distinctly realised, by the disappointment that overcame her, that she had been deceiving herself and that his pursuit was not only not distasteful to her, but was the whole interest of her life.[7]

Mr Pembroke was conscientious and romantic, and knew that marriage without love is intolerable. On the other hand, he could not admit that love had vanished from him. To admit this, would argue that he had deteriorated. Whereas he knew for a fact that he improved, year by year. Each year he grew more moral, more efficient, more learned, more genial. So how could he fail to be more loving? He did not speak to himself as follows, because he never spoke to himself; but the following notions moved in the recesses of his mind: 'It is not the fire of youth. But I am not sure that I approve of the fire of youth [...] I rather suspect that it is a nobler, riper emotion that I am laying at the feet of Mrs Orr.' It never took him long to get muddled, or to reverse cause and effect. In a short time he believed that he had been pining for years, and only waiting for this good fortune to ask the lady to share it with him.[8]

These cases share a structure. Both Anna Karenina and Pembroke are initially in conflict: each wants something which can only be pursued at a serious cost to themselves. Confronting Anna Karenina is the fact of her marriage; confronting Pembroke, that of his deterioration. For each, self-deception functions advantageously: Anna Karenina gets to meet Vronsky without recognising her danger of falling in love, and Pembroke marries without believing himself to be lacking in love. But it is not just Anna Karenina and Pembroke's good fortune that things turn out to their advantage. It is essential to grasp that, in both cases, self-deception is adduced, in preference to other possible interpretations that might have preserved the image of the characters' rationality intact, as a psychological *explanation*. It has the following form. Anna Karenina and Pembroke exercise preferences over the reasons on which they act, or over their beliefs about these: they prefer to believe that they are $\emptyset$-ing for reason R than R', because R' is discrepant with, whereas R accords with, how they want to think about themselves. Their irrationality consists in the fact that R, which is not their real reason for action, only has the role that it does because of R', with which it is in fact inconsistent. In the light of their preferences, Anna Karenina and Pembroke form intentions to determine their beliefs accordingly. Which means, in sum, that in deceiving themselves they secure their goals *through a process of practical reasoning*.

Although cases like Anna Karenina and Pembroke are highly familiar, some have denied the existence of strong self-deception, usually because it has been thought that nothing can, logically, satisfy such a description. I will now try to show in more detail how attributions of self-deception are genuinely explanatory, and argue that strong self-deception is indeed possible.

Strong self-deception, it has been claimed, hinges on the attribution of a distinctive kind of self-directed intention. Do we really need to attribute this arguably quite peculiar item? Can the operation of Anna Karenina and Pembroke's preferences not be accounted for in some other way – perhaps in terms of simple wishful thinking?

Wishful thinking has the following form. If I come to believe p, and this belief is formed either without evidence or against the evidence, then this will be wishful thinking if its best complete explanation has the following form: the desire that p causes me to believe that p. In wishful thinking, a desire either produces the congenial belief directly, or it reshapes evidence immediately related to it; no intention is involved. Perhaps, then, one could build up the phenomenon of strong self-deception by combining several processes of wishful thinking?[9]

The supposition that belief is directly vulnerable to desire in this way, and that there are simple mental dispositions (such as the brute magnetism of entertaining beliefs that represent the world in pleasing terms), are perfectly legitimate, and no doubt account for much weak self-deception. But no combination of them can account for strong self-deception, for the reason that strong self-deception manifests, we have seen, *practical rationality*, and exercising practical rationality requires an intention.

Let us call the psychological states S and S′ which are involved in strong self-deception the *promoted* and *buried* beliefs respectively. The two key causal sequences involved in strong self-deception run (i) from a first-order desire to a second-order desire (Anna Karenina's desire for Vronsky causes her to desire not-to-believe that she ought to renounce him); and (ii) from a second-order desire to bury a belief to a second-order desire to promote a belief (Anna Karenina's desire not-to-believe that she ought to renounce Vronsky, causes her to desire to believe that she is displeased with his pursuit of her). These are relations of instrumentality: the second-order desire to bury is instrumentally related to the first-order desire, and the desire to promote is instrumentally related to the desire to bury. What establishes that an intention is necessary for these connections is that rationality is required to account for the derivation of the instrumental term in each.[10] There is simply no other way of explicating the relations of instrumentality: sequences of the kind exemplified by (i) and (ii) are just what it is for something to occur through a person's intention. Any sparser story, that seeks to dispense with an intention in favour of wishful thinking and non-rational dispositions, will entail a conception of mental processing in which a desire can avail itself of the services of the right means miraculously – i.e. without need of reasoning to determine which are the right instruments for a desire to make use of. It follows that self-deceptive intent is required by the nature of practical reason.

Some important features and implications of this analysis should be noted. One, it accounts for our hesitation in attributing self-deception to children below a certain age. Although children can do something much like self-deceive – they can cover themselves by telling lies and then be utterly taken in by what they say – they lack the requisite grasp of the susceptibility of belief to manipulation in the first person case. They can identify interpersonal deception (and, correlatively, can attempt to deceive others), but they can not diagnose self-deception in adults, and are thus short of the piece of psychological 'theory' necessary for the formation of self-deceptive intent.[11]

Two, the subject of self-deception remains, logically, within a social interpretative context. This is so both in the obvious sense that Anna Karenina and Pembroke are conscious of the actual pressure of social judgement on them, and in the more interesting sense that the psychological forces at play in their self-deception do not lose touch with that context: they continue, in their thoughts, to envisage themselves as subjects of others' interpretation (indeed, they exploit the indeterminacy of such interpretation).

Three, a disanalogy between self-deceptive intent and ordinary propositional attitudes, regarding their attribution, should be conceded. For self-deception, we can not get the best proof, a thought or statement 'I mean to believe ... ' What we can however do instead is postpone the evidence: at some later time Anna Karenina will think, or be able to think, 'so that is why I told myself... ' And there is of course an explanation for why the intention does not show itself in the present tense: to do so would gain nothing for it, and risk its extinction.

Four, although self-deceptive intent is truth-*indifferent* in so far as the subject grasps the utility of the promotion-and-burial of belief, and truth-*violating* in so far as she grasps the falsity of the promoted belief, we do not have to think of the self-deceiver as intending to take the *falsehood* of a proposition as a *reason for believing it* – a psychological story which would indeed stretch credulity. Just as, in akrasia, there is no higher-order intention to contradict the general principle that one should do what one thinks it best to do, so in self-deception there is no need to attribute an 'intention to contradict the truth' or a 'preference for falsehood'.

All this has been said in defence of the explanatoriness of self-deceptive intent. I now want to make plain the two principal conceptual problems encountered by the concept of self-deceptive intent, and outline a defence of its intelligibility. This will lead to some general observations about the nature and workings of ordinary psychology.

(1) The first problem concerns *contradictory belief*. If there is, as appears to be the case, such a thing as sustained self-deception, it will require contradictory beliefs, since the belief that is buried will persist, contradicting the promoted belief, rather than be destroyed. Contradictory belief is however often considered problematic: how can someone believe opposites? The standard move to make at this juncture is to distinguish attributions of *contradictory belief* from *contradictory attributions* of belief.[12] Let us call the Principle of the Possibility of Contradictory Belief (PPCB), the view that the following is a consistent attribution:

A believes p and A believes not-p.

According to **PPCB** this attribution – of contradictory belief – is distinct from, and does not entail, the following, contradictory attribution of belief:

A believes p and A does not believe p,

which would indeed entail the contradiction:

It is the case that A believes p and it is not the case that A believes p.

Why might **PPCB** not be considered satisfactory? The following, epistemological objection might be made: any evidence there is for 'believes p' cancels out, and is in turn cancelled out by, whatever evidence there is for 'believes not-p'; so their product is an epistemic zero, i.e. no attribution of belief at all.

This objection succeeds only if evidence for 'believes p' either (i) entails or is equivalent to evidence for 'does not believe not-p'; and/or (ii) necessarily diminishes the value of evidence for 'believes not-p' in proportion to the degree to which it supports 'believes p'. But each of (i) and (ii) should be accepted only if it is assumed in advance that the states of affairs represented by 'believes p' and 'believes not-p' necessarily exclude one another; otherwise there is no motivation for viewing the units of evidence as working against one another.[13] So the epistemological objection begs the question: it rests on a false and crudely unilinear general view of the nature of evidence for psychological attributions, and it overlooks the specific reason we have for accepting PPCB, namely, the fact that the total phenomenon of self-deception is one in which we can see how and why a pair of contradictory beliefs should coexist.

Other, non-epistemological objections to PPCB may derive from views about the nature of either belief or believers. They will claim either (a) that what is attributed in self-deception is only partial, half- or pseudo-belief;[14] or (b) that what self-deceptive belief is attributed to must be a covert multiplicity of believers. The argument for (b) is held over for examination in chapters 2 and 3.

The argument for (a), rejecting PPCB on grounds having to do with the nature of belief, is that PPCB makes nonsense of all belief attribution: under PPCB any behaviour can be made to follow from any belief-attribution, and any belief-attribution made consistent with any behaviour; so belief-attribution ceases to be explanatory.

To succeed, this argument would have to show that the *global* requirement of consistency on belief filters down so far as to make any *localised* attributions of inconsistency impossible.[15] How could this be done? Only, surely, by defining belief in such a way that any inconsistency violates the nature of belief, treating beliefs as *ideal entities* deployed in a theory whose ultimate justification is instrumental, conventional or in some other way non-realistic – a view which PPCB itself gives no reason to accept.[16]

In conclusion, rejection of PPCB either begs the question or depends upon an idealised view of belief. There will be contradictory belief in self-deception as long as the phenomenon strikes us as unified in a way that can only be rationalised by a combination of contradictory beliefs, at least one of which is causally required to account for the role of the other. What is singular about the presence of contradictory belief in self-deception is that both beliefs show themselves in the very same piece of behaviour, in contrast with cases in which behaviour is fragmented in such a way that contradictory beliefs are only alternately or dispersedly manifest.

An important final point about PPCB is that propositional description alone should not be expected to make a self-deceiver fully intelligible: to achieve this, the pattern of inconsistent beliefs must be redescribed, making reference to different *ways of thinking* about the objects figuring in those beliefs. This point will be amplified below.

(2) The second problem concerns the conception of self-deception as a *doing*. The intention to bury and promote belief seems either to contradict the natural view (and perhaps conceptual truth) that believing is not an action;[17] or to require that one's beliefs be capable of figuring as immediate objects of manipulation, which seems to be false.

Self-deception is certainly not, as we would ordinarily put it, a *voluntary* matter, in the sense of issuing directly from reflective acts of choice. Reflective voluntariness is however a distinct property from being intentional, and only the latter is required for self-deception to qualify as a doing.[18]

To provide for self-deceptive intent, and at the same time avoid viewing self-deceptive promotion and burial as 'acts of believing', it needs to be assumed that there are some psychological entities, short of beliefs themselves, which intention can get a grip on and manipulate directly in such a way as to indirectly determine belief.[19] Suggestions for the family of entities which enables self-deception to be understood as a doing include: (i) *episodes of thought*, (ii) *representations* of objects, and (iii) a special sub-class of episodes of thought called *realisations*. These items hang together in obvious ways. All have to do with the manifestation of mental states in the stream of consciousness.

(i) Episodes of thought are related to beliefs in the right way to serve as manipulable instruments of belief-modification: thoughts give expression to beliefs, but need not be assertoric – they may entertain possibilities, rather than just reflect one's beliefs about how things actually are. Such uncommitted thoughts can furthermore be produced or blocked at will, and, because the direction of causation runs from thought to belief as well as the other way, a thought that p may feed back to form a belief that p.

(ii) The notion of a representation of an object is similar to that of a mode of presentation. Episodes of thought may express representations, rather than complete propositions (as is required for them to express beliefs). This enables them to bypass the requirement of truth-sensitivity constraining the network of beliefs,[20] so that in self-deception one's beliefs may be modified through episodes of thought expressing representations of an object: alteration of belief is achieved through targeting mental items one causal and evidential step below belief in the mental hierarchy.[21]

(iii) Realisation, an intriguing and distinctive phenomenon, is distinct from the ordinary formation or 'onset' of belief. Formation of belief is not sufficient for realisation, and vice versa: I can be struck by, and hence realise, something that I already know (something I have said and acted on for a long time). The topic of realisation – what one is struck by – again need not be a whole proposition: it may be only an 'aspect', as when one realises 'quite how dark' the sky is. Realisation characteristically involves bringing together two matters, in such a way as to yield the kind of combination which is exemplified when one thing is visually seen as another: typically it is realised that one thing is *also* something else (that two descriptions apply at once to the same object).[22] Realisation, along with noticing and remarking, is connected with the concept of attention, and also belongs in the class of such mental events as change of mind, surprise and deciding. In common with these, realisation carries implications for action: if p is some matter highly relevant to my conduct, then I can not be said to realise that p without this making a difference to my action-dispositions. Although realisation is intimately related to change in belief, what happens in realisation is therefore not just a change in the informational characterisation of the person, any more than making a decision is: if the words of realisation fly up, it is logically guaranteed that the thoughts do not remain below.

Realisation is pivotal for self-deception. This can be appreciated by noting that self-deceivers are often said to prevent themselves from realising things,[23] and that a realisation is what eventually releases someone from self-deception. Disappointment at Vronsky's absence triggers Anna Karenina's realisation. This sort of realisation has a structure. Let us suppose, as Tolstoy implies, that Anna Karenina, when self-deceived, experiences the world dividedly: different phenomenological worlds correspond to her domestic life and her time spent with Vronsky. In order to move towards a realisation that she is deceiving herself, Anna Karenina needs to undo this division. What would this amount to? She would need to think, when with Karenin, that she loves Vronsky; and, when with Vronsky, that she is also a wife and mother. But this is not just an external matter of having certain thoughts at particular times and places: what is necessary for realisation is that particular self-representations should be conjoined with particular self-ascribed predicates. Anna Karenina has one self-representation connected to Vronsky, and another connected to Karenin, and what is needed for realisation is that she should form the thought 'I love Vronsky' with her *Karenin* self-representation, and form the thought 'I am a wife and mother' with her *Vronsky* self-representation.

This may make it sound as if realisation consists in the acquisition of a new identity belief. But it can hardly be that 'Anna Karenina-with-Vronsky = Anna Karenina-with-Karenin' is something that Anna Karenina ever disbelieves! So it does not seem that Anna Karenina's realisation involves grasping a new proposition. Instead, the pulling together of descriptions involved in realisation may be thought of as a matter of identification: what Anna Karenina-with-Vronsky must do is *identify with* (the desires of) Anna Karenina-with-Karenin, and vice versa.

All this brings out another, essential, dimension of ordinary psychological explanation, which is highlighted in the context of self-deception: the presence and role of phenomenological factors. To the propositional sequence involved in strong self-deception there corresponds a phenomenology: we expect, crediting the self-deceiver with a stream of consciousness as well as a set of beliefs, desires and intentions, that each of their propositional attitudes will have phenomenological manifestations. So there will be *something it is like* for Anna Karenina to desire not to be aware of her desire for Vronsky: perhaps a flicker of disquiet when the thought of his attractiveness occurs. And it is partly in phenomenological terms that the terms of art, burial and promotion, should be understood: a belief that is buried is one that will not extend its influence across the stream of consciousness.

One aspect of the role of phenomenology, well recognised in ordinary psychology, can usefully be elaborated here. Proust talks about particular complexes of personal experience – as delivered through the workings of memory – as 'selves':

But if the context of sensations in which they ['the intermittencies of the heart'] are preserved is recaptured, they acquire in turn the same power of expelling everything that is incompatible with them, of installing alone in us the self that originally lived them [...] the self that I had just suddenly become once again had not existed since that evening long ago when my grandmother had undressed me after my arrival at Balbec[24]

It was perhaps because they were so diverse, the persons whom I used to contemplate in her at this period, that later I developed the habit of becoming myself a different person, according to the particular Albertine to whom my thoughts had turned; a jealous, an indifferent, a voluptuous, a melancholy, a frenzied person [...] I ought to give a different name to each of the selves that subsequently thought about Albertine[25]

Proust's selves are not persons, since their identity does not compete with, and in fact presupposes, ordinary personal identity. Rather, they form sub-divisions on the temporal axis of the person.[26] Such selves are exhibited in and partially constituted by what may be called *phenomenological sets*: that is, certain patterned, individually constituted and repeatable ways in which the world may appear to a person.

The notion of a phenomenological set has particular importance in the context of irrationality. A phenomenological set may bring a realisation in its wake, but it may equally effect the reverse of a realisation, as if closing the mind ('expelling everything that is incompatible' with it): as if undoing the knowledge that an object may fall under several descriptions, making it seem as if only one, particularly salient description can be true of an object. This means that, in order to escape from self-deception, what Anna Karenina needs to do is gain access, from the vantage point of her 'Vronsky' phenomenological set, to her other, 'conjugal' set, and identify with its subject.

1.4 ORDINARY PSYCHOLOGY AND ORDINARY IRRATIONALITY: SOME CONCLUSIONS

The account of strong self-deception has shown several very important things about the relation of ordinary irrationality and ordinary psychology. I will set these out.

(1) In distinguishing self-deception from neighbouring psychological conditions, the lines between the various categories are often hard to draw in practice, but we know in principle what to look for and how to go about trying to draw them. At each point where we want to contrast self-deception with other conditions, we have to cite nothing less than a complete propositional attitude;[27] there is no other way of getting necessary and sufficient conditions for self-deception. This is because there is no logical gap between recognising that the concept of self-deception has application, and knowing the kind of

psychological state of affairs that it consists in. Just as identifying a case as one of self-deception and knowing what sort of beliefs, desires and intentions it consists in are but one move, so there is no logical gap between making a judgement of self-deception and knowing an explanation of the phenomenon. Such proximity of description and explanation is a general characteristic of ordinary, propositional psychology. Hence the earlier description of self-deception as 'propositionally transparent' irrationality.

It follows, also, that self-deception does not allow for any finer set of attributions than those suggested above: it has no greater propositional depth than that which we ordinarily, pre-theoretically take it to have. And – an important associated point – it is part of the way in which ordinary irrationality is identified that it is distinct from madness.[28]

It is a consequence of all this (and further evidence for it) that scepticism about strong self-deception assumes the particular form that it does. By scepticism I mean here not the logical denial that anything can satisfy all of the conditions that the term implies, but the empirical denial that there is anything of such complexity as to *need* to be described in terms of self-deception.[29] The most likely target of sceptical simplification will be the promoted belief: the whole case for strong self-deception hinges on discerning self-deceptive intent behind it, and it is recognition of this that the sceptic will do best to withhold. Now, were it the case that a decent and determinate gap existed between explanans and explanandum in ordinary psychology, then it would be possible to *prove*, or disprove, the correctness of any given set of propositional attributions. But such a procedure does not exist, a fact which is reflected in the ineliminable possibility of sceptically simplifying the 'explanandum': it may always be roundly denied that anything as intricate as the promoted belief in fact exists, making any alleged proof of the concept's application circular.

We are put in a similar position by some novelists' psychological portrayals. Does anything correspond to Jamesian fineness of sensibility and appetite for motive, or Dostoyevskyan inscrutability of motivation – or are these conditions wholly fictitious? It is highly obscure what justification could be found in contexts of complex human behaviour for some such principle as one which enjoins us to be 'economical' in our attribution of psychological states. To describe an *apparent* degree of psychological complexity as 'only an illusion' would assume some external vantage point. But there is no a priori way of determining a limit to psychological complexity, or of deciding the maximal degree of complexity of which persons are capable. And even if there were such an external measure, by which a standard of 'needful' complexity could be established, still there would be no reason for assuming that people will in fact be any less complex than they are capable of being; since need is not the only determinant of propositional attitudes.

If Tolstoy and Forster are not engaged in fancifulness, there are situations where it makes more sense to attribute self-deception than anything else, and self-deception is real. If so, we are entitled to view the sceptic about strong self-deception as suffering from a kind of psychological aspect-blindness.

(2) Explanation in terms of self-deception consists in attributing a sequence of practical reasoning, one in which beliefs play the same role as they do in paradigm explanations of rational action. Self-deceptive intent does involve confusion, but this is a feature of the *content* of the propositional states comprising the sequence, and does not make it a different *kind* of sequence. This shows that self-deception can be explained without introducing anything worth calling psychological *theory*, or any kind of *innovation* of ordinary psychology.

(3) We also saw that phenomenological characterisation is essential for the propositional story of self-deception to go through. This complementarity of phenomenological and propositional characterisation is another general feature of ordinary psychology: phenomenology provides a certificate, and not a surrogate, for the attribution of propositional attitudes. Also, implicit in phenomenological characterisation, I suggested, is the Proustian idea of cohesive groupings of mental states, groupings which are to some degree mutually disintegrated.[30]

(4) It follows from the adequacy of ordinary psychology that the concept of a 'psychological mechanism' – understood as something alien to ordinary psychology – is of little or no relevance to the explanation of self-deception. Suppose scientific psychology offered a mechanistic theory of belief-manipulation. The question would then be, why the operation of such a mechanism should not be thought to *imply* the existence of self-deceptive intent. If postulating the mechanism does have that implication, then the mechanism just provides the contingent realisation of such intent. If, on the other hand, it does not have that implication, it follows that, if analogous

mechanisms operated in the rational case too, then it is – astonishingly – always a mechanism, and never a belief, that puts information to work in the service of rational action! So the upshot of claiming that mechanistic psychology explains self-deception in place of self-deceptive intent would be some sort of general eliminativism about ordinary psychology. Mechanistic explanation can not then have more relevance to self-deception than to anything else done under an intentional description.

(5) The discussion of ordinary irrationality also suggests an argument for realism about ordinary, propositional psychology. We have seen that the phrase, 'propositional explanation of self-deception', is misleading, if it is taken to suggest that self-deception is a non-propositional explanandum and that propositional attitudes are its explanans. If we generalise the case of self-deception, what we find is that propositional concepts *define their own topic*, in the following sense: propositional phenomena do not occur only on the side of explanation; there is in fact no 'side of explanation' to be set over and against a 'side of explananda', conceived in non-propositional terms, or even in propositional terms of reduced complexity. The line of 'explained/explains' does not coincide with that of 'non-propositional/propositional'. This suggests that some sort of direct realism is appropriate to the entities of ordinary psychology. This does not, of course, guarantee the reality of propositional phenomena, but the denial that propositional concepts occur only on a 'side of explanation' nevertheless exempts them, as original phenomena, from having to meet at least some requirements of explanatoriness in order to make their first bid to possession of reality; and it further suggests that assent to their reality might, up to a point, survive their failing to meet such requirements, if this proved to be the case. This cuts in favour of propositional realism to the extent that the arguments against it rely on considerations drawn up on the assumption that ordinary psychology is a form of theoretical explanation.

Strong self-deception is, no doubt, less common statistically than wishful thinking, akrasia and weak self-deception. But it is strong self-deception, more than any other form of irrationality, which invites the strategy of positing a division in the mind of the irrational person, an issue which is crucial for a proper understanding of psychoanalytic theory – Freud's theory of the unconscious having been viewed, it will be seen in 2.5, as pretending to offer a solution to the problem of understanding how a person can lie to himself, i.e. to the problem of strong self-deception. Further, it will be seen in chapter 4 that strong self-deception is what psychoanalytic interpretation would have to be understood as attributing, *if* it were a form of propositional attitude explanation. Also, as the 'most rational' irrationality, strong self-deception demonstrates, dramatically, one irrational possibility of the mind's – located, we will see, at the opposite end of the spectrum from those irrational phenomena to whose explanation psychoanalysis is directed.[31]

1.5 THE SPECIAL PROBLEM OF IRRATIONALITY

I have argued that the configuration of propositional attitudes in self-deception is not mysterious; the elements of self-deception, and their principles of combination, are drawn from familiar materials. I now want to identify the real problem in understanding self-deception.

In explaining self-deception, the motives usually adduced – the painfulness of certain thoughts, of moral conflict, etc. – are ones that also figure in the explanation of rational action. None of them is special to self-deception. A problem emerges when we now reflect that, precisely because of their familiarity, such motives fail to provide a sufficient explanation for what happens: they could equally have resulted in rational outcomes of various kinds, which would have been sufficiently explained by them. What is then left over from ordinary psychology's explanation of self-deception is the fact of irrationality itself: the fact that the subject's mental life takes an *irrational rather than rational* course, that self-deceptive intent is truth-violating. This I will call the Special Problem of irrationality. One does not have to idealise propositional attitudes to recognise this problem.

The Special Problem of irrationality assumes a sense in which an individual who is irrational could have not been so. The sense of 'could have', as it needs to be understood here, is very weak indeed, and does not even involve a denial that irrationality is causally determined. The claim is just that, if we go back far enough, wc will be able to uncover a specification of the prior conditions of irrationality that allow us to discern an alternative rational outcome available to the subject. This can be called the Assumption of Alternatives. It is not, it should be noted, the same as saying that an optimal solution or a solution without loss is always available. The situations that cue self-deception of course tend to make some loss inevitable, but the absence of a rational *solution* in that sense does not show that a rational *response* to the threat of loss was unavailable, and this is all that the Assumption of Alternatives requires.

The Assumption of Alternatives is built into the explanation of ordinary irrationality: unless we could construct specifications of antecedent problems for cases of self-deception – unless we were able to point to problems in rational life that self-deception addresses, and with respect to which it makes itself out to be some sort of solution[32] – we would be unable to identify them *as* cases of self-deception. More generally, if we were unable to indicate where irrationality begins in rational life, the rational and irrational worlds of the individual would begin to come wholly, and incomprehensibly, apart: all irrationality would then slide into madness, and there would be nothing to stand between the absolute obscurity of madness and the absolute lucidity of reason – a view which can not be right.[33]

A further, crucial presupposition of the Special Problem of irrationality should be spelled out. The Special Problem only makes sense if we think that ordinary psychology is bound by its general terms of employment to supply us with full explanations, such that it is obliged to answer questions such as, 'Why does A Ø, irrationally, rather than Ψ, rationally?' There are different views to be taken of the explanatory ambitions of ordinary psychology. On the Complete view, ordinary psychology is committed to there being in principle a full explanation in its own terms, or in terms congenial to it, for the psychological states that it cites as the proximal causes of action. On the Limited view, by contrast, ordinary psychology leaves undecided, and is indifferent to the existence of, explanation beyond a certain distance from its immediate point of application.[34] On the Limited view, there is no Special Problem in explaining irrationality. This enquiry will adopt the Complete view, with its implication that ordinary psychology must recognise the Special Problem of irrationality as a genuine explanandum. One reason for this is that tolerating incompleteness would jeopardise realism about ordinary psychology.[35]

1.6 AKRASIA

In this section I want to make a broad suggestion about the explanation of akrasia, and support the claim that akrasia, as a further form of propositionally transparent irrationality, displays the same relation to ordinary psychology as self-deception.

Akrasia, according to ordinary psychology, consists in failing to do what one knows it to be best to do; what one does instead is something that one desires to do, but believes it to be best not to do. Davidson puts it thus: in akrasia, the cause of my action is a desire which is a reason of a sort, but one that fails to reflect all of the considerations which I consider relevant to my choice of action; it represents only a limited, conditional judgement of my action's value. Akrasia consists in a failure to apply the Principle of Continence – 'act only on the product of all relevant considerations' – to the formation of one's ultimate intention.[36]

Like self-deception, akrasia can be rendered intelligible in terms of propositional attitudes, supplemented with phenomenological characterisation, without resort to psychological theory or innovation. And, again as with self-deception, an obvious further thing to do is to investigate the identity of the cohesive groupings of psychological states to which each of the akrates' divergent intentions belongs, in order to account for their plurality of desires. All this seems pellucid. So what in akrasia remains in need of explanation?

Akrasia differs from self-deception in an obvious and important respect. Self-deception involves doing something to oneself, as akrasia does not; the akrates does not *make* her will be weak. There is no analogue in akrasia of a self-deceptive 'plan' with which to tie up and make intelligible the akrates' divergent intentions: unlike the self-deceiver's buried and promoted beliefs, the akrates' inferior intention, the one on which she acts, is not the instrument of her superior intention. This difference – the 'purposelessness' of akrasia, the fact that the akrates is weak of will *for no reason* – means that something in it must take the place of self-deceptive intent. This is not hard to find. Self-deception is a distinctively *active* form of irrationality, and akrasia a *passive* form; what is then wanted for its explanation is something to play a passive role corresponding to the active role of self-deceptive intent.

Now it should be clear that the cause we are seeking can not be a propositional attitude. Recall that the problem is to find something that can cause a rational being *not* to relate its actions in the rationally required way to its rationally endorsed judgement of what it is best to do. No propositional attitude – an entity defined in terms of rational psychology – can possibly do this. If we attribute a propositional attitude, we commit ourselves to seeking to restore a coherent chain of thought, and this contradicts the very identification of akrasia as action whose antecedents involve a failure of thought. So the explanation of akrasia must lie in a relation between the propositional attitudes which constitute the agent's practical reasoning, and other, *non-propositional* psychological determinants, such that the latter can override the rationally dictated course of the former.

It is beyond doubt that there are in general causes of such a sort. Ordinary psychology includes within its scope numerous phenomena of *involuntariness*: force of habit, surrender to fatigue, illness, sexual attraction, physical appetite, and, most pertinently in the present context, emotional influence, i.e. cases of abandonment to, or being overwhelmed by, emotion. Recognition of such psychological patterns, more primitive than propositional sequences yet capable of affecting their course, is firmly entrenched in ordinary psychological understanding. Involuntariness manifests an underlying constitution, which forms the background to propositional attitudes. It is in this context that akrasia needs to be seen. Akratic action is, of course, not itself involuntary in any sense – it is every bit as intentional as ordinary rational action, hence the difficulty in understanding it – but involuntariness enters into its aetiology at the point where the inferior intention is adopted as the ground for action.[37]

Following Aristotle, the idea can be put in a slightly stronger form, by developing the analogy of akrasia with emotional influence.[38] It is a general truth that emotion is constitutively linked with passivity.[39] Now akrasia, it may be claimed, involves the same kind of involuntary structure as is constitutive of emotion, and whose causal power we experience directly when we experience ourselves as subject to an emotion. The involuntary structures manifested in emotions are the causes of akrasia. This would imply – as seems correct – that only where motivation has the capacity to produce affective phenomena does it also have the capacity to cause akrasia.

Where does this leave us? Three things should be noted. First, this perspective on akrasia differs from many analyses in not seeking to provide it with a propositional decomposition, and it has the implication that such accounts do not provide sufficient explanation. But a propositional analysis of akrasia is not thereby made otiose: for it is still necessary to isolate the akrates' particular point of propositional fracture, and integrate akrasia into the general picture of practical reasoning.[40]

Second, although ordinary psychology can explain the generation of contradictory intentions in akrasia (just as it explains the production and coexistence of contradictory beliefs in self-deception), there remains for it a Special Problem: the failure of application of the Principle of Continence. The notion of an involuntary structure is helpful as far as it goes, but its nature remains unspecified, and to this extent the Special Problem therefore remains unsolved. In 7.4 I will suggest how psychoanalytic explanation may be thought to bear on the Special Problem of akrasia.

The third thing to emphasise is the general character of the strategy used to explain akrasia: namely, that of viewing propositional attitudes as embedded in a structure, a constitution, which is psychological but not propositional, and capable of influencing propositional attitudes in organised ways. Exactly this strategy, we will see, is deployed on a large scale in psychoanalytic explanation.

1.7 BAD FAITH: METAPHYSICAL MOTIVATION AND THE ORIGINS OF IRRATIONALITY

The explanation of irrationality offered by ordinary psychology relies, fundamentally, on such basic notions as mental conflict and the power of desire to malform belief. Psychoanalytic theory exploits, with much greater intensity, the same resources. In this final section I wish to draw attention to – not in order to explore in any depth, but for purposes of contrast – a form of explanation of irrationality which differs fundamentally from both ordinary and psychoanalytic psychology. It is exemplified by Sartre's famous account of bad faith.

Highly schematically, Sartre's concept of bad faith is constructed as follows. We begin with the assumption that there are two modes of being: that of consciousness, for-itself, and that of the physical world, in-itself.[41] Both are possessed by persons. The distinction between for-itself and in-itself cuts across persons, and supplies them with two sets of properties: persons as for-itself are transcendent (they are free, spontaneous, active, engaged with possibility, lack enduring properties), and as in-itself they have facticity (they are also objective, embodied, public, situated, open to characterisation). The basic human motivational story, or 'fundamental project', arises from the necessity of persons' reconciling these two radically different modes of being. This necessity comes about because consciousness, which is for-itself, experiences itself as 'lack(ing)', as an 'insufficiency' of being, relative to in-itself, and is compelled to try to rectify this deficiency. The fundamental human project, undertaken in response to the initial condition of ontological inequality, has as its goal overcoming the disparity of modes of being. Such a resolution is however a metaphysical impossibility, which means that the project is strictly futile, and its manifestations necessarily irrational.[42] Sartre maintains nevertheless that to a limited extent the two modes of being of persons, transcendence and facticity, 'are and ought to be capable of a valid coordination'; bad faith is distinguished by the fact that the individual in bad faith 'does not wish either to coordinate them or to surmount them in a higher synthesis'; contradictorily, they 'affirm facticity as being transcendence and transcendence as being facticity'.[43]

Consider the waiter, in the famous passage from Sartre, who is 'playing *at being* a waiter', and 'plays with his condition in order to *realise* it'; he seeks to 'be immediately a café waiter in the sense that this inkwell *is* an inkwell', to realise 'a being-in-itself of the café waiter'.[44] The properties of his behaviour 'jar' with those of consciousness; consciousness is ill-expressed in his behaviour. The kernel of bad faith consists then in representing oneself in thing-like terms, i.e. representing the relation between oneself and one's states and actions as if it were the same sort of relation as holds between a physical object and its properties. Forms of behaviour manifesting bad faith mimic thinghood because they misexpress one's nature as a conscious being. Bad faith is therefore a structure of motivated self-misrepresentation defined not by a configuration of propositional attitudes, as is strong self-deception, but by a certain species of motive (the fundamental project) and means (the refusal to effect a coordination of modes of being; self-thingification). Its connection with self-deception is consequently contingent: bad faith, as in the case of the waiter, is fundamentally a form of *self-misexpression*, and this need imply only the faintest of propositional inconsistencies, or none at all.

Only the general shape of Sartre's account matters for present purposes. Its differences from ordinary psychology are deep and evident. First, Sartre's is a view of human irrationality as motivated by *metaphysics*, rather than psychology. Put another way: psychology is for Sartre the *vehicle* of metaphysics. Whereas the metaphysical characterisations of persons typically considered in analytical philosophy (such as those of Descartes and Locke) do no more than set the scene for psychology, and leave questions of motivation open, Sartre's wholly determines motivation. It does this because specific motivational axioms follow directly from Sartre's metaphysic of persons. Sartre's vision can therefore soak up, explanatorily, any given instance of human behaviour; particularly, of course, irrational phenomena, since these, involving as they do self-contradiction, stand out as emblems of the contradiction which is constitutive of human existence (and thereby, for Sartre, serve to confirm his metaphysic of persons).[45]

Second, whereas in ordinary psychology the origin of irrationality is located in the *conative* powers of the mind, for Sartre it is located in the mind's *representational* powers: specifically, in persons' representation of themselves. All that is needed for Sartre's account is bare self-consciousness, which implies that even if persons had neither infancy nor biological identity – that is, neither an opaque past nor needs – they would still be irrational.

Third, Sartre's explanation posits *irrational desire*, in the sense of desire whose *content* is irrational, in the form of desire for the metaphysically impossible transformation of for-itself into in-itself. Ordinary psychology, by contrast, assumes for the greater part only desires whose content is roughly rational, and explains irrationality by assigning *deviant causal histories* to such desires.

In the first two respects, psychoanalytic theory is aligned with ordinary psychology: its motivational assumptions do not derive from metaphysical commitments, and it explains irrationality by referring primarily to conation rather than cognition. However, psychoanalytic explanation shares the third feature of Sartreian explanation: at least in its full Kleinian form, psychoanalytic theory posits irrational desires, under the name of phantasies. Chapter 4 will argue that this departure from ordinary psychology is warranted by the distinct grade of irrationality with which psychoanalytic theory is concerned.

Sartre's account of bad faith can be read as exemplifying a general method of metaphysical explanation of irrationality. On such accounts, the origin of irrationality is something like a *contradiction in reality*, in the following sense: irrationality is explained by the incapacity of persons' powers of representation to provide a consistent representation of reality, the inconsistent representation which produces irrational phenomena being germane to, and systematically caused by, the very attempt to represent. On such a view, inconsistent representation is not optional for the mind, but forced upon it: persons are brought viciously into contradiction with themselves and made to be irrational through being made to misrepresent reality. In Sartre's account, the relevant bit of representation-recalcitrant reality is one's own nature as a person.

There is no space to spell this out, but other instances of the same strategy can be found in Hegel (from whom Sartre takes much of his conception of the fundamental project[46]); Nietzsche (at the time of *The birth of tragedy*: the world's own irrationality feeds directly the irrational Dionysian 'art-states' of the human subject[47]); Heidegger (who suggests that, because Being is 'concealed', Dasein is '*especially* subjected to the rule of mystery and the oppression of errancy'[48]); Merleau-Ponty ('there is in human existence a principle of indeterminacy');[49] and, arguably, Lacan.[50] Whatever one may think of such accounts, there is undoubtedly something compelling about the underlying conception of irrationality to which they give expression. It is both a *romantic* and a *tragic* perspective: it suggests that irrationality is so deeply bound up with what it is to be a person that irrationality is a necessary, legitimate way of pursuing one's destiny as a human being.[51]

Metaphysical accounts of motivation have other, more logical attractions: they solve the Special Problem of irrationality; provide determinate explanations of all human desire; and, with their addition, ordinary psychology is guaranteed to be Complete rather than Limited. But, for obvious reasons, unless one accepts in full the metaphysics behind such stories, not much can be taken from them. They can not be joined to other depth explanations of human motivation, such as those of psychoanalysis. This is not because psychoanalytic explanation precludes sources of motivation arising autonomously in consciousness, which it does not, but that metaphysical pictures such as Sartre's are necessarily monolithic – they can not be made to occupy less than all the space of explanation that there is. Which leaves, for non-participants, the prospect of attempting to render metaphysics of motivation such as Sartre's in psychological terms. Whether it is necessary to do this, i.e. postulate a source of explanation of irrationality which draws only on the bare nature of self-consciousness, will depend upon how much – if anything – is judged to be left over from ordinary psychology conjoined with psychoanalytic explanation. This enquiry will suggest that such is not necessary.

CHAPTER 2

Persons in parts

2.1 PARTITION

It is often thought that irrationality shows the mind to be *partitioned*, or divided into parts. This chapter and the next discuss the idea that this description of the irrational person is more than an eliminable metaphor.

This topic deserves detailed treatment, for two reasons. One is that partitive explanation offers itself as a unitary, general solution to the problem of explaining irrationality – a proposal that it is evidently important to evaluate. The other is that psychoanalytic explanation is widely thought – mostly by its critics – to be a form of partitive explanation.[1]

Since the claim that irrationality is associated with partition is conceptual, it predates, and can be made out independently from, the specific claims of psychoanalytic theory. Nevertheless, it is Freud who provides the modern paradigm of such a form of explanation. Sartre's discussion of psychoanalysis in *Being and nothingness* assumes that Freudian explanation is partitive, and he goes on to charge Freud with conceptual confusion. I leave until Part II all questions about the accuracy of Sartre's reading of psychoanalytic theory, in order to discuss on its own terms the model of explanation that Sartre identifies as a target; even if that model does not ultimately provide a correct conceptualisation of Freud's thinking, it has powerful attractions, and deserves to be considered in its own right. Claims made on its behalf by Davidson and Pears are scrutinised in the next chapter.

The final sections of this chapter consider the involvements of cognitive psychology with partitive explanation and psychoanalytic theory.

40

2.2 IRRATIONALITY AND PARTITION: FREUD'S UNCONSCIOUS AS A SECOND MIND

There are two basic, intuitive ways of establishing the connection between irrationality and partition.

The first is made as soon as behaviour is characterised as irrational, and its kind specified: in self-deception, the subject divides into deceiver and deceived; in akrasia, into subjects of higher and lower preferences. The principle of partition consists here in simple relations of inconsistency between propositional attitudes. This provides a first and weak sense of part.[2]

The second connection is established as soon as we follow out a natural train of thought regarding the explanation of irrationality. It is natural to think: If I am irrational, then the cause of my deviation from the norm of rationality must lie – given that I am essentially rational – in some source other than myself;[3] but since this source of my irrationality can not be external to me in any ordinary sense of 'external', it must be 'within' me, but be only some part of me.[4]

The second connection can also be spelled out in another way, which coincides with Freud's argument in his 'Justification for the concept of the unconscious'. In any irrational set of propositional attitudes, there is incompleteness, and completing the set is a matter of identifying the part of the person responsible for his irrationality, a task which is much like trying to work out what another person is thinking. This form of reasoning is argued by Freud to legitimate psychoanalytic theory's postulation of the unconscious:

> The assumption of an unconscious is, moreover, a perfectly legitimate one, inasmuch as in postulating it we are not departing a single step from our customary and generally accepted mode of thinking [...] that other people, too, possess a consciousness is an inference which we draw by analogy from their observable utterances and actions, in order to make this behaviour of theirs intelligible to us [...] Psycho-analysis demands nothing more than that we should apply this process of inference to ourselves also [...] If we do this, we must say: all the acts and manifestations which I notice in myself and do not know how to link up with the rest of my mental life must be judged as if they belonged to someone else: they are to be explained by a mental life ascribed to this other person.[5]

The problem lies of course with what seems to be the unpalatable consequence that we bear within our bodies unmanifest pseudo-persons, essentially like us but lacking, for example, access to a voice:

This process of inference [...] leads logically to the assumption of another, second consciousness which is united in one's self with the consciousness one knows.[6]

Presumably things could, in some sense, have been like that – a second, conscious mind is a logical possibility. The existence of such a mind is in fact canvassed as an empirical theory by Janet,[7] and it has even been alleged that we are pre-theoretically familiar with instances of it in cases of 'multiple personality'.[8] But introducing a Second Mind into all irrational contexts is self-evidently unwelcome, as Freud recognises. Freud therefore says:

we have grounds for modifying our inference about ourselves and saying that what is proved is not the existence of a second consciousness in us, but the existence of psychical acts which lack consciousness.[9]

Freud's concept of the unconscious can, for present purposes, be seen as a compromise, which results from applying the argument for the existence of other minds to the context of irrationality, and modifying its conclusion: a Second Mind is warranted and acceptable so long as it is not a conscious mind. What seems to mark logically Freud's acceptance of a Second Mind in some form is the nominalisation, his talk of *the* unconscious.[10] Although the theory of the Second Mind so far lacks detail, it displays the virtues of simplicity and ready applicability. This interpretation of Freud's concept of the unconscious matches Sartre's understanding of psychoanalysis. It implies that psychoanalytic theory is committed to dividing the person into parts in a very serious sense.[11]

2.3 MEREOLOGY: ASPECTS AND COMPONENTS

It will help to distinguish different senses of part. At one end of the spectrum, there are what may be called *aspects*; at the other, *components*. The idea of an aspect trades off that of a perspective, suggesting that what parts something has depends to some degree on how it is viewed, what experiences there are of it: the contribution of the viewer, and the variable condition of the object, co-determine what features of the object are grasped as aspects of it. Aspects fuse appearances of objects with the real features in which these are grounded. The clearest examples of aspects are perceptual. Aspects are referred to by picking out the object under some description.

At the other end of the spectrum, there are parts which are components, entities that yield the whole of which they are parts as a causal or logical product. They can be referred to without the whole being referred to, and may be able to exist independently from the whole. Examples of components are material parts of machines.

Undoubtedly persons have aspects. If the Second Mind hypothesis is correct, then they also, at least whilst they are irrational, have components.

2.4 SARTRE'S ARGUMENT IN OUTLINE

Sartre does not distinguish the different forms that Freud's theories of the unconscious took. His critique of Freud is stated in such a way as to make the entity which Freud calls the censor mechanism an important part of the theory under attack, whereas this concept had in fact a relatively short life-span in Freud's work. Despite these limiting features, Sartre's argument can be restated so as to have application to partitive theory in general.

By the distinction between the 'id' and the 'ego', Freud has cut the psychic whole into two. I *am* the ego but I *am not* the id. [...] Thus psychoanalysis substitutes for the notion of bad faith, the idea of a lie without a liar; it allows me to understand how it is possible for me to be lied to without lying to myself since it places me in the same relation to myself that the Other is in respect to me; it replaces the duality of the deceiver and the deceived, the essential condition of the lie, by that of the 'id' and the 'ego'. It introduces into my subjectivity the deepest intersubjective structure [...] Can this explanation satisfy us?[12]

In reply to this question Sartre writes:

Psychoanalysis has not gained anything for us since in order to overcome bad faith, it has established between the unconscious and consciousness an autonomous consciousness in bad faith. The effort to establish a veritable duality and even a trinity (*Es, Ich, Überich* expressing themselves through the censor) has resulted in a mere verbal terminology. The very essence of the reflexive idea of hiding something from oneself implies the unity of one and the same psychic mechanism and consequently a double activity in the heart of unity, tending on the one hand to maintain and locate the thing to be concealed and on the other to repress and disguise it [...] By rejecting the conscious unity of the psyche, Freud is obliged to imply everywhere a magic unity linking distant phenomena across obstacles [...] on the one hand the explanation by means of the unconscious, due to the fact that it breaks the psychic unity, cannot account for the facts which at first sight it appeared to explain. And on the other hand, there exists an infinity of types of behaviour in bad faith which explicitly reject this kind of explanation because their essence implies that they can appear only in the translucency of consciousness. We find that the problem [of motivated self-misrepresentation] which we had attempted to resolve is still untouched.[13]

Sartre's argument rests on no special or exaggerated assumptions about personal unity or the necessary minimal degree of mental integration,[14] but instead tries to show that partitive explanation fails on its own terms. Sartre aims to show that any theory that postulates distinct parts in order to explain motivated failures of self-knowledge must logically assume, even if it does not do so explicitly, the existence of an entity with the logical properties of the censor mechanism. These centre on a capacity for rationally manipulating mental contents. Any theory that has to make that assumption, Sartre argues, falls into explanatory vacuity or incoherence. His argument shows this in two stages. Freud's modification of the argument from analogy and description of what it yields as an 'unconscious mind' is first rejected, as a purely nominal change: if the Second Mind is different in no other respect from the conscious mind, it might as well – and indeed must – also be a consciousness. The Second Mind, with consciousness restored to it, is then shown to collapse, once its claims to explanation are conscientiously followed out, into identity with the first mind of the person. The individual's partitioning is thereby undone. Sartre's argument may be viewed as attempting to demonstrate the untenability of Freud's crucial move, in his 'Justification', of forming the concept of the unconscious by subtracting consciousness from mentality.

2.5 UNCONSCIOUS RATIONALITY

Sartre focuses his argument on the phenomena of resistance and repression:

Freud in fact reports resistance when at the end of the first period the doctor is approaching the truth. This resistance is objective behaviour apprehended from without: the patient shows defiance, refuses to speak, gives fantastic accounts of his dreams, sometimes even removes himself completely from the psychoanalytic treatment. It is a fair question to ask *what part of himself* can thus resist [italics added] [...] The only level on which we can locate the refusal of the subject is that of the censor. It alone can comprehend the questions or revelations of the psychoanalyst as approaching more or less near to the real drives which it strives to repress – it alone because it alone *knows* what it is repressing [...] how could the censor discern the impulses needing to be repressed without being conscious of discerning them? [...] These various operations in their turn imply that the censor is conscious (of) itself. But what type of self-consciousness can the censor have? It must be the consciousness (of) being conscious of the drive to be repressed, but precisely *in order not to be conscious of it.* What does this mean if not that the censor is in bad faith?[15]

Let us fit to this some details from an actual case history of Freud's. Freud's case-notes for a patient read: 'Resistance, because I requested him yesterday to bring a photograph of the lady with him – i.e. to give up his reticence about her. Conflict as to whether he should abandon treatment or surrender his secrets.'[16] At a later point in his treatment, the patient is invited by Freud to recount the events that led him to undertake psychoanalysis. As he describes the important and complex fantasy which precipitated his crisis, 'his face showed every sign of resistance'; he identifies a woman in the fantasy, but it is only when Freud reminds him that that he had on an earlier occasion described the fantasy as including not one, but two figures, that he admits to the presence of his father in the fantasy. Here the patient had resisted Freud's efforts to identify unconscious material manifested in the fantasy, by repressing part of its content.

Sartre is right to regard resistance and repression as essential concepts in psychoanalytic theory. Freud writes:

The theory of repression is the corner-stone on which the whole structure of psycho-analysis rests [...] It may thus be said that the theory of psycho-analysis is an attempt to account for two striking and unexpected facts of observation which emerge whenever an attempt is made to trace the symptoms of a neurotic back to their sources in his past life: the facts of transference and of resistance.[17]

And Freud views resistance as a cue for partitive theory:

his resistance was unconscious too, just as unconscious as the repressed [...] We should long ago have asked the question: from *what part of his mind* does an unconscious resistance like this arise? [italics added][18]

Freud describes resistance and repression as distinct but correlative operations; the strength of resistance is a measure of the strength of repression.[19] Furthermore, he suggests that resistance is an action, one which is motivated by, and undertaken with a view to protecting, repression: 'This action ['a permanent expenditure of energy'] undertaken to protect repression is observable in analytic treatment as *resistance.*'[20] The model of explanation proposed by Freud, and targeted by Sartre, looks like this:

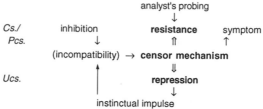

Resistance and repression are thus interlocked so as to form a structure of motivated self-misrepresentation. On Sartre's view, the particular kind of structure exemplified by resistance is self-deceptive. On one view of what goes on in psychoanalysis, this is easily shown. The motive that Freud's patient originally had for not recalling his fantasy was that doing so would border on repeating it, which would have been painful. His further motive, determined by the analytic setting, is that full recall of the fantasy would result in disclosure of his motive for entertaining it. Outside the analytic setting, the object of defence would be simply the desires connected with the fantasy; within analysis, it becomes *knowledge* of those desires. This is shown above all when the patient withholds material that would have served as helpful evidence for psychoanalytic interpretations. Within analysis, the maintenance of self-ignorance requires increasingly complex and differential responses to the analyst's probings; the promoted states become increasingly numerous until their architecture evidences the rationality of self-deceptive intent. If self-knowledge is the patient's goal, and mental operations which impede it are correctly describable as means to avoid it, then Sartre's identification of resistance as a form of self-deception is correct: without awareness of the object of defence under a specific description, the patient would betray herself to the analyst.

Two issues are now sharply in focus. One concerns the object of psychoanalytic interpretation. If Sartre is right, then the immediate clinical datum for psychoanalytic interpretation – its explanandum – is nothing other than self-deception.[21]

The other issue concerns the nature of psychoanalytic theory. If Sartre is right, then the concept of the unconscious is, logically, a hypothesis advanced in order to explain self-deception. The next question to be pursued is then: Can psychoanalytic theory, understood as a Second Mind theory, explain unconscious rationality?

2.6 THE CENSOR CRITICISM

Sartre's detailed argument against psychoanalytic theory – which will be called the Censor Criticism – is compressed into the following passage:

The very essence of the reflexive idea of hiding something from oneself implies the unity of one and the same psychic mechanism and consequently a double activity in the heart of unity, tending on the one hand to maintain and locate the thing to be concealed and on the other to repress and disguise it. Each of the two aspects of this activity is complementary to the other; that is, it implies the other in its being. By separating consciousness from the unconscious by means of the censor, psychoanalysis has not succeeded in dissociating the two phases of the act, since the libido is a blind conatus toward conscious expression and since the conscious phenomenon is a passive, faked result. Psychoanalysis has merely localized this double activity of repulsion and attraction on the level of the censor.

Furthermore the problem still remains of accounting for the unity of the total phenomenon (repression of the drive which disguises itself and 'passes' in symbolic form), to establish comprehensible connections among its different phases. How can the repressed drive 'disguise itself' if it does not include (1) the consciousness of being repressed, (2) the consciousness of having been pushed back because of what it is, (3) a project of disguise? No mechanistic theory of condensation or of transference can explain these modifications by which the drive itself is affected, for the description of the process of disguise implies a veiled appeal to finality [...] By rejecting the conscious unity of the psyche, Freud is obliged to imply everywhere a magic unity linking distant phenomena across obstacles, just as sympathetic magic unites the spellbound person and the wax image fashioned in his likeness. The unconscious drive (*Trieb*) through magic is endowed with the character 'repressed' or 'condemned', which completely pervades it, colours it, and magically provokes its symbolisation. Similarly the conscious phenomenon is entirely coloured by its symbolic meaning although it can not apprehend this meaning by itself in clear consciousness.

Aside from its inferiority in principle, the explanation by magic does not avoid the coexistence – on the level of the unconscious, on that of the censor, and on that of consciousness – of two contradictory, complementary structures which reciprocally imply and destroy each other.[22]

Sartre and Freud concur, then, in asking of the analysand who resists, '*what part of themselves* can thus resist?' Carrying over the action-predicate 'resists' from person to part raises, however, complex issues, and in order not to have to go into these yet, the question may be rewritten in the following, more neutral form: What part of the analysand is in a state, call it R, such that the part's being in state R explains the person's manifesting resistance?

Sartre discusses the various options suggested by psychoanalytic theory concerning the identity of the part and the nature of R.[23]

R can not be a state of the ego, Sartre argues, so long as the ego is 'envisaged as a psychic totality of the facts of consciousness'.[24] The point is that if we take the ego as represented – if only in part – by the states that figure in the person's conscious life, then we can not ascribe to it any states inconsistent with these, without creating a further need for explanation. So R must be consistent with the person's conscious states. No such condition can be met by the ego, Sartre argues. The analysand in his conscious capacity has a desire to discover and eliminate the unconscious cause of his suffering – to the extent that he resists, it must be assumed not just that he encounters difficulty in realising this end, but that he *desires* to frustrate it. (He does not at any rate resist *in order to* discover his unconscious state.) If the ego is both colluding, and refusing to cooperate, with the analyst, then it is itself divided, and further partitive discrimination within the ego is called for.

Put slightly differently, the person aims to share at all times the viewpoint of the analyst, in an attempt to gain information about herself. If the ego resists, then either it is electing to hold back information, or it is being made to do so. But we do not picture the analysand as *lying* to the analyst, and if the ego is *coerced*, then some further entity is required to do the coercing.

Nor can R be a state of the id's, for simpler reasons. The id is characterised by Sartre as 'blind conatus', making it ex hypothesi incapable of rational resistance.[25]

The only remaining candidate considered by Sartre is the censor mechanism.[26] The part responsible for resistance must serve as a *medium of exchange* between other parts, as the id and the ego can not. Call this part C. It must have a greater capacity than any other part of the mind for (i) representing the contents of other mental parts, and (ii) controlling mental events. These conditions must be met for the following reasons. For C to cause resistance, it must represent the unconscious motive alongside the desire to reject it: R involves representing the motive as 'to be repressed'. Furthermore, the maintenance of self-ignorance requires more than just excluding the motive from consciousness: C must operate the mental levers of self-misrepresentation, which involves having a picture of the mind's differentiation into parts, grasping some representations in consciousness as threatening the revelation of the motive, and installing misrepresentations in consciousness as means to the burial of others. So C has a grasp of evidential relations and an *ability to manipulate representations rationally.*[27]

If C's role requires *this* much, then R involves having beliefs and desires, and exercising rational capacities. C is therefore a Second Mind. It is in fact just what Freud's iterated argument from analogy first arrived at, before the modulation to 'unconscious mind'. This means that, as Sartre says, the truly explanatory item in Freud's theory – the real Second Mind – is not *Ucs.*, but the censor.

Sartre's next step is to show that there is no real difference between C and the first mind of the person.

If C is now reconsidered, we see that it amounts to an *approximate reduplication of the entire person*: C *is* the whole person, seen through the lens of partitive redescription. The only differences between C and the whole person are that (i) C knows, as the person does not, of the existence and content of the repressed motive, and (ii) C is sympathetic to the cause of id-expression in a way that the person is not. But these differences are not substantial: postulating C yields an abiding illusion of explanation – it appears to explain 'the person's getting himself not to know of something about himself' – only because C is a redescription of the person *minus* his rejected motive, and *plus* belief about the existence of that same element. The reflexive dimension of the person's resistance is hidden from view when relations that are apparently irreflexive, between parts, and between person and parts, are substituted. Partitive redescription seeks to explain an effect at the level of the person by shifting onto a plane that is supposedly, in some sense, 'less than' that of the whole person. But it introduces as a putatively sub-personal part an entity which stands in the same relations to the other parts as does the person, and thereby reintroduces the level of the person at the level of putatively sub-personal description. It is, therefore, only through the optical-illusory device of partitive redescription that C can be made to *seem* to be only a part: C is, in fact, a reduplication of the person at a putatively sub-personal level.[28]

Another way of assessing the tactic of partition is by considering how it would look in a rational context. Any rational action of a person's could also be partitively 'explained'. I desire to smoke, believe this to be a cigarette, and light it. Partitive explanation says:

there is a part of me that does not have my desire to smoke, but shares all my beliefs, and desires that my desire to smoke be satisfied. It reasons that getting me to light the cigarette will satisfy my desire to smoke, and therefore causes that action. Clearly, this is harmless partitive explanation, which will always 'succeed', because it is not really explanation at all. That minds can always, logically, be redescribed as communities of rational homunculi shows nothing important.[29]

Since partitive explanation of rational action does not catch our interest, why does that of irrational action do so? We must remind ourselves of the intuitions in favour of partition spelled out in 2.2. Suppose that, instead of lighting a cigarette, 'this mouth should tear this hand for lifting food to't' (Lear's image of filial ingratitude). In this case I do something irrational and, apparently, something reflexive. Partitive explanation naturally suggests itself: if we postulate something less than myself, which is me minus my hand, and call this 'part' of me 'this mouth', then we can say that my biting my hand is to be explained by some state and operation of the part, 'this mouth'. The action may then seem to have been made less strange, but its position as regards explanation is formally identical with that of the partitive explanation of my rationally lighting a cigarette: for all that has been said of the 'part', 'this mouth', is that it is me-minus-my-hand! Whatever momentary impression of explanation there is here clearly derives from the substitution of an irreflexive for a reflexive description: the strangeness that attached to the original reflexive description has just been pushed out of sight, through being built definitionally into the identities of the hypothesised parts. Thus the tactic of partition fails to resolve the puzzle of reflexivity which lies at the heart of irrationality.[30]

For partition to explain irrationality, there would have to be an asymmetry with its application to rational action; but no relevant difference suggests itself, and the 'hand/mouth' example implies that the appearance of explanation is illusory. If Sartre's argument is correct, any entity in partitive theory fitting the description of C - such as Freud's censor – embodies an *extra-systemic principle*, and is not a genuine part:[31] C can not be regarded as a logical product or function of the relations between mental parts, since it is precisely their interacting so as to yield a system-transcendent outcome which C is invoked to explain.[32]

The argument has revolved so far around the logical status of C.

Now this somewhat aprioristic objection to partitive explanation would look a lot less impressive, if C were empirically identified and accounted for. And, conversely, if C really does, as alleged, involve a conceptual confusion, there will be no empirical evidence for it.

Cases of multiple personality, such as Hervey Cleckley and Corbett Thigpen's Eve,[33] suggest the kind of empirical grounds there might have been for believing in the existence of C. In Cleckley and Thigpen's case, Eve Black is revealed to have had, without being present to an external observer, access to Eve White's thoughts, and to have conspired against her, sometimes by interfering with her thoughts and intentions. This is of course just the role wanted for a Second Mind. But the reason for believing in the existence of Eve Black is that this entity at some point identified itself to the clinical investigator and exhibited all the properties of a self-conscious subject in charge of a voice. There is no such evidence for Second Minds.[34]

There is, in any case, a positive argument against the possibility of accounting empirically for C. How can C have been brought about, so as to save the person from knowledge of her buried motive?[35] It can not have been generated from the motive itself, nor from its repudiation: mental states alone do not give rise to mental parts. Nor can C have issued from the conjunctive interaction of the motive and its repudiation: two desires are here no better than one; all that we have a right to expect to result from their conjunction is conflict, the existence of which does not, on its own, suffice to generate a device for its solution.

We do not, however, want to say that the person *himself* is causally responsible for the existence of C; although this seems to be the only remaining option. If we allow that the person *creates* C, then this is an action of his, explained by a reason: he views C as a means to solving his conflict. Parts then come out as instruments of self-deception: self-deception consists in *literal* mental self-division, whereby the person hands down the job of burial and promotion to an intentionally created part of himself. This circuitous story does succeed in explaining how motivation can be transmitted downwards, from person to part, but at the cost of making parts redundant: the story at the level of the person does all the work, and the postulation of C merely detours self-deceptive intent through speculative sub-personal channels. Our understanding of how self-deceptive intentions are executed is not aided by supposing that there is an action of literal self-division.

It seems that no causal story can account satisfactorily for C's existence. Stories which begin at the level of the person return us to a non-partitive form of explanation in terms of self-deception. The genesis of C therefore needs to be located at the sub-personal level, in such a way that the causation is 'bottom-up', rather than intentionally initiated and 'top-down'. But we do not know of any story at the sub-personal level which avoids generating a regress of demands for explanation. (It will be argued later that there is no reason to think that cognitive psychology is in a position to supply the missing piece.)

To recapitulate, there are two ways – which are complementary, and can be pressed simultaneously – in which the Censor Criticism can be formulated. (i) As a charge of *contradiction* or *logical confusion*: the partitive form of explanation is obliged to view the mental parts that it postulates as both separate and conjoined, in a mind that is both integrated and disintegrated. The Second Mind model must suppose both that the relevant mental parts are wholly discrete, and coordinated in the way ordinarily supposed for a single mind. This means describing the person as having both many minds and a single mind. Equally, partitive explanation must view the key mental part that it postulates as simultaneously personal and sub-personal. (ii) As a charge of *triviality* or *redundancy*: the partitive form of explanation is non-explanatory in the rational case, and there is no asymmetry between its application there and to the irrational case.

2.7 PARTITION: THE ARGUMENT SO FAR

Sartre's argument against the censor has been unpacked and presented in as strong a form as possible. Although the burden of proof has been located firmly on the side of the proponent of partitive explanation, so far nothing has been settled definitively: the argument has identified mistakes that partitive explanation *could* be in the business of making, but it has not been shown that each instance of such explanation *must* make them. We have as yet only a systematic statement of the view that partitive explanation is contradictory or trivial, not a proof of it.

Chapter 3 will carry the argument against partition to a firmer conclusion. In the rest of this chapter I will consider how cognitive psychology bears on the question of partition and, more generally, the problem of irrationality.

2.8 COGNITIVE PSYCHOLOGY

Cognitive psychology postulates mental parts liberally. Sometimes this is only implicit, as in talk of 'information processing', where reference to the processor itself is elided, but mostly the commitment is blatant. For example, in analysing word-recall, scanners of word-lists are hypothesised; in perception, a homunculoid device composed of receptors and emitters negotiates environmental input and motor output; a series of 'boxes' registers and responds to bodily events involving pain; a 'speech-centre' governs current verbal behaviour; and a 'semantic intent' surveyor registers what operations underlie what one means to do next.[36] These bits and pieces seem on first glance to correspond to parts of the person that respectively remember names, perceive objects, feel pain, talk, and introspect.

Cognitive psychology thus seems to be a theory of second, third and nth minds. Sub-personal entities are postulated to account for each state or capacity of the person's: for any state S, there is an 'S-producer', and for any capacity to Ø, there is a 'Ø-er'.

Such a system of modules would on the face of it seem to be vulnerable in the same way as Freud's censor. Indeed, Fodor records Locke's objection to faculty psychology, a precursor of Sartre's Censor Criticism: 'we may as properly say that the singing faculty sings, and the dancing faculty dances, as that the will chooses, or that the understanding conceives'.[37] Does cognitive psychology postulate faculties *trivially*? If not, how does it escape Locke's charge?

What saves cognitive-psychological theory from paradox or triviality is its reducibility. Fodor says that it is an error to suppose that 'the understanding' conceives: it is the *organism* which conceives, and it does so *by virtue of* the operations of its faculty of under-standing.[38] These operations are specified in terms that do not simply recapitulate the activity of the person receiving explanation, and are analysed in terms that reduce all the way down, to a level that does not presuppose intelligence. Fodor gives as an example the ability to tie one's shoes, which is explained by 'a little man who lives in one's head. The little man keeps a library. When one acts on the intention to tie one's shoes, the little man takes down a volume entitled *Tying One's Shoes*.'[39] This homunculus contains a list of instructions for tying shoes, but psychological theory will proceed by replacing the little man with 'less global' little men, to each of whom less intelligent predicates are applicable than to their predecessor, until an end is reached by postulating 'elementary' units about which psychological 'how' questions do not arise.[40] These terminal 'operations' are nothing but neural firings, which are not in any sense homunculoid.[41]

2.9 THE CHARGE OF ANTHROPOMORPHISM

This is the proper point at which to mention – in order to set aside – an objection to the enterprise of giving the mind decompositional descriptions of any kind. The objection, which concerns both psychoanalytic theory and cognitive psychology, is that such descriptions are necessarily *anthropomorphic*. Anthropomorphic theories are either meaningless or false.[42]

Irving Thalberg, discussing Freudian theory, complains that to describe 'egos, neurones and machines' as repressing, retrieving, devising and so on turns the entity in question into a 'counterpart of a human agent'. Since a range of questions that would have been meaningful in the case of whole persons do not remain so with respect to their counterparts ('do computers play chess for the prize money or renown? are they sore losers?'), we do not know 'what the verbs and adverbs do or could mean' in their new usage. Thus 'animistic stories of our mental life are incoherent'.[43]

This objection is obviously close in spirit to Sartre's Censor Criticism. But it is pitched at a more basic, semantic level, and does not hang on the intricacies of partitive explanation. Effectively, the objection says that any term that *can* be employed as a psychological predicate of whole persons can be employed *only* in this way, guaranteeing that every time a predicate is carried from a person to a person-part, an anthropomorphic statement results. But this principle seems plainly false. First, ordinary psychology talks non-theoretically of thoughts, emotions and desires – rather than persons – as forceful, persuasive and so on, in ways that are perfectly intelligible. Second, the predicates applied to Fodor's shoe-lace-tier are theoretical terms, and the difference in their employment here from that which they enjoy with respect to whole persons, is accounted for in terms of the theory in which they have their place: the non-applicability of 'further questions' that Thalberg observes is an upshot of the programme of progressively analysing out the intelligence of homunculi.

The charge of anthropomorphism therefore rests on a false view of meaning as rigidly circumscribed by paradigm cases or primary contexts of usage. This arbitrarily debars words from having uses which are genuine and literal although not primary.[44]

2.10 PERSONAL AND SUB-PERSONAL PSYCHOLOGY

Cognitive-psychological speculation does not founder on semantic considerations. But it does lead to a difficult metaphysical issue. Fodor says that propositional attitudes and cognitive-psychological states are *identical*.[45] Thomas Nagel describes the question which this raises:

How much of all that a man's body and mind do, can *he* be said to do? [...] At some point it will be clear to everyone that by traveling deep enough inside the person we have lost him, and are dealing not with the means by which he ties his shoes, but with the physiological and mental substructure of his actions. If there is a line between a person and the rest of that elaborately organized organic system in which his life proceeds, where does the line fall, and what kind of line is it?[46]

Nagel's argument is that Fodor's position is incoherent because, for him, statements which imply 'a line between a person and the rest of that elaborately organised organic system' are ultimately reducible to others in which this distinction is lost. Identifying something *as* an intentional doing (a tying-of-shoes rather than an organic change) is the indispensable starting point of empirical psychology, and this identification is effectively, and inconsistently, revoked, if the notion of agency becomes so extended in the theory that seeks to explain doings that the fundamental condition underlying their identification – the distinction of an 'inner boundary of the self' – is obliterated.[47]

What Fodor says about agency is this:

There is, obviously, a horribly difficult problem about what determines what a person (as distinct from his body, or parts of his body) did. Many philosophers care terrifically about drawing this distinction, and so they should: It can be crucial in such contexts as the assessment of legal and moral responsibility. It can also be crucial where the goal is phenomenology [...] But whatever relevance the distinction [...] may have for *some* purposes, there is no particular reason to suppose that it is relevant to the purposes of cognitive psychology [...] What *is* implied (and all that is implied) is just that the distinction between actions and happenings isn't a *psychological* distinction. Lots of very fine distinctions, after all, are not.[48]

What should be made of the disagreement between Nagel and Fodor? On the one hand, Nagel does not *prove* the irreducibility of ordinary psychology, since cognitive psychology *might* identify a sub-personal property exactly matching, and (perhaps) appropriately elucidating, attributions of agency. Ordinary and cognitive psychology would then form some sort of partnership. So Fodor's position is not necessarily self-defeating in the way that Nagel implies.

On the other hand, it is by no means clear that Fodor's statement is adequate. Fodor *appears* to rely on the ('special sciences') tactic of relativising predicates to different levels of enquiry and generalisation, as a way of safeguarding the reality of the properties in question.[49] But that is not in fact what is happening here: law and morality are normative contexts, not special sciences, and phenomenology, as Fodor understands it,[50] is not a science of the mind. From which it follows plainly that a distinction expressed only in such contexts, and not in psychology, will lack reality. This supports Nagel's claim that Fodor is 'out to scrap the concept of a person', as a 'dying notion not likely to survive the advances of scientific psychology'.[51] Something is needed to show that, in this context, indifference does not amount to elimination,[52] and this Fodor does not provide. If cognitive psychology does pose the threat to ordinary psychology which Nagel describes, and ordinary psychology is not to be eliminated (or, at least, realism abandoned for it), then the only remaining option is to weaken suitably the philosophical claims made for cognitive psychology.[53]

The whole question of ordinary and cognitive psychology is obviously enormously complex, and there is no space to pursue it here. The point of discussing it is not to take a stand on the reducibility of ordinary psychology, which is unnecessary for the purposes of this enquiry. It is to indicate the warrant for adopting a firm distinction between personal and sub-personal psychologies: personal psychology is constituted by, amongst other things, the concept of agency, which has essentially a phenomenological dimension. This concept does not figure in cognitive psychology, which is consequently sub-personal rather than personal.

The exact nature of the personal/sub-personal distinction is again too large a question to be dealt with properly here. The following points may nevertheless be made. We want to say that the mental states ascribed by a personal psychology are *owned* by the person, as sub-personal psychological states are not. Some sort of criterion for ownership is however needed. Consciousness seems to provide the natural criterion: a mental state is personal if it is of a kind which can be consciously self-ascribed. This, however, would exclude the unconscious mental states attributed by psychoanalytic theory, which, it will be argued in 7.6, is a form of personal psychology.

A less restrictive, more liberal way of handling the personal/sub-personal distinction is the following. Personal states are constitutive of personhood, in two senses: they allow themselves to be thought of as 'mine'; and they enable their subject to think of themselves as a person.[54] Sub-personal states are those whose self-ascription is not required for, and does not make possible, grasping oneself as a person. Sub-personal postulations contribute instead to the causal explanation of persons' propositional attitudes, and other psychological features. Cognitive-psychological parts explain these features, but are not themselves subjects of propositional attitudes, or other properly personal psychological features. Because the content-involving predicates applied to cognitive-psychological parts are neologised theoretical terms, these parts are not Second Minds. The territory that these parts occupy may be named the *properly sub-personal*. Properly sub-personal psychological theories are, in essence, distinguished by their *not* asserting a relation of ownership between persons and what they postulate. So if parts are properly sub-personal, they are logically disqualified from competing with persons for the authorship of conception or agency. Defining sub-personal psychology in this way removes cognitive psychology from the scope of the Censor Criticism, which has application only to theories at the personal level.

2.11 COGNITIVE PSYCHOLOGY AND IRRATIONALITY

What bearing does cognitive psychology have on the explanation of irrationality?

First, it should be noted that the reasons, given in 1.4, for denying that mechanisms could have special pertinence to the explanation of irrationality, carry over to cognitive psychology. Another point to be made – with reference back to the Censor Criticism – is that even a universally accepted scientific theory of mental parts could not give us reason for believing in the existence of C. Any mental part that cognitive psychology comes up with will be defined in terms of either a general mental capacity, or a *type* of propositional attitude. C, by contrast, is invoked with reference to *token* configurations of propositional attitudes, and without reference to anything that counts as a general capacity (irrational phenomena do not imply, and need not be accompanied by, general failures of competence). There is in fact positive reason for expecting cognitive-psychological parts *not* to converge with C-parts: whereas cognitive psychology is concerned with successful, i.e. rational, mental functioning, C is connected uniquely with irrational mental functioning. Furthermore, C is bound up with complex, high-level propositional attitudes, and Fodor concedes that these are unlikely to yield much to cognitive-psychological analysis.[55]

It is then probable that cognitive psychology will leave a lacuna with regard to irrationality. Of course, it *may* turn out that cognitive psychology suggests good explanations for irrationality. But we have as yet no clear grasp of what form these could take. It would, for example, be absurd to suppose that cognitive psychology will simply identify an 'irrationalising' module. In any case, no philosophical account of irrationality should allow itself to rest on a half-promise pinned on a future psychology; and there is a legitimate interest in exploring personal psychology on its own terms.

For these reasons, and others that will emerge later, I will take it that the general position of psychoanalytic theory *vis-à-vis* cognitive psychology, and any other form of properly sub-personal psychology, is no different from that of ordinary psychology. This means, first, declining the invitation to view psychoanalytic theory as proto-cognitive psychology.[56] Second, it means not pushing specific hypotheses pretending to integrate cognitive psychology with psycho-analytic explanation. These could only avoid appearing hopelessly ad hoc against the background of a general theory telling us how the claims of personal and sub-personal psychologies are linked; which we do not have, as yet. So it will be assumed that psychoanalytic theory and cognitive psychology are independent: neither hinders nor advances the other's development and application.[57] For similar reasons, this enquiry does not give a role to cognitive dissonance theory.[58]

It is worth noting that, even with cognitive psychology shelved in this way, the enquiry that follows still holds some interest for those who are committed to viewing it as the only significant form of psychological explanation: if the project of explaining irrationality at the personal level fails, to a greater or lesser extent, this will show that the explanation of irrationality *must*, to that extent, be supplied by cognitive or some other form of sub-personal psychology. That would be an important result.

CHAPTER 3

Persons and sub-systems

But man is so partial to systems and abstract deduction that in order to justify his logic he is often prepared to distort the truth intentionally.

Dostoyevsky

3.1 THE THEORY: DAVIDSON

This chapter continues the discussion of persons and their parts, in the form of Davidson and Pears' theory of sub-systems. What has to be determined is whether or not sub-systemic theory, which is founded on and elaborates the two intuitions for partition presented in 2.2, provides a successful form of explanation of irrationality.

Davidson says that cases of irrationality 'may be characterised by the fact that there is a mental cause that is not a reason' for the mental state that it causes.[1] The appropriate move to make when confronted with such a cause is to 'partition the mind' in such a way that the 'breakdown of reason-relations defines the boundary of a subdivision'. Parts emerge, through conceptual analysis, from the definition of irrationality as intentional behaviour that runs contrary to reason: they are 'defined in terms of function; ultimately, in terms of the concepts of reason and of cause'.[2]

Mental parts have three essential features:

First, the mind contains a number of semi-independent structures, these structures being characterized by mental attributes like thoughts, desires, and memories.

Second, parts of the mind are in important respects like people, not only in having (or consisting of) beliefs, wants and other psychological traits, but in that these factors can combine, as in intentional action, to cause further events in the mind and outside it.

Third, some of the dispositions, attitudes, and events that characterize the various substructures in the mind must be viewed on the model of physical

59

dispositions and forces when they affect, or are affected by, other substructures in the mind.[3]

Like Sartre, Davidson takes psychoanalytic theory to depend fundamentally on partition.

The second feature of Davidson's sub-systems – resemblance to a Second Mind – is to be noted in particular.[4] Davidson says that the elements within sub-systems may combine with one another 'as in intentional action' to cause further events in the mind; a sub-system is 'a structure similar to that needed to explain ordinary actions',[5] an 'agency' which is 'relatively autonomous'. But a suggestion of full mental agency is explicitly denied by Davidson: 'the analogy does not have to be carried so far as to demand that we speak of parts of the mind as independent agents'.[6] This leaves an ambiguity – or at least, raises an issue – that will become very important later.

3.2 SUB-SYSTEMS AS CHARACTERISED COMPARTMENTS

Davidson's presentation of his theory is austere, and I mean now to extend his remarks in what seem to be appropriate directions.

In a simple case of akrasia – having adhered all day to a strict dietary regime, at midnight I go downstairs and eat chocolate – an obvious first point of entry for sub-systemic theory is provided by relations of inconsistency between propositional attitudes: one sub-system contains a desire to eat, another a desire to lose weight. The sub-systems are defined by the exclusivity of the desires' conditions of satisfaction. Similarly in self-deception: one sub-system contains the buried belief, another the promoted belief; the line between them reflects the impossibility of both beliefs' being true.

If inconsistency were however sufficient for sub-systems, they would also exist in cases of straightforward conflict of desire and unwitting incompatibility of belief. To reserve sub-systems for irrational contexts, a further condition must be added: as Davidson put it, there must be a mental cause that is not a reason for its effect. Sub-systems are then postulated liberally – since nothing more than simple akrasia is required for them – but not gratuitously.

The concept of a sub-system, which is so far quite minimal, comes from conjoining the conditions of inconsistency and non-rational causation. The problem is that this association is, so far, completely arbitrary: no reason has yet been given for talking of sub-systems *only* in cases of irrationality, rather than either not at all, or in every case of propositional inconsistency. Put another way, sub-systemic language is so far only weakly redescriptive, in a sense which falls short of being explanatory. This state of play is closely connected with the fact that, so far, belonging to a sub-system is just a bare relation of *set membership*.

If sub-systems are to be explanatory, they need to play a role in the *causation* of irrationality, rather than just recapitulate the fact of its existence: the inconsistencies which sub-systems reflect must also be ones which are due to the existence of sub-systems. This means that, in the case of akrasia, the akrates' sub-systems must causally explain the inconsistency between their intention to diet and their intention to eat. Sub-systems can do this if they are conceived in richer terms. So let us fill out the description of the akrates' sub-systems by supposing that one of them contains a lot of information about diet and health, an image of an attractively slim physique etc., and the other an assailing desire for chocolate, a thought about the importance of occasional self-indulgence, and so on. The akrates' inconsistent intentions coexist in the person, despite their inconsistency, because each is generated by a different sub-system.[7] Our grasp of sub-systems is now significantly extended: they are coherent groupings of propositional attitudes and *real unities*, belonging to which is more than a matter of set membership.[8]

It can now be seen that the problem originally facing sub-systems was none other than the ancient, and entirely general problem of analyticity in action explanation: the link between effect (inconsistent intentions) and cause (sub-systems) was analytic on account of the original means of individuation of sub-systems. The problem has been solved, here as it is in general, by individuating sub-systems in terms of other mental states that are logically remote from the effect to be explained, making the link non-logical and potentially explanatory.[9]

The explanatory value of sub-systems depends on, first, the relations of *cohesion* between members of each sub-system, the centripetal force exerted by the internal agreement of a set of propositional attitudes; and, second, the relations of non-integration or, as I will call it, the *mental distance* between members of different sub-systems. For Davidson, this is primarily an effect of policy in interpretation: rather than attribute one all-inclusive but unstable set of propositional attitudes, we prefer to attribute multiple stable sets. But there is another, more immediately realistic way of understanding the explanatoriness of cohesion and mental distance: it is explanatory to construct taxonomies of a person's propositional attitudes because kindred propositional attitudes causally reinforce one another – the mutual coherence of beliefs causes them to be more deeply entrenched and thus more causally effective.[10]

It should be noted that the concepts of internal cohesion and mental distance are equally primitive, and conceptually connected. Internal cohesion necessarily contributes to mental distance: if mental item A coheres with B but not C, and B is inconsistent or conflicts with C, then there will be a tendency for A not to integrate with C. And mental distance in turn implies the existence of internally cohesive structures, for holistic reasons: if an isolated mental item fails to integrate with the bulk of the mind, this must be because it derives support from other mental items, whose magnetism helps to draw it apart (in other terms, there are no atomic unintegrated elements).

There is a natural way of extending this perspective on sub-systems, which is consonant with the usual ways of deepening action explanation. This is to *characterise* sub-systems: to provide them with non-propositional mental attributes, after the manner in which agents are assigned character traits. This involves regarding groupings of propositional attitudes as more than just sources for the derivation of syllogisms in practical reasoning. In the ordinary explanation of rational action, we refer to persons' changing frames of mind, the relativity of their beliefs and desires to circumstance (introducing a lot of tacit role psychology), their competences, moods and humours, and of how these vary with time and topic; we single out styles and patterns, and not just propositional objects, of beliefs. This miscellany of factors in the background to a person's propositional attitudes can be carried over to sub-systems. This goes some of the way towards providing what Davidson has in mind by the third of his features, the attribution of physical-like dispositions to sub-systems.

Sub-systems may now be described as *rational goal-structures*.[11] In characterising a sub-system motivationally, as libidinal, or achievement-orientated, or bourgeois, we assign to it a 'goal', specified in very general terms, and thereby set up expectations about the person's behaviour, through the assumption that the sub-system will aim at realising that goal. Describing persons' characters, and interpreting them sub-systemically, therefore go together naturally, since anything of sufficient psychological complexity to be recognisable as a person will not be characterisable in terms of a single goal, and characterising them in terms of multiple goals immediately makes room for sub-systems.[12] The case for the explanatory value of sub-systems, identified as rational goal-structures, is then just as good as the case for propositional attitude explanation conjoined with character-trait attribution in general, such that an attack on the former would involve an attack on the latter.

It should be emphasised that rational goal-structures are not merely abstract entities. They are aspectual parts of persons, and have experiential realisations. Their experiential realisations are Proust's 'selves', whose phenomenological sets provide persons with perspectives on their aspects, the perspective which they afford being that of the aspect raised to consciousness. A phenomenological set provides a person with an experiential point of view on themselves, qua one of their aspects.[13]

The following, *compartmental thesis*, assembles all that has been said so far:

the mind has aspectual parts, which are internally cohesive sets of propositional attitudes, structured by non-propositional mental characteristics, which can be thought of as rational goal-structures, and are realised in phenomenological sets.

These sub-systems, which I shall call *characterised compartments*, provide a firm sense in which persons have aspects.

The compartmental thesis, it should be observed, uses the first and third of Davidson's features, but not the second, 'likeness to people', for which no use has been found so far. It would consequently be wrong to think that the picture of the mind obtained by supplementing ordinary psychology with characterised compartments is en route to the Second Mind model. It is, metaphysically, firmly on the side of the ordinary single mind.

It is important to note that conceiving sub-systems as characterised compartments largely undoes Davidson's specific connection of them with irrationality: characterised compartments are brought to bear on cases of irrationality just as they are in any other context of psychological explanation. So, for example, characterised compartments might contribute to the explanation of Anna Karenina's self-deception in this sort of way: her conjugal aspect recognises the danger of her attraction to Vronsky, her libidinal aspect endorses the attraction, and her self-deceptive burial and promotion of belief issues from the conjunction of these two aspects. The boundaries of sub-systems conceived as characterised compartments are no longer *defined* by the breakdown of reason-relations, although such breakdowns will indeed align with distinctions between different characterised compartments. Characterised compartments are as well connected to, and widely present in, the explanation of rational as of irrational action. To insist on a condition of irrational causation would be an improper restriction on their reality, given that, as it has been seen, sub-systems' claims to explanation require precisely that they pre-exist the occurrence of irrationality. Severing any exclusive connection between irrationality and sub-systems is the price paid for making them explanatory.

This point has an important consequence. If sub-systems are logically independent of irrationality, they can not help with the Special Problem of irrationality. Any attempt to exploit sub-systems to that end would mean regressing to a weakly redescriptive conception of sub-systems and re-encounter the problem of analyticity. The measure employed to rescue sub-systemic explanation from analyticity – transforming them into characterised compartments – debars them from solving the Special Problem of irrationality.

Pears' sub-systemic theory advances the discussion in two ways: it brings the second of Davidson's features into focus, and it seeks to address the Special Problem of irrationality.

3.3 THE THEORY: PEARS

Pears accepts as axiomatic Davidson's formula that 'the breakdown of reason-relations defines the boundary of a subdivision', but, unlike Davidson, he views the introduction of sub-systems as an 'apparently drastic hypothesis', and thinks that the explanatory credentials of sub-systems are not easy to secure.

Pears postulates sub-systems only when there is a piece of irrationality that 'the person is competent to avoid'.[14] This makes his position less liberal than Davidson's, since not all failures of reason-relation will be avoidable. Pears' sub-systems will nevertheless, like Davidson's, apply to both self-deception and akrasia.[15] Sub-systems come in for Pears when (i) one mental state causes another in a way that violates a rational constraint, (ii) the subject has the capacity to prevent or to correct the causation, which presupposes that (iii) the person has a belief to the effect that the causation violates a rational constraint. Pears calls the item in this last condition a *cautionary belief*. The fault that Pears wishes to isolate and treat with the theory of sub-systems is more finely specified than Davidson's target: it is not so much the fact that a mental state deviates from its ideal rational course, as that nothing is done to correct its aberration.[16]

Emphasis on the cautionary belief is bound up with a distinction that Pears makes, between the permissive and productive causes of irrationality. To cite the *productive* cause of malformation of belief is to identify what Davidson calls the cause that is not a reason for what it causes. Where the irrationality is motivated, this will be a desire.[17] To cite the *permissive* cause is to 'identify the thing that allows irrationality to occur'.[18]

Pears sees Freudian theory as 'primarily concerned with the permissive cause of irrationality',[19] in the form of unconsciousness, and says that what we need instead is a theory of the productive cause. This is provided by a theory of sub-systems defined by a 'functional' criterion, which assigns propositional attitudes to sub-systems on the basis of their causal role. Pears says that there can be two understandings of what constitutes a 'breakdown of reason-relations', to each of which there corresponds a different criterion for sub-systemic membership. By the *positive* criterion, mental states will be assigned to a sub-system if they intervene irrationally; by the *negative* criterion, they will be assigned to a sub-system if they fail to intervene rationally.[20] Pears favours the negative criterion. If we now recall that irrationality consists, for Pears, in the inertness of the cautionary belief, we find that the first role for a Pearsian sub-system will be to contain the cautionary belief.[21]

3.4 SUB-SYSTEMS AS RATIONAL CENTRES OF AGENCY

Pears does not give an extended example showing the application of sub-systemic theory, but we can project how his theory would model a case such as Anna Karenina's.[22]

To postulate a sub-system in a person's mind is, to start with, for Pears, to hive off selected propositional attitudes from the bulk that constitute what he refers to as the 'main system'. Pears says that it is usually not the existence of a desire, but its operation, that is screened from the main system. So we should allow that Anna Karenina's desire for Vronsky is, in most respects, a member of the main system. What the main system misses is Anna Karenina's recognition that her desire for Vronsky has malformed her beliefs. This, her cautionary belief, is entered – by Pears' negative criterion – into the sub-system.

At this point Pears' doubts emerge. The problem is that 'the thesis, that no degree of avoidable irrationality is possible without a schism, will be true by definition of the word "schism"'.[23] Unlike Freudian theory, which uses consciousness as an independent criterion for drawing the line between main and sub-system, the functional theory only makes reference to facts of interaction and non-interaction.[24] It follows, Pears thinks, that the language of mental partition is so far only metaphorical: 'the separateness of the two systems is really only another piece of theatre',[25] 'it is just a technical way of restating the facts to be explained'.[26]

This contradicts the view we arrived at in the previous section, according to which facts of cohesion and (non-)integration are primitive and explanatory. For Pears, by contrast, at all points where mental distance enters into psychological explanation, there must be an accompanying explanation for how this distance is maintained; which is as much as to say that mental distance itself drops out of the story.

Pears reaches his conclusions for the simple reason that the only kind of separateness he considers is that of persons. From the correct observation that we lack what is needed to make a good analogy hold between separate persons and separate sub-systems – namely an independent means of identification of sub-systems, to correspond to the bodily individuation of persons – Pears infers that the first of Davidson's features, which we expressed in the thesis of compartmentalisation, must, if it is to be worth anything, depend wholly for its explanatory value upon Davidson's second feature, the likeness of mental parts to people. In this way, Pears thinks, sub-systemic theory can be repaired. Pears therefore makes a fundamental change to the basis of sub-systemic explanation, by exploiting the analogy of sub-systems with persons by considering persons as *rational agents*:

There is only one possible remaining source of the explanatory power of the functional theory and that is in the sub-system itself. The sub-system is built around the nucleus of the wish for the irrational belief and it is organized like a person. Although it is a separate centre of agency within the whole person, it is, from its own point of view, entirely rational.[27]

The full consequences of this crucial move will unfold under investigation. Its importance is testified by the fact that Pears affirms explicitly what Davidson denies: granting or withholding the further description of sub-systems as 'rational centres of agency' is not therefore a minor issue, and whatever they may be, rational centres of agency are not just what have been called rational goal-structures or characterised compartments.

Pears' reconception of sub-systems as rational agents brings in its wake further psychological attributions to them. Sub-systems can not merely subsist as characterised compartments for Pears, since for him it means nothing to say that Anna Karenina's cautionary belief is 'sub-systemically separated' from her promoted beliefs, unless this state of affairs is pictured as an effect of the sub-system's identity as a rational agent. This means that the inertness of the cautionary belief must be viewed as an effect of the sub-system's having a *reason for action*. A 'wish for the irrational belief', causing the inertness of the cautionary belief, is consequently introduced into the sub-system, to provide the desire-component of its reason for action.[28]

In conclusion, Pears can be seen as having taken the second of Davidson's features and refined it into the following thesis:[29]

the mind is divided into parts, which are numerically distinct centres of rational agency, each of which has its own reasons for action, in which respect they are related to one another in the way that different persons, considered as rational agents, are.

This thesis posits mental parts which are components rather than aspects of persons. Since they, unlike characterised compartments, are posited only in cases of irrationality, they may be claimed to provide, as characterised compartments do not, some sort of solution to the Special Problem of irrationality. Pears' strong reconception of sub-systems dissociates them, however, from the modes of ordinary psychological explanation with which the conception of sub-systems as characterised compartments is in harmony, and this, I will argue later, is its weakness.

Pears' sub-systems are Second Minds, and Sartre's Censor Criticism therefore applies to them. Before returning to the question, which was left unresolved, of its accuracy, I want to consider in more depth the conception of sub-systems as rational centres of agency.

3.5 SUB-SYSTEMS EXAMINED: THE LANGUAGE OF SUB-SYSTEMS

Sub-systems are hard to keep in focus. At one moment the language of sub-systems seems obviously appropriate, at another, an extraordinary metaphor. Which indicates that we do not know well what is being said in that language.

Having distinguished two very different logical conceptions of sub-systems, a fresh reconstruction of the overall claims of sub-systemic explanation, with a view to separating out obvious truths from extreme claims, may be undertaken.

Let us begin by comparing two, corresponding pairs of statements:

(P_1) Anna Karenina refused to recognise her feelings for Vronsky;

(P_2) Anna Karenina told herself that she was averse to Vronsky.

(S_1) Anna Karenina's sub-system prevented the formation in her main system of a belief about her attraction to Vronsky;

(S_2) Anna Karenina's sub-system produced in her main system the belief that she was averse to Vronsky.

The first pair, the P-statements, are personal – they are clearly about, and at the level of, the person – and the second pair, the S-statements, are sub-systemic, seemingly about, and at the level of, something 'less than' the whole person. What relations hold between the two kinds of statement?

It is clear that the relation of sub-systemic theory to personal psychology can not be the same as that of cognitive psychology, because sub-systems, unlike the modules of cognitive psychology, are logical subjects of propositional attitudes. So the first observation to be made is that sub-systemic theory is not properly sub-personal.

Since the compatibility of P- and S-statements is not guaranteed by the latter's being properly sub-personal, it may be that they are incompatible. Then, whenever an S-statement is true, its P-statement counterpart is false. This is Sartre's view of psychoanalytic explanation: psychoanalytic statements are S-statements which falsify their P-counterparts. Sartre thinks this because the explicit irreflexivity of S-statements (main system $\neq$ sub-system) is,[30] for Sartre, inconsistent with the implicit reflexivity of P-statements.

This, however, is certainly not how Davidson and Pears wish sub-systems to be understood. Their view is instead that corresponding P-

and S-statements may both be true: sub-systemic analyses are meant to agree, and not conflict with, statements about the person as deceiving themselves.[31] Let us proceed on the assumption that this is so: the truth of an irreflexive S-statement does not falsify its reflexive P-counterpart.

Which of P- and S-statements *explains* (or provides for the truth of) the other? Obviously, S-statements are meant to explain P-statements. This means that the relation between P- and S-statements can not just be one of 'mutual illumination': if S-statements do not say something that is not said by P-statements, then sub-systems are redundant and lack reality.[32]

With the rules thus set out, let us compare the contributions of P- and S-statements to the explanation of Anna Karenina's irrationality. Her desire not to believe herself in danger of falling in love caused her to desire to believe that she was averse to Vronsky. This complex second-order attribution can, according to (S_1) and (S_2), be represented sub-systemically:

> (1) Anna Karenina's desire to believe herself averse to Vronsky belongs to one sub-system, her belief that this is so to another.

Sub-systems conceived as reflections of propositional inconsistencies, we know from 3.2, require characterisation. So from (1) we get:

> (2) Anna Karenina's desire to believe herself averse to Vronsky is motivated by a different (dutiful) sub-system from the (libidinal) sub-system which motivates her desire for Vronsky.

Sub-systemic analysis thus indicates a connection between the failure of reason-relations indicated in (1), and the motivational contrast described in (2): the particular fault-lines of reason-relations correspond to contrasting features in the characterisation of the person. A further element in the analysis is then:

> (3) Anna Karenina's sub-systems individuated in (2) are identical with those individuated in (1).

This might be amplified in terms of a psychological law holding for the individual Anna Karenina,[33] relating her particular kind of failure of awareness to her particular kind of emotional conflict.

At this point, S-statements are still formally reducible to statements about persons and characterised compartments (which reduce in turn to statements about reasons, causes and nomologies of character). Sub-systemic language nevertheless provides a profitable expression of the facts, and sub-systems may be viewed as real unities.

Sub-systems as envisaged by Pears, however, are meant to do more than this. For Pears, there is a further content to (S_1) and (S_2):

(4) Anna Karenina's sub-systems individuated in (1) and (2) are distinct 'rational centres of agency',

and:

(5) they are 'related to one another in the way that different persons are'.

At this point, sub-systemic language starts to reveal its potential for wild ambiguity. Now, it *could* be that what it is for Anna Karenina's 'main system to represent her sub-system' is just for her to have some thought in which relations between different characterised compartments can be discerned (e.g. 'I must not let my desires mislead me'); and what it is for her 'sub-system to act on her main system' is just for a desire (e.g. to be free of anxiety regarding Vronsky) to lead to a thought (e.g. that she is averse to him). Then, talk of sub-systems in (4) and (5) means *nothing more* than that the person thinks about and bears certain attitudes towards herself. So if being a centre of rational activity in (4) is explained in terms of (5), and if (5) is just a way of talking about how the person's different characteristics condition her thoughts and intentions, then sub-systemic language in (4) and (5) returns – much too quickly, and without any gains being made – to the level of the person.

A dilemma facing S-statements now emerges. Because S-statements are 'read through' the level of the person, in the sense that we understand them and test them for truth in terms of ordinary psychology's picture of the person, their specifically sub-systemic content gets lost in being filtered through P-statements, and what survives merely recapitulates what we already know of the person. So either S-statements are readily understood simply because they mean the same as P-statements that we already grasp, or, in trying to offer more than their P-counterparts, they fail to make sense. This difficulty may be highlighted by making the contrast with cognitive psychology, whose attributions are not constrained by any similar requirement of intelligibility: properly sub-personal attributions have only to explain causally, and do not themselves count among, the person's propositional attitudes.

The dilemma comes about for the following reason. Sub-systems are not (ordinary) persons, but (ordinary) persons are our more or less exclusive model for 'centres of rational agency'. This creates the following difficulty for (5): How is its description of the relations between sub-systems as 'interpersonal' distinguished from a trivial interpersonal characterisation of psychological relations (the conception of the rational psyche as a perfectly cooperative community of homunculi, considered in 2.6)? Given that, for the sub-systemic theorist, 'interpersonal' does not mean 'holding between persons' – since for them the terms of interpersonal relations are to consist with as much logical propriety in collections of psychological states as persons – what does sub-systemic 'interpersonality' consist in? The sub-systemic theorist needs to be able to define this relation intrinsically, without reference to the kind of individual that it holds between. This – a metaphysical picture in which 'interpersonal' relations are logically prior to persons! – seems unpromising.

Sub-systemic theory is therefore obliged to ground its use of interpersonality, in (5), on (4): inter-sub-systemic relations can be regarded as truly interpersonal, if the terms between which they hold really are *person-like*. But the person-like terms in (4) can not be identified with the whole person Anna Karenina; nor will it do to identify a person-like 'rational centre' with either a particular catalogue of desires, or an abstract 'motivational structure'.[34] So the question is, what reading of (4) will secure a sense for (5)?

It should now be recalled that the whole point of talking about sub-systems is to try and explain how what it is apparently impossible to do at the level of the person ('lying to oneself') can nevertheless be done, through being *done sub-systemically* – just as cognitive psychology holds out the promise of explaining intelligence, the tying of shoes, and other matters which can not be explained at the personal level. With this in mind, the question becomes: Can S-statements tap sources of explanation not available to P-statements?

The difficulty is acute. What would *alone* establish definitively a sense for (4) that would distinguish it from a corresponding P-statement, and break the circle of uninformative mutual definition formed by (4) and (5), is the following claim: a sub-system is something that *can have the representation 'other sub-system' in a sense in which the person can not*. This would entail the existence of facts which can only be conceptualised (or modes of presentation which can only be grasped) at the level of sub-systems, by 'Anna-Karenina-at-a-sub-systemic-level' and not by Anna Karenina in full. Such facts (or modes of presentation) can only be made available at the personal level indirectly, through employing sub-systemic analyses. This is the deep (inexplicit) thought underlying sub-systemic theory, and it represents the crux of the matter: sub-systems do not think as we do, and it is because they 'think differently' that they can do what we can not.[35]

There is a logical connection between conceiving sub-systems in this way, and thinking of them as agents rather than compartments. None of the propositional attitudes that a compartment contains depends for its content on the concepts of sub-systemic theory, and a compartment is 'internally rational' so long as the beliefs it contains are consistent. By contrast, for a sub-system to be shown to be internally rational after the manner of an agent, it must manifest behaviour which needs to be rationalised – that is, it must act. The opportunity for introducing special sub-systemic concepts can therefore occur only in rationalising actions of the sub-system's that are *not actions of the person's*.[36]

It is now possible to see how sub-systemic theory may claim to solve the Special Problem of irrationality: it is licensed to issue S-statements which *have no P-counterparts*, which makes a sub-systemic explanation of what is inexplicable by P-statements a genuine possibility. In the next section we will see how Pears explores exactly this route.

The claims made by Pears' version of sub-systemic theory can now be summarised in the following *sub-systemic thesis*:

Sub-systems deploy the explanatory resource of internal rationality rather than separateness; their logical mark is *mutual representation* as sub-systems; if and only if sub-systems are attributed with the capacity to represent one another in a way that the person can not represent herself, are they envisaged as rational agents; being a rational centre of agency does not reduce to facts about the person's rational agency and must be understood realistically.

Henceforth I will use 'sub-system' to refer only to entities with these properties. They are of course, more clearly than ever, the very kind of thing which the Censor Criticism targeted, and it must now be considered how that argument applies to Pears' account, bearing in mind that all claims for the reality of sub-systems, as opposed to that of characterised compartments, rest on the basis just made out.

3.6 SARTREIAN PARADOX

Pears' explanation of self-deception[37] exploits (4) and (5). He says that the sub-system, S, stands in relation to the main system, O, as a subject to an object of deception. The interpersonal analogy is rigorously followed out. S promotes in O a belief to which S itself does not assent. S is internally rational: all its beliefs are consistent and all its operations are rational means to achieving its ends. Pears attempts to defend this picture against the Censor Criticism.[38]

First Objection: 'S is really the person, and is self-deceived.' If S is internally rational, why does it not replicate the main system within itself? S has access to all of the main system's contents, and is itself a belief-former; given that its rational capacities are not inferior to those of O, it ought to share any beliefs in the main system to which it has access.

This turns the tables against describing S as just a 'sub'-system: S has all (but one) of the main system's beliefs and can dominate that system by generating false beliefs in it. We are owed some description of S that would show there to be an error, or at least loss of intelligibility, in thinking of the putative component S *more simply* as the aspect, 'Anna Karenina in so far as she means to deceive herself' (and of O as 'Anna Karenina in so far as she believes what she wants to believe').

But if, on the one hand, S *is* the person, S is also, and inconsistently, attributed with an intention toward O. This can not take the form of an intention 'that *Anna Karenina* believe ... ', because S is itself part of Anna Karenina, and has all of the evidence against the belief it has to promote: such an intention would consequently be self-deceptive, and being internally rational, S can not self-deceive. In order to promote the belief in the main system, S needs to represent O *under the description* 'main system'. It needs this in order to form the more precise intention, 'that Anna Karenina's *main system* believe ... ' Thus we see how S's possession of a specifically sub-systemic concept, 'main system', a concept that Anna Karenina lacks, is essential to the sub-systemic story.

The problem of weakness of redescription has now given way to a contradiction: that of being asked to think of S both as equivalent to the person, and as something decidedly less than the person. This is certainly no less paradoxical than thinking of a person as 'lying to themselves'. (So, if that is a paradox, it has not been removed.)

Reply: 'O is S's environment.' Pears attempts to rebut the First Objection by creating an asymmetry between the epistemological viewpoints of main and sub-system, that will block the reduplication of O in S: he says that 'the sub-system has the main system as its environment'; 'The sub-system looks out on to the main system and the main system looks out onto the world.'[39] Since the circumstances, or input, of main and sub-system are so fundamentally different, their output will diverge, even when they are granted equal rationality – S and O will form different beliefs.

Pears' proposal does not just mean that whereas the main system happens to be interested in the world (Vronsky), the sub-system happens to be interested in the psyche (beliefs about Vronsky): for this divergence of interest is itself an explanandum. Pears' claim about 'environment' has to be taken more literally. When so taken, Pears' Reply requires a highly problematic notion: that of understanding a second-order representation without understanding what it is a representation *of*. We are required to suppose that the sub-system can, with full rationality, manipulate representations of Vronsky without understanding who or what Vronsky is. But this is impossible, just as pictures can not be sorted into landscapes and seascapes by a person who is not sighted. To get semantics, S must take the world as its environment in the same sense as O does.

Should Pears' asymmetry then be restated as, 'the sub-system has both the world and the main system as its environment, whereas the main system has only the world'? That would be to concede Sartre's point, that S is in fact extra-systemic. (S is really the person in so far as he knows both the world *and* himself.)[40]

Second Objection: 'S has no origin.' If the input and capacities of S and O are identical, why should S's motivation differ from that of O, such that they end up doing different things? More specifically, what is the origin of S, a part of the mind that is as if specifically programmed to get Anna Karenina to promote a certain belief? S needs an origin, or it looks like a theoretical deus ex machina. For reasons given earlier, cognitive psychology can not help. Nor can the characterisation of compartments account for the divergence of causal role between S and O, since, as also argued earlier, motivational contrasts within a person do not explain the existence of multiple rational agencies within him.

Reply: 'The wish secedes.' Pears therefore says that the wish 'secedes from the main system and sets up a sympathetic sub-system', and takes 'an egoistic form in the main system but a semi-altruistic form in the sub-system':[41] the wish that the main system believe 'is the force that produces the secession of S and motivates all its operations'.[42]

Again, Pears' suggestion (in responding to the severity of the problem) encounters a fundamental difficulty: the wish *itself* is required to perform all of the operations involving the crucial exercises of rationality. It must 'secede' (thereby exploiting mental distance before any has been created, on Pears' own account), 'set up' a sub-system (ex nihilo), and within that sub-system change its form (rewriting its own propositional content). Any attempt to cash all of this out will inevitably invest a desire with the properties of a rational centre of agency (the capacity to grasp a sub-system as a means to an end, and so on). The only way of getting a desire to do the work that Pears requires of it would be to build the means that it employs into its content, i.e. pre-programme it as 'the desire to see-Vronsky-by-setting-up-a-sub-system ...'; taking us firmly back to square one.

It should be emphasised that sub-systems can not be extracted directly from the concept of mental distance: lest it be thought that sub-systems just automatically come into existence once non-integration reaches a sufficiently high degree. Mental distance is admitted in ordinary psychology against the background of a *single* mind. The sub-systemic model obliterates this background, and promotes an alternative background with an interpersonal, *multi-*mind character. Because of this metaphysical shift, there can be no direct route from the concept of mental distance to sub-systemic theory.[43]

At this point, it might be wondered whether the solution might lie in an innate mechanism, perhaps supplied by evolution, that would take over the job of getting the wish to secede.[44]

An innate mechanism of sub-system creation is not the sort of thing that figures in ordinary psychology, and introducing it would involve mixing sharply discontinuous styles of psychological explanation. Should we tolerate this? Sub-systems possess concepts, and are constituted out of propositional attitudes. This means that the proposed innate mechanism must, without any kind of propositional background, directly institute a structure of propositional attitudes which possesses concepts and rational powers. This seems unacceptable.

The innatist proposal would have to cohere with more general psychological theory.[45] As things stand, there is every reason for resisting it: there is no independent evidence for an innate mechanism, making the innatist strategy arbitrary and ad hoc.

One possibility remains. It is that sub-systems are always present in human personality, in some actual or immanent form. To say this would be to claim that, from manifest mental disunity in certain contexts, the concealed existence of two or more mind-like entities at all times is to be inferred.[46] This would solve the problem of causal genesis: if rational existence is in fact no different fundamentally, no special explanation is owed for the appearance of sub-systems in irrationality. That this – evidently drastic – proposal can not be taken on board will be argued in 3.8.

It should be noted that the Second Objection is more fundamental than the First, since, if S has no origin, the sub-systemic story collapses en bloc, however plausible the operations of S, once established, could be made to seem.[47]

3.7 MENTAL DISTANCE

In conclusion: Sartre's argument succeeds against Pears' sub-systemic theory. Self-deception, and unconscious rationality in general, can not be partitively explained.[48] Since the Censor Criticism has application to all sub-systems that have the feature of mutual representation, it is reasonable to infer that any sub-systemic story that trades off the second of Davidson's features, reformulated as Pears' sub-systemic thesis, will fail.

Does the argument allege a logical, or a causal mistake in sub-systemic theory? In effect it combines logical and causal considerations; these are intimately bound up together, each either leading into or mirroring the other. For example, the logical necessity of treating the censor, or S, as occupying an extra-systemic vantage point, is at the end of the day re-expressed in causal terms when this vantage point is shifted back into the desire which is supposed to generate S. And the causal objection, that S will necessarily replicate the main system within itself, reflects the logical objection that talk of a sub-system is really nothing but talk of an aspect of the person, viewed with reference to certain of her propositional attitudes.

The overall argument therefore has the following shape. Problems of circularity, part-whole confusion and so forth carry over from Sartre's analysis of Second Mind modelling, and imply that the sub-systemic picture is logically confused. This objection would be undermined, however, if an adequate explanation of the sub-system's causal genesis could be provided. But no explanation – one that avoids either creating a regress or positing residual irrational attitudes – has been forthcoming; and since it has not, it is appropriate to affirm the first result, and conclude that the causal unaccountability of sub-systems gives expression to a logical error in their design. The logical objection follows on from the success of the causal objection.

It has not been argued that sub-systemic explanation fails simply because it is incomplete. That would be a mistake, since explanation can be incomplete and yet, as far as it goes, successful (which is the situation in much ordinary psychology, including explanation by self-deceptive intent). Rather, the argument has been that sub-systemic explanation fails because of its implication of paradox: in this particular case, incompleteness entails failure of explanation. The point is important, because it means that the sub-systemic theorist can not block the Second Objection by pointing out that – whether one opts for the Complete or the Limited view, described in 1.5 – there is always some sort of 'tailoring off' in propositional attitude explanation. This response is unavailable, for two reasons. First, sub-systemic theory is introduced precisely in order to compensate for the tailoring off in the ordinary explanation of self-deception. Second, the particular form of tailoring off in sub-systemic theory is not ordinary: the problem with which the sub-systemic theorist ends his story is not just a reproduction of the original problem in ordinary psychology, but an aggravated form of that problem.[49]

What has been made of the two intuitions in favour of partition described in 2.2? Effectively, the first intuition – that partition guided by relations of inconsistency between propositional attitudes provides a weak sense of part – has been endorsed, in the form of characterised compartments; whilst the second intuition – that the cause of irrationality must lie in something which is external to, by way of being only a part of, the person – in so far as it is expressed in

Pearsian sub-systems, has been rejected. Persons do have parts, in the sense that their personalities comprehend contrasting sources of motivation; but not in the sense that their minds have parts which function like agents.

Davidson's formula that irrationality involves 'a cause that is not a reason for what it causes' does not imply a divided mind. What it does imply is *mental distance*.[50] Mental distance is entailed by the concept of irrationality: (1) irrationality involves necessarily, as Davidson says, 'a cause that is not a reason for what it causes', since if every mental cause were a reason for what it caused there would be no irrationality; (2) given such a cause, an explanation is required for why the mind does not correct the causation (the question to which Pears' concept of the cautionary belief draws attention); which implies (3) that there are mental states which ought to have corrected the irrational process; which in turn implies (4) that there is mental distance between those states and the irrational cause. So, if what it is for the mind to be divided is just for there to be mental distance, then irrational minds are indeed necessarily divided: but only in the sense that they possess a feature shared by every mind, irrational or not, that falls short of perfect integration. The idea that there are cohesive groupings of mental states, which are internally integrated and to some degree mutually disintegrated, is immanent, although not fully explicit, in ordinary psychology.[51]

How has the explanation of irrationality been advanced in this chapter? It has been shown that the concept of mental distance is primitive, and that characterised compartments, which use the concepts of mental distance and cohesion, are explanatory. But the most important result of this chapter is negative: if Second Mind modelling is not explanatory, then psychoanalytic theory should be made independent from it; and a sure way of doing this will be to dispute the assumption that unconscious rationality is an object of, or that its existence is assumed by, psychoanalytic interpretation.

3.8 PERSONS IN WHOLE: THE NATURE OF PERSONAL UNITY

The case against partition could be left as it stands. But, if we step back from the argument, the following thought presents itself. Ordinary psychology forbids partition not merely for 'technical' reasons, related to the 'logic' of propositional attitude explanation, but because there lies in its background a metaphysical picture of persons – tacitly drawn on in the argument against sub-systems – as *unities*.

Recall Descartes' assertion: 'I am unable to distinguish any parts within myself; I understand myself to be something quite single and complete.'[52] Now anyone, however wary of Cartesian claims in general, should admit to having some idea of this kind of self-apprehension.[53] The issue may accordingly be defined in the following terms. The necessary and sufficient condition of personal unity is *indivisibility*. Persons are *divisible* if they have, or can have, parts of a kind the self-ascription of which would contradict the self-conception articulated by Descartes; if they do not and can not have such parts, they are *indivisible*.

Note that, so defined, division has nothing to do with psychological conflict, and the question of personal unity is distinct from non-logical questions about psychological unity in the sense of freedom from psychological conflict. Whether a psychological theory is person-divisive depends upon the kind of parts that it postulates; more precisely, upon how these are logically related to the sortal concepts which are employed in, at a fundamental level, individuating persons. *Non-person-divisive* theories are of two kinds. (i) They postulate parts which are only mental *faculties or functions* (such as the memory and will). Or (ii) they postulate parts which fall under a sortal concept which is not given application at the point at which a person is individuated, but whose employment is consistent with everything involved at that point. *Person-divisive* theories postulate parts falling under sortal concepts that are necessarily given only a single application at the point at which a person is individuated, from which it follows that such theories show us to be multiples of that of which we previously took ourselves to be single instances; they postulate a 'multiple self'.[54]

That persons are unities is something that we seem to believe – it shapes our motives and reactive attitudes to one another. Self-deceivers, for instance, in forming pictures of themselves as undivided by conflict, display a *concern for unity*: theirs is not so much the motive of avoiding conflict (which would lead them to form rational, conflict-resolving preferences), but of avoiding *realising that they are in conflict*. This sort of concern is equally presupposed by our characteristic attitude of disapprobation towards self-deception and other tactics of personal division by means of which persons seek to escape their responsibilities: self-deception is condemnable because, in order to make a superficial gain in the cohesion of conscious thought, it treats the person as if she could be decomposed into independent parts, each being allowed to go its own way.[55] It is therefore no accident that the phenomenon should invite the kind of modelling that sub-systemic explanation provides for it: sub-systemic theory accords with the self-deceiver's own self-*mis*representation.[56]

Now it is clear that sub-systems violate the concern for unity, on at least three counts. Sub-systems *have their own points of view*: as concept-possessing subjects of propositional attitudes, sub-systems require a special metaphysical setting, which grants them perspectives on one another. That they individuate themselves thus means that sub-systems have a subjectivity which is necessarily not that of a person, yet contained within persons.[57] Furthermore, sub-systems are *subjects of agency*: for if sub-systems' concepts are not directly available to the person, then nor are the action-descriptions under which sub-systems do what they do; their doings are logically of a kind that the person could not undertake.[58] And, lastly, sub-systems are *subjects of ascription*: given that belonging to a sub-system is a relation of the kind envisaged when a thought or feeling is said to belong to one person rather than another, and that in our present conceptual scheme one token mental state can not be ascribed to two subjects,[59] ascription of mental states to persons and to sub-systems would seem to *exclude one another*; mental states belong to either the person or their sub-system, but *not both*.[60]

Sub-systems therefore entail radical conceptual revision: equipped with their own point of view, they think, intend and act, and in so doing compete with persons for the ownership of mental states. Sub-systemic theory is therefore person-divisive.

Now, it might be felt that we can and should tolerate such a revision *for limited purposes*: such as the explanation of irrationality. But, if sub-systems are posited in the irrational case, then a conditional holds true of the ordinary case: 'were sub-systems explanatorily needful, they could be posited legitimately'. This implies that a person is a sort of thing to which sub-systemic analysis can legitimately apply. This imputes an *immanent multiplicity* to persons, contradicting the conception of them as indivisible. That sub-systems are in fact explanatorily redundant in the rational case is therefore irrelevant: what is significant is sub-systemic theory's admission of metaphysical possibility. And, if sub-systemic analysis is, as it seems, unacceptably metaphysically immoderate, then the sub-systemic theorist's final remaining response to the problem of causal genesis – the claim that sub-systems are always present in human personality – must also be rejected.

It may be thought, however, that the notion of personal unity is in any case under threat from empirical quarters, to such an extent that it ought to be abandoned. In particular, multiple personality may impress one as conceptually explosive.[61]

On examination, multiple personality cases fail to show that the unity we naturally grant ourselves is illusory.[62] Multiple personality controverts personal unity only if Cartesian self-consciousness is that in which personal indivisibility *consists*, or the unique *ground of inference* to it. But this is to misunderstand the contribution of self-consciousness to personal unity. Cartesian self-consciousness can not predetermine the degrees of psychological disintegration to which persons are susceptible: at the level of bare self-consciousness, there is no complete or even comprehensive knowledge of the nature of persons. So if someone like Eve White – the original presenting subject of Cleckley and Thigpen's case – has false beliefs about her mental unity, this is because she is ignorant of her peculiar condition, and not because phenomenological conditions have 'misled' her into a false view of her unity. Self-consciousness should then be regarded as a sign, manifestation, or expression of personal unity, rather than its essence. That self-consciousness is, in highly abnormal conditions, such as multiple personality, unable to inform a person of their non-integration does not mean that, *under normal circumstances*, it is not correctly informative of a person's ordinary unity.[63]

Nor does multiple personality provide conceptual motivation for sub-systemic theory. The kind of non-integration exhibited in multiple personality is irrelevant to sub-systemic theory, since the *structural conditions* – absolute discontinuities of consciousness, distinctions of memory stores, alternation of access to physical motility and so forth – that form the background to deception between Eve Black and Eve White are altogether absent from, indeed precluded by, self-deception. Attributions of irrationality are premised on judgements of basic integration, the erosion of which is constitutive of the phenomenon of multiple personality. So it can not be said that multiple personality presents in a fully developed form what exists in self-deception in an incipient form, and thereby offers a model for partition. An Eve-personality is not a theoretically inferred Second Mind: the latter is an explanans in a case of unconscious rationality, the former an explanandum in a case of multiple personality. Multiple personality gives no evidence for Second Minds, or for thinking that Second Minds can exist without self-consciousness.[64]

Finally, consider how hard it is to imagine a phenomenology of multiple selfhood. How could one experience oneself in a form midway between regarding oneself as a single person, and as many persons? Any attempt to describe what it is like to be many selves would immediately become a description of what it is like to be one self among many.[65] If there is no phenomenology capable of providing multiple selfhood with a distinctive realisation, then the psychological reality to which sub-systems would have to answer is not one that we could ever be in a position to think of as our own.

What is the nature of personal unity?

There is, first, an obvious negative connection between a certain view of personal identity and the presuppositions of the concern for unity. What is wrong with self-division is that one takes oneself to constitute *no more than a set of desires*: self-division manifests a Humean conception of persons as constructed out of relations between mental states.[66] For the Humean, any statement that a person has conflicting desires will reduce to a statement that there is a relation of conflict between desires; that a person is in conflict, to a statement that there exists a relation of conflict. So the Humean conception is unable to explicate the content of motives and attitudes displaying a concern for unity.

The Humean conception is interdependent with the division of the person into components, and prepares the ground metaphysically for sub-systemic theory. If relational description is complete, then relations between sub-systems, and between person and sub-systems, can all be logically represented in terms of relations of set membership; entailing that no radical revision of the logic of personal agency or ascription is entailed by sub-systemic theory. The Humean conception implies that ordinary rational agency, self-deception, multiple personality, and the case of two persons should all be traced as lying at successive points on a logical continuum, mapped in terms of degrees of integration of mental states. This contradicts our pretheoretical view that moving along the spectrum is not an equable experience: at some point we are lost, only to reappear later as one of two. For ordinary thought, the cases of one and two persons are conceptually fundamental, and the 'intermediate' cases more or less puzzling deviations from one or other of these.

If persons are indivisible, it is however not for Descartes' reasons: belief in personal indivisibility goes deeper than the Cartesian or phenomenological reasons that may be advanced in its support. Personal indivisibility does not consist in the unity of consciousness or the existence of an ego conceived as a bare particular. The right view is surely that it consists in *the natural kind of unity appropriate to a psycho-physical substance.*[67] The unity of consciousness expresses a nomological unity, determined by the life-principle of the natural kind of persons, and ordinary psychology is inseparably bound up with this meta-physical conception of persons.

This conclusion will be carried over to the discussion of the philosophy of psychoanalysis in Parts II and III.

3.9 PERSONS AND MINDS

It might be objected that the discussion of partition in this chapter and the last suffers from a failure to draw a basic distinction, regarding the identity of that which is being said to have parts. The distinction is between *persons* and *minds*. Drawing it – so the proposal goes – enables us to say that minds have parts of the kind that sub-systemic theory describes, and at the same time deny that this carries over to persons: partitioned minds may belong to undivided persons. In this way sub-systemic theory is released from any revisionary metaphysical implications.

The distinction between persons and minds may seem to accord with some of the grammar surrounding our use of the word 'mind': we speak colloquially of 'what our minds do', and even of what they 'do to us', apparently contrasting us, as persons, with our minds.

However, the proposal is really just a way of postponing difficulties. The general relationship between minds and persons, as we ordinarily understand it, may well not be fully perspicuous,[68] but it does not encourage the proposal. We do refer to groups of mental states as minds, but in so doing surely do not think of minds as so to speak the *spiritual bodies* (or organs) of persons. But this is just what the proposal demands: in permitting the mind, like the body, to be divisible into parts, without these being parts of *us*, it tells us to think of our relations to our minds as just like our relations to our bodies. But body and mind are not symmetrical in this way, and so – without a thorough (and revisionary) reconception of the relation of mind and person – it will remain inexplicable why partitioning of the mind should not be thought, with justice, to imply division of the person.

The situation with regard to cognitive psychology is of course quite different. There can be no objection to saying that cognitive psychology attributes parts to the mind but not to the person, on the condition that 'mind' is understood in this context as referring to the *theoretical* entity constituted by a person's system of sub-personal states.

PART II

Psychoanalytic concepts

CHAPTER 4

Unconscious motives and Freudian concepts

Our Prince, suddenly and for no reason at all, committed two or three shocking outrages on various persons. The striking thing about them was that they were so utterly shocking, so unlike anything anyone could have expected, not at all what usually happens, absolutely idiotic and puerile, committed goodness only knows why, without rhyme or reason.

Dostoyevsky

The mind of man is capable of anything – because everything is in it, all the past as well as all the future.

Conrad

4.1 'RADICAL HETEROGENEITY'

Part II will set out the basic concepts of psychoanalytic theory.[1] The relation of psychoanalytic theory to ordinary psychology is not easy to describe accurately. On the one hand, it will be stressed that psychoanalytic concepts are natural extensions of the ways of thinking of ordinary psychology. This extension is independent from the line of reasoning that leads to the unconscious being conceived as a Second Mind – making the Censor Criticism irrelevant to psychoanalytic theory. On the other hand, psychoanalytic theory is not just a terminological reformulation of ordinary psychology: it explains things that ordinary psychology can not explain, and does so by employing a distinctive form of explanation which is foreign to ordinary psychology. This second claim is well expressed in the following passage:

In Sartre, for instance, the critique of the psychoanalytic unconscious misconstrues the latter's radical heterogeneity by reducing unconscious contents to the misunderstood fringes and implications of present intention [...] The questions thus posed (bad faith, conscious reticence, misunder-

87

standing-pathology of the field of consciousness, etc.) [...] we characterise [...] as marginal in relation to a domain which is properly psychoanalytic.[2]

To say that the properly psychoanalytic domain possesses a 'radical heterogeneity' is to reject Sartre's assumption, in 2.5, that psychoanalytic theory is a theory of self-deception. Sartre's basic error is to have supposed, in taking Freudian explanation to rival explanation by bad faith, that there is *but one* range of irrational phenomena to be accounted for; in fact, self-deception and psycho-analytic pathology are very different and can not both be spanned by one theory.[3] To establish this, however, it must be shown that psychoanalytic explananda and explanations are at a significant remove from self-deception, for, it will also be suggested, Sartre is at least correct in thinking that the combination of ignorance and motivation uncovered in psychoanalytic interpretation has the outward appearance of self-deception.[4]

In sum, it needs to be shown both why it would be wrong to dissolve psychoanalytic concepts back into the terms of ordinary psychology[5] (which are, after all, familiar, simpler and already known to be sound); and how it is possible for ordinary psychology to provide the basis for a theory of the mind which, in some respects, may appear to revise it.

4.2 INACCESSIBILITY

There is a class of irrational phenomena which stand on the borderline between self-deception and the properly psychoanalytic domain. They are ambiguous because the subject's motive for misrepresenting herself is obscure. In a case like that of Anna Karenina, it is easy to identify the buried motive. But people often act from motives suggesting that they envisage the world in ways that it would be extremely difficult for them to articulate; particularly in irrational contexts, they are unable to recognise and identify the motives that move them. In such cases, the stretch of mental distance between a person's motive and her self-awareness is unusually great. There are then structures of motivated self-misrepresentation where, even if the subject had not misrepresented herself, she would still have lacked self-knowledge. Hard though it is to classify such cases, they are obviously very common.[6] Often in cases of this kind, there is a sort of detachment from reality: the person 'imagines', 'seems to think', 'behaves as if', 'appears to suppose', that something, which does not match reality, is the case, and this unreal envisagement of theirs is integral to their unavowed motive. Because of the difficulty we think the subject would have in articulating her motive, we would hold back from saying that they *believe* the relevant proposition. This suggests an attitude on the part of the irrational subject which is akin, but not straightforwardly equivalent to belief (an idea which will be made more definite later).

These conditions of first personal mental opacity, which are recognised in ordinary psychology, suggest a rudimentary sense in which mental states, without being self-deceptively buried, may nevertheless be inaccessible to their owner. They may be unlike those psychological states – paradigmatically, current perceptual beliefs – that we self-ascribe immediately, and their self-ascription may require their being *found out*. This can take one of two distinctive routes: a sudden flash of realisation, or interpretation. We reserve a special sense of interpretation for those attributions that are intuitively discontinuous with quotidian psychological attributions; they are built on the more basic attributions of mental states which are read off more or less directly from behaviour.[7]

The concept of inaccessibility is worth expanding on. Mental states differ in the facility with which they become topics of self-knowledge. This epistemic property is their *accessibility*. It can be determined in two ways. First, a token mental state may be inaccessible because of some *accidental* property that it has: its having been simply forgotten, or buried in self-deception, or belonging to a currently excluded characterised compartment and phenomenological set, and so on. The second cause of inaccessibility is provided by a *non-accidental* property of mental state: i.e. its inaccessibility may derive from its being a mental state of a certain *type*. This provides a further, and deeper, way of conceiving the unconscious; it will be suggested in later chapters that the states fundamental to psychoanalytic explanation, in its most developed form, are, as types, minimally accessible. The rest of this chapter will be concerned with the determinants of accidental inaccessibility proposed by Freud.

4.3 THE RATMAN: NEUROTIC SYMPTOMS AND THEIR INTERPRETATION

Freud describes the Ratman as an obsessional neurotic: he is irrational because he exhibits 'symptoms'.[8] An inventory of these includes: compulsive impulses (to cut his throat, and undertake a near-fatal diet); groundless fears that terrible things will happen to the people he loves, and corresponding obsessive desires to protect them (he removes a stone from the road so that it will not bring harm to his beloved, who will later be passing in a carriage); chronic indecision (over his choice of marriage partners); absurd, ill-conceived projects (he undertakes a train journey in order to repay a trivial debt, knowing it to be erroneous, and suffers a mental breakdown en route); and barely intelligible, violent and emotionally overwhelming trains of thought, that he finds foreign and repugnant, on themes of death and torture. We call such things symptoms because they are such aberrant kinds of psychological phenomena. The Ratman's feelings and actions appear to 'lack all reason', and Freud has to coin the term 'obsessional structures' to refer to them. These phenomena, it should be emphasised, present themselves as differing in kind from the ordinary constituents of mental life. They strain the Ratman's ordinary way of viewing himself, and create in him a corresponding need for self-explanation.

Although the Ratman's symptoms are contra-rational and not understood by him, they can still not be viewed as complete psychological freaks: they are after all embedded in his stream of consciousness, and given in some connection, however obscure, with the rest of his mental life. They fall short of being completely alien, out-of-the-blue psychological occurrences; these would signify madness, and hence lie altogether outside the scope of, not putting stress on, our ordinary perspective on ourselves.[9] The Ratman's irrational phenomena do not just 'befall' him: they manifest mental states that must indeed be *his*, but whose nature and content he is unable to grasp. This puts him in the contradictory situation of knowing that his symptoms manifest mental states which are his own, but of not knowing what these states are. That he is unable to 'read' his own mind produces, in a more extreme form than ordinary irrationality, the self-contradiction constitutive of irrational phenomena. The Ratman can not be asked to think of his symptoms in a way that would exile them, conceptually, from the rest of his experience. They need to be found a place compatible with his ordinary perspective on himself, or some acceptable extension thereof: he is crying out to be made intelligible to himself, at whatever conceptual price is compatible with his continuing to view himself in intentional terms, that is, as a person.

The severity of the Ratman's condition disposes him to undertake psychoanalysis. This does not mean, however, that the demand created by the Ratman's condition is merely practical or therapeutic. The demand that his irrational phenomena be intentionally accommodated is in the first instance a demand for explanation; if benefits such as relief from his symptoms accrue to the Ratman by way of his achieving self-understanding, that will be, we are entitled to assume, because it embodies correct explanations, and identifies his symptoms' true causes.

The Ratman's irrational phenomena clearly do not exhibit the immediate intelligibility, and unity of identification and explanation which, we saw, characterises ordinary irrationality. The Ratman's is a different and deeper grade of irrationality, which is propositionally *opaque*, rather than transparent. That his irrational phenomena can not be viewed as constituted by, and explained in terms of, configurations of propositional attitudes, has the highest importance for their correct explanation: How can the Ratman – as a rational believer and desirer, possessed of a single mind belonging to a psychophysical unity – contain enough mental richness and disorder to generate the confusions and disintegrations involved in his deeper and distinct grade of psychoanalytic irrationality? What extension of the ordinary view of persons could account for this, without losing focus on, or actually controverting, the image of persons as rational unities?

Although nothing would appear to be further from the hyperrationalism of the self-deceiver, or less susceptible to explanation in terms of wants, Freud succeeds in making the Ratman's obsessional structures intelligible by showing them to derive from, through being motivated by, a strikingly simple set of underlying conflicts. The central motive that Freud uncovers in the Ratman is hatred of his father. This hatred is located in a matrix of contrary but symmetrically ordered attitudes: his hatred for his father, who has in fact been dead for some time, is opposed by an idealising love for him, and this love enters into competition with the Ratman's love for women, who are themselves also objects of his hostility.[10]

The full details of the case and its interpretation are too complex to survive summary, but I will describe the central issue: what Freud calls the Ratman's 'great obsessive fear'. The Ratman tells Freud how, when in the army, his military superior, the Captain, once related the administration of a criminal punishment, in which rats were inserted into the victim's anus. The anecdote provoked overwhelming horror in the Ratman – apparently a direct reaction to the cruelty of the punishment (or so he thought at the time). Yet, as he heard this story, there had intruded into the Ratman's mind, unaccountably, the thought of the same punishment being applied to his father. Whilst telling all this to Freud, the Ratman showed 'every sign of horror'. But he also betrayed quite opposite feelings: 'At all the more important moments while he was telling his story his face took on a very strange, composite expression.' Freud was therefore presented, at the level of pre-interpretative, physiognomic understanding, with definite but conflicting data. He diagnoses the Ratman's total reaction as '*horror at pleasure of his own of which he was unaware*'.[11] From this, together with other material, Freud infers the Ratman's unconscious hatred of his father, and his equally unconscious repudiation of it. The next question is: What is responsible for the Ratman's unconscious hatred of his father?

The answer to this question, and the explanation of the Ratman's response to the Captain's story, is only arrived at later, once Freud has uncovered the Ratman's memory of a traumatic beating, received as an infant, at the hands of his father, to which the Ratman had responded with an outburst of infantile abuse, so vehement that his father had been shocked into breaking off the punishment. His father had then pronounced that his son would become either a great man or a great criminal. The beating was originally hypothesised by Freud to have been administered in connection with masturbation, a suggestion that led the Ratman to recollect that his mother had told him many times of an incident in which he had been punished for biting. In Freud's interpretation, the beating had had the general and profound effect of putting an end to the child's constitutional auto-erotic enjoyments.[12] This led the Ratman to perceive his father as wishing to deny him sensory pleasure.

Out of this fusion of elements, the Ratman's conflict between his love for his father and his adult love for women issues: to satisfy the latter, he must sacrifice the former, and vice versa. What the Ratman called only a 'train of thought', the idea of the rat-torture being applied to his father, is in fact the expression of something that the Ratman *wants*. The stage had been set for the Ratman to form his sadistic father-torturing thought by his prior representation of the Captain: 'The captain – a man who could defend such punishments – had become a substitute for his father, and had thus drawn down upon himself a part of the reviving animosity which had burst out, on the original occasion, against his cruel father.'[13]

Freud uses the same material to account for the Ratman's peculiar behaviour in the analytical session. When originally asked about his great obsessive fear, the Ratman cowered before Freud: 'the patient broke off, got up from the sofa, and begged me to spare him the recital of the details'.[14] Freud says that, as the Ratman recounted his 'train of thought', the result was, once again, the *fulfilment of a wish*. The Ratman's illicit pleasure in imagining the fulfilment of his sadistic wish was something that he also wished himself to be punished for; and here the analyst himself had entered his thoughts – the Ratman's parricidal thought was overlaid by another, in which Freud, in the capacity of his father, beat him for his sadistic wish; causing him to retreat physically before Freud.

The reason for the Ratman's original reluctance to rehearse the Captain's story – his inability to think of it without massive conscious anxiety – is then that doing so gives expression to a wish which is repudiated, this repudiation being expressed in turn by the Ratman's wish to be punished. This second wish motivates, and draws on, the Ratman's portrayal of Freud as being simultaneously his father (administering the punishment which he received as an infant) and the Captain (administering the military punishment to the criminal), and reverses the situation represented by the first wish: now it is the Ratman who is made to suffer.

Freud's interpretation thus refers to a complex of interlocked motives which are inaccessible to the Ratman: his hatred of his father, conflict about his erotic life, and sadistic and self-punitive wishes. Through the interpolation of these motives, and by means of certain crucial interpretative moves, Freud arrives at a causal connection between the Ratman's infantile beating, and his present irrational phenomena. The nuclear psychoanalytic concepts are exhibited in these moves, but their true theoretical form is best approached through an examination of something else that Freud's interpretation suggests: the kinship of unconscious motivation and self-deception.

4.4 NEUROTIC SELF-MISREPRESENTATION

Neurotic symptoms are structures of motivated self-misrepresentation that pervert the ways in which the world appears to the person, and in which they appear to themselves. Examples are provided by the Ratman.

Freud speaks of neurotics' 'need for *uncertainty* in their life', which draws them 'away from *reality*': 'it is only too obvious what efforts are made by the patients themselves in order to be able to avoid certainty and remain in doubt'.[15] The Ratman exhibits this in the 'indeterminacy' of his mental processes. Freud explains these 'efforts' of the neurotic as follows: it is as if, by putting *all* in doubt, they can avoid certainty with regard to the particular matters which cause them anxiety; and, by stripping thoughts of their 'direction of fit', they can disguise their desires. This is a structure of motivated self-misrepresentation: states of incertitude and indeterminacy are promoted in order to bury memories, and block the realisation of parricidal impulses.

A second example is provided by the Ratman's response to the problem that his choice of a marriage partner conflicts with what he believes would have been his father's preference. Freud says: 'he resolved this conflict [...] by falling ill; or, to put it more correctly, by falling ill he avoided the task of resolving it in real life'.[16] Illness, misrepresented by the Ratman as unmotivated, is the promoted condition, which serves to bury the anxiety associated with disobeying his father; they too are related to one another in the way defined for a structure of motivated self-misrepresentation.

A third example is the Ratman's masochism. Freud tells him: 'you derive pleasure from your self-reproaches as a means of self-punishment'.[17] Masochism has a self-misrepresentational form: suffering is promoted so as to bury feelings of guilt, the operation's success again requiring this connection to remain unrecognised.

On one occasion the Ratman exhibits the more familiar sort of self-deception. When the Captain instructs him to repay a debt to a certain Lieutenant, the Ratman knows perfectly well that the Captain has made a mistake, and that the money is in fact owed to someone else. Yet he makes himself believe what the Captain says. As Freud's interpretation runs, he promotes the belief that the Captain is right in order not to disobey his father, whom the Captain represents to him.[18]

Now, such neurotic structures of motivated self-misrepresentation surely do not come about through an intention of the subject's, and hence do not qualify as self-deceptive. If this is right, the self-knowledge required for self-deceptive intent is absent from neurotic structures, which must consequently operate through non-intentional processes, without knowledge of their operation.

This can be shown by applying in reverse the argument (in 1.3) that strong self-deception necessarily involves rationality, intention and self-knowledge. If the Ratman's symptoms issue from self-deceptive intentions, there must be beliefs correlative with those intentions. Such as: the belief that making thoughts appear indeterminate is a way of disguising their desirousness; that arbitrary self-reproach is a means of self-punishment; that obeying the Captain is a way of atoning for hating his father – and so on! Now, whereas the beliefs required for self-deceptive intent usually present no difficulty, these so-called beliefs are very different: they do not belong to, and can not be derived from, the stock of 'core' beliefs that everyone may be assumed to share. Since there is no way in which they could have been rationally formed, their explanation must be sought elsewhere. And if we must look elsewhere, it seems that we must enquire into a special domain of causes of these 'beliefs'. These causes can not be of any familiar kind, and they must be assumed to achieve their effects without the medium of intentions. This opens up the crucially important possibility that such a domain, of irrational causes, explains the irrational phenomena of neurotic self-misrepresentation *directly*, and not via the intermediary of beliefs and self-deceptive intentions. The task is set of developing the hypothesis that neurotic self-misrepresentation occurs without self-knowledge to engineer it.

To illustrate what sort of thing an irrational cause of irrationality might be: in the discussion of obsessional neurosis that follows the Ratman's case history, Freud advances the view that '*an obsessive or compulsive thought is one whose function it is to represent an act regressively*'. This is explained by the mechanical redirection of energy that would otherwise have gone into action into the realm of mental events; as Freud more specifically puts it, thinking becomes 'sexualised'.[19] The concepts needed for this to be properly intelligible have not yet been set out, but it is worth noting the extent to which the weight of argument *already* favours some such hypothesis, i.e. one that can take over where attributions of belief must either leave off or become tortuous and implausible. The substantial question is the coherence and nature of the general picture of the mind implied by the preferred theory of the domain of irrational causes.

4.5 EMOTION AND AMBIVALENCE

Three inter-locking features are responsible for the unconsciousness, and hence inaccessibility, of the Ratman's hatred for his father: the emotion's special, infantile character; its engagement in what Freud calls 'chronic conflict'; and its being repressed. The first and second features are what make repression necessary. Conflict and repression will be discussed in later sections. Here we need to ascertain what differentiates the Ratman's hatred from ordinary hatred.

At one point, the Ratman puts the following pertinent question to Freud: How *can* he hate his father, given that this is inconsistent with everything that he knows about his feelings towards his father? 'He wondered how he could possibly have had such a wish, considering that he loved his father more than any one else in the world.' Freud replied: 'I answered that it was precisely such intense love as his that was the necessary precondition of the repressed hatred.'[20]

Freud contrasts the combination of love and hatred found in the Ratman with ordinary emotional ambivalence.[21] His argument is as follows. The Ratman's hatred could only have become available for self-knowledge if it had been *of a kind* that would have allowed for combination with love in a composite attitude, one of ambivalence, towards his father; had it been of such a kind, it would not have become unconscious, and the outcome would not have been pathological – it would have been something closer to the self-deception which characteristically accompanies ambivalence, where one of the contrary attitudes is simply buried. But because the Ratman's hatred was not of such a kind, it had to be removed from the sphere of self-knowledge and control necessary to yield a non-pathological solution.

The crucial feature that differentiates the Ratman's unconscious hatred from ordinary hatred is its unconditional, and hence total, character. To see what this involves, a logical distinction is helpful.

The formal objects of emotions may be *particulars*, or they may be *states of affairs*. The former are given by noun-phrases ('X hates a'), the latter by propositional expressions ('X hates its being the case that a is F').[22] Ordinary emotional states are properly and typically reported in the second, propositional form. Reporting emotions in this form is connected with assessing them for appropriateness: propositional expressions embody judgements about objects which provide prima facie justifications for emotions.[23] Reporting an emotion's object merely by a noun-phrase, by contrast, does not establish any such justification.

That ordinary emotional states are properly and typically reported in a propositional form explains how ordinary emotional ambivalence is possible, and why there is nothing inherently irrational about it. A case of rivalry provides an illustration. Suppose a friend's success in getting the job for which I also competed is something towards which I have mixed feelings.[24] Spelling out these feelings will involve bringing to the fore different desires and evaluative dispositions: my own desire to succeed, and my desire that my friend should succeed. Contrary emotions towards a single object are therefore compatible with rationality, so long as each is associated with a different description of the object, in a way which explains how one state of affairs may be experienced and judged as both desirable and undesirable. Ordinary ambivalent attitudes are irrational only if the contrariety they contain can not be elucidated in this way.

The Ratman's hatred of his father is altogether cruder than the emotions which enter into ambivalent attitudes: it is correctly reported by a noun-phrase, and not a propositional expression. It is this logical feature which permits its exaggerated magnitude. The Ratman's hatred stems from the infantile beating, and it is in the nature of infantile emotion to be unconditional: the child's grasp of its pain as inflicted on account of the commission of a particular offence is tenuous. The Ratman's retaliatory emotion, the hostility subsequently felt towards his father, similarly does not take up and express what causes it through a propositional characterisation of its object. So the Ratman's infantile hatred is not hatred of his father *as* one who administers punishment, but of his father tout court; yielding a response of matching crudity, a wish for his father's annihilation. Uninformed and unmoderated by judgement, the hatred is not in touch with thoughts about its cause that would make it appropriate (other than, trivially, the self-confirming thought of his father's hatefulness). Insulated in the unconscious, such emotions may survive into adulthood with their infantile character intact and without loss of potency. When they do so, they can not be combined in ambivalent formations, since these presuppose a coordinated network of thoughts. Such networks supply emotions with propositional objects, keep them in touch with the thoughts that provide their grounds, and enable the identity of individuals across contrary emotions to be properly appreciated.[25] It follows that ordinary emotional ambivalence is a rational luxury denied to the Ratman.

4.6 CONFLICT WITHOUT PREFERENCE

It was claimed (in 4.4) that neurotic structures of motivated self-misrepresentation do not operate through intentions. Here I want to pursue and strengthen the argument that neurosis does not conform to the mould of ordinary psychology.

Freud is explicit that the 'chronic conflict' to which the Ratman is subject is different in kind from ordinary conflict: 'the pathogenic conflict in neurotics is not to be confused with a normal struggle between mental impulses both of which are on the same psychological footing'.[26] As with the Ratman's hatred, we need to know what makes the difference from the ordinary. My suggestion is that the concept of preference provides the key.[27] The Ratman shares with the self-deceiver the motive of aversion to conflict, but the resemblance is limited in this crucial respect: the Ratman does not exercise a preference for neurosis over awareness of conflict.

It is not just ill-luck of the Ratman's that every significant desire of his should generate an impulse to its opposite: he is constitutionally conflicted. A purely propositional perspective on the Ratman would omit constitutional factors and thereby make him forever unintelligible. Something is therefore gained for explanation as soon as it is hypothesised that constitutional, non-propositional structures dominate the Ratman's mental life and determine the fundamental lines of his mental conflict. This tells us why the 'psychological footing' of the Ratman's conflict is different from the ordinary. To explain more, it would be necessary to know more about the nature of the structures.

When we say that neurotic symptoms stem from conflict, we are thinking of conflict in a very literal sense. Let us call the sense in which a person's desires may conflict solely by virtue of their joint content being unsatisfiable – whether or not the person knows this – *objective* conflict. There is *subjective* conflict of desires, by contrast, when the interaction of conflicting desires involves appreciation of their objective conflict. Subjective conflict takes two forms. Usually, subjective conflict issues in practical reasoning, about which desire to satisfy. Then, the relations between desires are mediated by representations of them: what in fact interacts causally is not the desires themselves, but beliefs about them (the desirability, probability, cost, etc. of satisfying one rather than the other). But we have a grasp of another kind of subjective conflict, in which the desires themselves, and not just representations of them, interact causally: a conception which shows itself in our talk of one desire as defeating another. Here we estimate desires in quantitative terms and liken them to vectors of physical forces.[28]

The distinction between the two kinds of subjective conflict enables a sharp line to be drawn between the kind of conflict that issues in neurosis, and that which issues in self-deception. Self-deception requires the interaction of desires negotiated by beliefs about them: consequently it is able to provide solutions, of a sort (albeit often unstable and temporary ones), and to give expression to preferences, which may or may not be akratic. Neurosis, by contrast, represents a 'solution' only in the attenuated sense that the triumph of one force over another can be said to represent a solution. This is because the Ratman's love and hatred for his father enter into conflictual relations with one another directly.[29] Neurotic conflicts are therefore ones whose true solution would require the outright extinction of one of a pair of powerful desires. Neurosis results when this is not possible. It follows that, if the Assumption of Alternatives can guide our understanding of neurosis at all, its application in that context is – by comparison with self-deception and akrasia – highly strained: no alternative rational outcome, or response to the threat of suffering, is available to the subject.

This claim is supported by, and bears out, our intuitions about when it is and is not appropriate to view a piece of behaviour as reflecting a person's judgement of their interest, i.e. their preference. The rough rule we follow is this: the more desires are satisfied through behaviour, and the more we can imagine performing operations of thought that make the selected course of behaviour seem attractive, the more it can be supposed to manifest a preference. Self-deception can be seen in such a light: Anna Karenina gains time to allow the mutual interest she shares with Vronsky to grow. By contrast, there is little inclination to say that the Ratman prefers neurotic suffering to yielding to hatred of his father.[30]

Of course, it remains logically possible to enforce explanation in terms of preferences. We could, for example, suppose that the Ratman judged that a realisation of the hatred he bears towards his father would endanger his sanity: so at all costs he must do whatever is necessary to bury it. Such a construction is, however, objectionable, because it imports a vantage point that – unlike the point of choice in self-deception – we can not coherently imagine occupying. 'I prefer to forget' is intelligible, but 'I prefer to form symptoms' is not. Any subjective vantage point where there is enough organised information about choices for the outcome to be describable as expressing a preference, must also be one that is sufficiently rational for symptom-formation not to be recognisable, from that vantage point, as an alternative. And unless there is such a master-point – a complex psychological state that can represent itself under a single description which enables the coordinative identification of conflict as problem and neurosis as solution – there can be no understanding of what results as truly revealing a preference.

The argument applies equally, and perhaps even more clearly, to the somatic symptoms of conversion hysteria, with which obsessional thoughts have much in common. In Freud's interpretations, hysterical symptoms, like dream presentations, combine contradictory meanings, derived from different desires. The fact of combination is itself without purpose; meanings are not combined to any end. Dora, for example, suffers from irritations of the chest and throat. These are analysed by Freud as deriving from her experience of being sexually assaulted by a man, Herr K., conjoined with a buried fantasy of sex with her father.[31] The symptom then 'reads': 'I wish to have sex with my father, and I reject this wish just as I rejected Herr K.' Now, if we adopt the model of preferences, then this interpretation of Freud's must be entered into the content of an intention of Dora's, that her irritations should have that meaning. But, once again, we can not coherently suppose a vantage point where Dora's knowledge of her memory of Herr K. and of her conflicting desires could converge with a judgement that hysteria is a suitable course of action; nor can we find intelligible a preference for hysterical 'expression' over the disabling cost of its symptoms.

These points are sufficiently important to deserve amplification. It might be thought: neurosis is an alternative to madness or even greater suffering; so it may be explained by a preference for neurosis over madness or greater suffering. But the description of X, an actual state of affairs, as *preferable to* Y, a counterfactual state of affairs, does not show X to have *been preferred* to Y. If someone is credited with exercising a preference, they must have known how to execute it. For which reason, psychosomatic disorders are not possible objects of preference. Nor is neurosis: it outstrips what can be imagined about persons to suppose that they could know how to induce symptoms in themselves. The reason why neurosis can not be explained by preference is not, then, that this would have to be unconscious, for people do indeed exercise non-conscious preferences (e.g. to self-deceive). It is because they can not be credited with the appropriate beliefs ('By forming symptoms, madness can be avoided'), without overstraining the concept of belief by removing from it all connection with justification; and because, if beliefs and desires sufficient to rationalise neurosis are attributed ('Let me form symptoms, lest I go mad'), it becomes incomprehensible that the rationality which is the conceptual concomitant of belief and desire does not lead the neurotic to exercise a better preference – or does not simply dispel the irrational hatred which makes the neurosis necessary in the first place.

The preference reconstruction of neurosis therefore founders. Whereas the attribution of self-deceptive intent encounters only the semi-technical difficulties examined in 1.3, the conceptual stage for the attribution of preference in neurosis collapses as soon as the attempt is made to set it up.[32]

4.7 REPRESSION

The account so far of the Ratman's hatred leaves the problem that he ought, by virtue of its powerful influence on his life, to feel it intensely, which he does not. An explanation is therefore owed to account for this conjunction of effectiveness and ignorance. According to psychoanalytic explanation, repression is called down on the emotion by its original crudity, and maintains its lack of connection with judgement. The characterisation of the Ratman's hatred as repressed introduces a *dynamic* characterisation of the unconscious: it is thought of as active with respect to mental contents. This section considers the essentials of the theory of repression: the evidence for repression, the nature of what is repressed, and the two philosophical ideas at the core of the theory.

As is well-known, the first class of clinical data to which Freud's theory of repression was addressed concerned the unretrieved memories of hysterics, around which failures of self-knowledge formed penumbrae: '*Hysterics suffer mainly from reminiscences.*'[33] This class also includes the forgetting of names and other interruptions to normal functioning.[34] These warrant the inference to something's having been repressed at some earlier time.

A second class of data is created in the context of analysis: when suggestions of the analyst (such as Freud's suggestion of infantile masturbation to the Ratman) are resisted, it is inferred that something is being currently repressed.

The phenomenon is deepened, at a third stage, when an interpretation is no longer resisted but its acceptance is purely nominal: the analysand's assent to propositions fails to produce the appropriate effects, and thus falls short of realisation, in the sense of 1.3.[35]

Repression refers then both to a kind of event, and a condition of mental state created by such events. Whether or not the specification of repressed events and states requires reference to real events, or can proceed 'solipsistically', is left open. The theory of repression is consequently neutral between acceptance and rejection of Freud's early seduction theory: this is an entirely separate question, which concerns the contribution and importance of real events (such as war trauma, and physical and sexual abuse) to psychological events.[36]

The psychological material of repression includes not just particular memories (e.g. a particular explosion of infantile anger), but also the conative dispositions crystallised around them (the feeling of anger and all that goes with it). For which reason, Freud's talk of 'impulses' as repressed is consistent with his equally frequent talk of 'ideas' (*Vorstellungen*) as repressed.[37] The material of repression requires a desire-like as well as a memory-like characterisation: repression has elements of both forgetting, and inhibition of desire.

The first challenge facing the theory of repression is to show that Freud's concept does not just recapitulate the commonsensical fact that persons are able, by redirecting their attention, to make themselves unaware of what they do not wish to be aware of – an ordinary phenomenon, not necessarily irrational, which might be called suppression.[38] If it can be shown that repression is something other than suppression, and that it is postulated only in contexts where it explains more than ordinary psychology can explain, the term will acquire meaning as a theoretical concept, on account of which its attribution will be explanatory.[39]

Certain features in contexts of failures of self-knowledge provide criteria to distinguish repression from other conditions. They revolve around the person's *inability to come to a realisation*, i.e. to form a self-ascribing belief that is effective in correcting their behaviour.[40] The starting point for an attribution of repression is a situation in which a person's behaviour manifests differential sensitivity to some object, and bears such marks as anxiety, flight or aggression. Such behaviour discloses a thought, as, for example, of a particular person as hostile. Further criteria and procedures – such as interrogation and probing in analysis – may determine that the person is unable to form appropriate awareness of that thought, and that this is not due to wilful perversity, self-deception, or otherwise explicable by ordinary psychology, but comes about because *the thought itself can not be manifested* in consciousness. The criteria used to identify this state of affairs may be limitlessly subtle, but a clear example is the Ratman's fierce idealisation of his father at the beginning of his treatment, which makes it impossible for any antagonistic feelings towards his father to manifest themselves, entailing a consequent inability on his part to form the belief that he also perceives his father as hostile.

A judgement of inability propels us into the concept of a *mechanism*: repression is the mechanism which makes it impossible for the Ratman, at that stage, to co-realise his love and hatred. It explains the inaccessibility of mental states without imputing an intention.[41] Its non-rational character is confirmed by the fact that no benefits accrue to the subject other than relief from anxiety; unlike the self-deceiver, nothing in his behaviour shows that he draws on knowledge of the repressed.

How does repression work? The theory, I will suggest, is best reconstructed philosophically in two parts. The first exploits the concepts of ideas and mental distance. The second rests on the notion of a special sort of psychological temporality.

I Freud's various descriptions of repression fall into two classes, each concerned with a different conceptual feature of the process.

(1) Freud emphasises that what is repressed is never an instinctual impulse itself, but always its 'ideational representative'.[42] Ideas are akin to memory-traces or linguistic units, and in repression, they are pulled apart from their associated 'affects', and made unconscious.[43] Freud also theorises repression as consisting in a split within ideas

themselves, between the 'word-presentation' or linguistic representation of the object, and the 'thing-presentation' or experiential representation of the object, the latter becoming unconscious.[44]

We get the following picture of repression. The divorce of idea from affect consists in the break-up of a judgement, such as 'My father is a hateful tyrant', into two components, the linguistic representation 'father', and the experiential representation of the father as hateful; the latter, and its correlated impulses, become unconscious. The experiential representation may then combine with some other linguistic unit (such as 'rat'), to produce symptoms, via the circuitous, non-rational routes retraced in psychoanalytic interpretation.

The basic philosophical intuition behind Freud's account is not hard to discern. Consciousness is bound up with the predominantly *propositional* character of its contents, so a good way of accounting for the impossibility of something's becoming conscious is to suppose that it is prevented from assuming a propositional form. The contents of the unconscious are then not judgements but ideas, whose relations to one another are not such as to form propositions, but rather Humean relations of association. Identifying the material of repression as ideas makes it possible to understand how repression can occur without the instrument of conscious thought: in Freud's later theory,[45] anxiety is the signal which causes repression, and it is triggered by ideas, not judgements.

To say this is not to deny that forming a belief, e.g. that one's sexual excitement is illicit, may contribute causally to repression. But the sense in which a condemnatory belief may cause repression is not by directly providing a *reason* for it, but by cueing the formation of an idea of the object as shameful, abhorrent etc.; the resulting abhorrent idea – not the original belief – then does the work of causing anxiety and, thereby, repression.

What happens in repression is that a propositional mental state disintegrates into more primitive, *pre-propositional components*; these are blocked from recombining in a propositional form and being manifested in consciousness. This reconstruction accords with Freud's description of repression as 'something between flight and condemnation',[46] and his most general description of the motive for repression as an impulse's 'incompatibility' with the ego,[47] which is clearly concerned with something below the level of propositional inconsistency; and with his statement that '[b]elief (and doubt) is a phenomenon that belongs wholly to the system of the ego (the *Cs.*) and has no counterpart in the *Ucs.*'[48]

(2) The second conceptual feature of repression consists in Freud's *topography*: it can be said that, in repression, an idea alters location, for example from consciousness (*Cs.*) to the unconscious (*Ucs.*), or that there are multiple 'registrations' of an idea, one in *Cs.* and another in *Ucs.*[49] Topographic characterisation of the mind, and the individuation of mental systems such as *Ucs.* and *Cs.*, are conceptually interdependent sets of terms.

Freud says that the concept of topography is necessarily connected to that of repression.[50] But topography clearly takes off from the ordinary idea of mental distance. So, it might be wondered, does topography amount to anything more than talk of mental distance, in the pretheoretical sense discussed in 3.7? It does, for the reason that psychoanalytic theory builds its concept of the unconscious as a mental location out of several, independent contexts. The difference between the condition of an idea that is repressed, and one that is only buried or suppressed, is that repressed items belong in *Ucs.*, as merely buried or suppressed items do not; and what it means to 'belong in *Ucs.*' can be explained in terms of further roles – e.g. in relation to dreams – which ideas in *Ucs.* have, and merely buried or suppressed ideas do not have. This means that repressed ideas can be identified from several angles. Topographic characterisation therefore underpins causal role across a variety of contexts.

Topographic characterisation requires an innovation in the individuation of mental items, and it is important to get clear about what this involves.

Normally, we do not individuate different representations of a concept (either general or particular) within one person. For example, we do not ask if someone uses the same or different representations of the number 2 in performing several arithmetical computations, any more than we attach sense to the question of how many beliefs that $2 + 2 = 4$ a person holds.

That the theory of repression does innovate the individuation of mental items can be seen by bringing out an unexpected consequence of the description of repression as the 'destruction of propositional form'. What such a description seems to imply, and what it would at first glance lead us to expect, is that the Ratman will as a result of repressing some such idea as that of 'my father as a hateful tyrant', become aphasic or exhibit conceptual 'blindness' regarding at least some propositions about fathers and tyrants.[51] But of course this is not what happens: the disappearance of the Ratman's hatred from his consciousness does not damage his ability to understand the word 'father' or even the sentence 'I hate my tyrannical father'.

The inertness of thought caused by repression confirms this point: when the Ratman accepts Freud's parricidal interpretation of his symptoms, but his neurosis continues, conscious thought fails to get hold of the 'same idea', in some sense, as the persisting and recalcitrant unconscious idea. As Freud puts it: '*Our* knowledge about the unconscious is not equivalent to *his* knowledge: if we communicate our knowledge to him, he does not receive it *instead of* his unconscious material, but *beside* it; and that makes very little change in it.'[52] Since repression does not consist in the loss of a concept, or inability to apply a concept, what is lost in repression must be an 'idea' in another sense.

Nor, at the other extreme, can repressed ideas be mental items in an *episodic* sense, for a very simple reason. Memory-images, let us agree, are individuated by episodes of remembering. Suppose we individuate the Ratman's 'ideas' of his hated father in the same way: we then find the Ratman required to perform a limitless number of acts of repression, since repressing one idea of his father in a given burst of hatred will do nothing to impede the recurrence of another idea of his father in a second wave of hatred – since, if ideas are individuated like memory-images, the second episode will employ a qualitatively identical yet numerically different idea, one that has yet to be repressed!

So we need another logical understanding of idea, closer to that in which a memory may be said to be lost, or recur in several episodes of remembering, and in which representations (as described in 1.3) enter into the formation of beliefs. This will provide a sense in which the Ratman may be said to fail to form the 'right' belief that he thinks of his father as a hateful tyrant, if he does not form it with the 'right' representation: there can be as many representations as one likes in *Cs.*, but unless the Ratman's conscious thought succeeds in harpooning the right representation in *Ucs.*, nothing will change for him. Getting the right representation will result in realisation: it will involve the Ratman's thinking of his father under several descriptions, in a way that brings all the relevant data to bear: 'as the person who beat me in my fifth year, as the figure I now identify with Freud, etc.'

Considered in terms of the distinction of types and tokens, the ideas of repression are therefore types: it is explanatory to say that an idea fails to surface in awareness, or does so only inertly, because it is *of a type that is repressed*. Here, type of idea is defined by a complex of criteria, including content, affective role (which makes reference to the subject's motivation), and the episode of thought which identifies the original event of repression.[53] So an 'idea' – that which in falling victim to repression becomes unable to recur freely – is like a concept which can only be specified in terms of an individual history, in which it is anchored; and it is one of the goals of analysis to reconstruct the right idiosyncratic 'concept'.[54] Although this is indeed an innovation, we are not altogether unfamiliar with similar notions outside the theory of repression. Proust provides an illustration, focusing on the distance between childhood and adult experience of the same object:

since I had seen Gilberte again, Swann had become to me pre-eminently her father, and no longer the Combray Swann; since the ideas to which I now connected his name were different from the ideas in the system of which it was formerly comprised, ideas which I no longer utilised when I had occasion to think of him, he had become a new, another person[55]

In sum, repression is a state in which an idea, defined by content plus affective role plus event-memory, is prevented from manifesting itself in conscious thought. Although this concept of a mental particular is coherent, it gives the theory a somewhat contrived air: tailor-made for the theory of repression, it seems to have restricted use outside that context.[56]

II The second part of the theory of repression, in my reconstruction, has to do with psychological temporality.[57] Repression understood in the way about to be suggested involves no new theoretical psychological concept, and leans instead on philosophical categories. It complements (and does not replace) the account of repression in terms of ideas and topography.

Familiar ways in which the present is related psychologically to the past include memory and learning. Sketchily, memory fixes beliefs about the past, and does so directly, on the immediate basis of past experience; and learning involves a transformation of past experience into present competence. In these cases, no present experience is required conceptually for the subject to have a relation to past experience. Memory *may* of course take an experiential form, and when it does, its object is represented experientially *as* past; but such experience is not necessary for memory. Something similar is true of learning.

Memory and experience do not however exhaust the conceptual possibilities regarding the relation of present to past. There is also room for the idea of a relation to the past that is *directly experiential*: in which present experience has a past object, without the object's being represented *as* past, and without the experience's representing itself *as* a memory. This, I contend, is involved in the concept of repression. Dora, for example, in repressing her experience of Herr K.'s sexual assault and her surge of revulsion, is in the terms suggested continuing to experience that scene.

Direct relations to the past of this kind are not already part of commonsense.[58] Ordinary psychology admits, of course, the idea that persons have feelings directed toward the past; they do so when, for example, past events, through being remembered, cause present emotions. But here the relation to the past is *in*direct, in that it holds by virtue of a memory. The same goes for the sense in which ordinary psychology allows persons to be related to the past by way of still 'undergoing its effects', past events continuing to 'have psychological repercussions' in the present.

The psychoanalytic concept of repression, by contrast, involves the concept of *temporally extended experience*, rather than that of experience as *having effects across time*: it claims the possibility of an experiential relation to a past event which involves no more mediation or intervening representation than enters into present experience of a present object.[59]

There are two reasons why this concept does not occur in ordinary psychology. First, it requires the concept of unconscious mentality in a strong sense[60] – since there can be no conscious self-ascription of a direct experiential relation to the past – which is not available in ordinary psychology. Second, the explanatory resources of ordinary psychology make it unable to conceptualise the direct relation to the past as anything but a 'magical' relation (i.e. as if present consciousness, despite having moved on in time, were able to time-travel, back to a past event). Freud however has a non-magical account of the relation, in terms of the mind's failure to 'date' its experience. This is expressed in his conception of the unconscious as *achronological*. The discovery of the unconscious was first formulated in terms of deviant vicissitudes of memory, but the formulation which

Freud later substituted sees the unconscious instead as a time-insensitive alternative to memory.[61]

The two parts of the theory of repression come together in the following formulation: repression is a psychological process which detours experience into the achronological unconscious, preventing it from being dated and given a propositional form, which would facilitate its becoming an object of memory and being consciously manifested; the resulting repressed ideas constitute a direct relation to the past.[62]

The discussion of repression leaves us with a theory that is workable, but has several weaknesses. One, the concept of repressed ideas is, as conceded earlier, inelegant. Two, mental place is an independent variable in the theory of repression, and whilst this notion is, it has been argued, unobjectionable, its explanatory burden in this context may seem excessive. Three, it remains unclear why the mere absence of consciousness should be a primary goal of irrational mental functioning, as the theory of repression implies;[63] particularly given that, on the account given here, experience that is repressed will in any case persist in the unconscious, rather than be destroyed. Even if it is allowed that the mechanical character of repression absolves it from having to make sense as a stratagem, the sufficiency of unconsciousness for the wide range of effects that Freud supposes is not secure. In 7.1 it will be suggested that Kleinian theory resolves these difficulties.

4.8 INTERPRETING THE RATMAN: THEORETICAL CONCLUSIONS

We have seen that, in order to explain irrational phenomena of a grade transcending ordinary psychology, psychoanalytic explanation attributes motives, such as hatred and its conflict with love, and assigns a function to self-misrepresentation. Although this gives neurotic symptoms the appearance of self-deception, the crucial ingredients of intention and preference are missing: in so far as a person is self-deceived, she knows what she is up to, but in so far as she is neurotic, she does not. That preferential modelling deforms psychoanalytic explanation is the second fundamental lesson of the Censor Criticism. The essential nature of psychoanalytic explanation remains to be identified, but it is already clear that Sartre's allegation of logical confusion in psychoanalytic theory is a consequence of his false assumption that it is only a semi-disguised exercise in ordinary psychology.

The three features of the Ratman's motive – its crudity, conflict and repression – make it accidentally inaccessible. This answers his question, 'how can I not know ... ?': the greater his cultivated love of his father and repression of his hatred, the more isolated his hatred becomes and the less it is worked over by adulterating rational processes, increasing its crudity and further intensifying his mental conflict. So it is explained why an ordinary psychological law – the stronger an emotion, the more prominent it will be in consciousness – does not hold in this case.

The Ratman's failure of self-knowledge has been accounted for,[64] but what has not yet been explained is how and why the Ratman's motives issued in his symptoms – the productive aspect of the dynamism of the unconscious. Also, it was said earlier that a theory of what the non-propositional structures dominating the Ratman's mental life consist in is needed. Both of these tasks will be taken up in chapter 6, which moves from Freudian metapsychology, in which the unconscious is thought of chiefly negatively, in terms of failure to assume propositional form, to Kleinian metapsychology, in which the unconscious, viewed as formed out of states that are non-accidentally inaccessible, is given its own positive description, and its dynamism explained in terms of the nature of the mental states which compose it.

4.9 CONCEPTUALISING UNCONSCIOUS MOTIVES: HOMOGENEITY VERSUS HETEROGENEITY

The rest of this chapter will begin to discuss the philosophical issues thrown up by psychoanalytic concepts. The first is a very basic question about the nature of the unconscious motives attributed in psychoanalytic explanation.

Calling something a motive provides it with only a minimally informative description: a motive is pretty much anything that plays a relatively basic, conative role in psychological explanation. But Freud says of the Ratman's central motive, his hatred, that 'to give it such a name was to caricature the feeling'.[65] Now to call something a caricature is to suggest more than exaggeration of scale. Freud's implication is that referring to unconscious states in terms drawn from ordinary psychology is, in some sense, to misrepresent them.

This would show that Freud recognised the 'radical heterogeneity' of unconscious motives.

However, Freud also says that

all the categories which we employ to describe conscious mental acts, such as ideas, purposes, resolutions and so on, can be applied to them. Indeed, we are obliged to say of some of these latent states that the only respect in which they differ from conscious states is precisely in the absence of consciousness.[66]

Now I want to trace the lines of thought which led Freud to these opposite ways of thinking about the nature of unconscious motives, and pursue the argument – already begun in discussing the Ratman – for the claim that we should come down on the side of heterogeneity.

Freud employs a wide vocabulary to report the contents of the unconscious: he talks of unconscious motives, impulses, emotions, desires, beliefs, thoughts, intentions, and memories. This encourages what is perhaps the most natural way of proceeding in the philosophical discussion of psychoanalysis, which is to ask, with regard to each species of unconscious state, how it compares with a conscious version of a state of the same kind. So there is, paralleling Freud's usage, an extensive philosophical literature taking up the question of each kind of unconscious state in turn.[67] Alvin Goldman draws an analogy that illustrates this approach:

An unconscious want is related to a normal want in the way that a sweet lemon is related to a normal lemon. One of the usual criteria of lemonhood is a sour taste, but we can decide to call fruit which is not sour but which is otherwise like a lemon a 'sweet lemon'.

Goldman says that we should then go on to ask: 'What is the relevant respect in which unconscious wants are *like* normal wants?'[68]

This assumption leads directly to the *homogeneous* view of unconscious motives.[69] For here the assumption is that 'unconscious want' is not just a convenient way of referring to a psychoanalytic state that will serve to identify it until a more accurate description is found, but that it picks out the state under two independent and correct descriptions, as a *want*, and as *unconscious*, only the first of these giving its essential nature. I now want to spell out the corollaries and difficulties of this assumption.

One corollary is that, because the theory of the unconscious is to be provided piecemeal, by taking each kind of state in turn, it reduces to many theories, of unconscious wants, unconscious beliefs, unconscious intentions and so on. The tendency of this approach will be to divert attention from a unifying explanation of the common status of psychoanalytic states.

Second, it means that 'unconscious' in psychoanalytic expressions is relegated to indicating only an epistemic feature of mental states, their inaccessibility. This suggests that other differences between conscious and unconscious instances of the same kind of mental state must somehow be derived from their epistemic difference, since, ex hypothesi, it will not be derivable from their nature as wants, beliefs, etc. Clearly, there is something strange in the supposition that the distinguishing features of psychoanalytic states could be effects of their inaccessibility; since, as has already been seen with regard to the Ratman's hatred, the inaccessibility of psychoanalytic states only becomes intelligible once they have been shown to differ in non-epistemic respects from ordinary conscious states.[70]

Third, psychoanalytic claims are thereby made vulnerable to the sceptical objection that the subtraction of consciousness discards an *essential dimension* of all mental states.[71] Now, psychoanalysis will of course at some point have to challenge this Cartesian axiom; but it would be better to conceptualise psychoanalytic states at the outset in terms of more basic, non-epistemic features (as it were, to find a property of 'sweet lemons' that will explain their sweetness).

Fourth, the natural companion to Goldman's assumption is, of course, the Second Mind: for if psychoanalytic explanation is centrally concerned with 'wants' as ordinarily understood, then it requires a background of the kind standardly supposed by the ordinary use of such a concept – most readily supplied by a Second Mind.

Of course, there could be a psychological theory whose explanatory claims centred on the postulation of states which are in all essential respects identical with those attributed in ordinary psychology, but for their being unconscious, in the sense of not being avowed by their subjects. Decision-theory, as employed in for example the analysis of economic behaviour, fits this description, to the extent that it imputes unconscious preferences. But the explanatory ambitions of such a theory are utterly remote from those of psychoanalysis.

In proposing that Goldman's assumption be rejected, some qualifications are needed. Denying Goldman's assumption does not preclude unconscious versions of familiar kinds of mental state from having some role in psychoanalytic interpretations: it is being denied only that they stand at its core. Nor is it being argued that any mistake necessarily occurs in the clinical, as opposed to the theoretical, language of psychoanalysis, when interpretations are couched in terms like 'unconsciously want'. Such locutions are appropriate to the extent that a psychoanalytic motive appears to be, with reference to a certain set of its effects, more desire-like than belief-like. But the existence of semi-heuristic reasons for getting the analysand to think of his unconscious mental states in terms drawn from ordinary psychological language does not commit the meta-psychology to doing likewise.

Goldman's assumption, and the homogeneity view which it entails, create unwelcome conceptual difficulties. Yet it is not hard to understand why Freud should have wanted to claim that psycho-analytic states differ only in their absence of consciousness: he wanted to insist on the fully *psychological* nature of unconscious motivation. The homogeneity view is motivated by the worry that psychoanalytic states, if allowed to stray from the familiar, will lose this title, and may as well be regarded as physical (brain) states. But to qualify, or even dispute, the assumption that the unconscious is composed of beliefs, desires and so forth, is not necessarily to fly in the face of Freud's intent: the psychological reality of the unconscious does not guarantee the conceptual homeliness of its contents, for there are ways of asserting both the unconscious' radical het-erogeneity and its psychologicality.

4.10 PSYCHOANALYTIC STRATEGY: IRRATIONAL CAUSES

In the rest of this chapter I want to make out a case for the concepts that will appear in the following chapters in such a way as to make them seem, as far as possible, inevitable. In this section I will argue for the strategy that I favour, and in the next set out the central range of tactics which it involves.

Three opposing strategies stand out, on first reflection, as candi-dates for responding to the massive degree of incoherence that we encounter when we describe the Ratman as thinking that Freud is his father and tormentor, i.e. irrational phenomena that are propo-sitionally opaque.

(A) As noted earlier, nothing prevents us outright from persevering in attributing beliefs, desires and preferences:[72] any instance of behaviour can after all be read in such terms (we can do it for slugs). So, we can get the result that the Ratman's father-torturing phantasy resulted from either (i) a direct preference for *imagining* torturing his father, or (ii) a preference for *really* torturing his father, in combination with a delusion that he is actually doing so when in fact he only thinks he is doing so – rationalised perhaps by a belief that his thoughts have unlimited potency, which gives him reason to select imagination, as the course of action with the best chance of success.[73] We might add that the Ratman puts a value on father-torturing that outweighs the cost of neurosis. Were the Ratman himself to contest all this, as he would be certain to do, we would simply call his preference unconscious.

The preference model can always – in a barren sense of 'can' – be imposed; but the upshot is a reductio.[74]

(B) A second strategy is provided by sub-systems. Encouraged by the intuition that there is a sense in which the satisfaction of sadistic desire has a kind of independence from, and occurs at the expense of, the Ratman himself, we might reapply the model of preferences across two or more analogues of persons: insulating some of the Ratman's extravagant beliefs and desires in a sub-system.

Leaving aside the conceptual precariousness of sub-systemic theory, the strategy of redistributing propositional attitudes across multiple subjects of preference faces the conclusive objection that it does nothing to explain how sub-systems come to have such irrational contents – which is the real explanandum.

(C) A third response, suggested by Daniel Dennett,[75] sees the Ratman as but an aggravated instance of the general problem of what explanation to offer when a rational creature displays either imperfection or breakdown in its mental functioning. Dennett takes seriously the observation that, as long as we continue to attribute propositional attitudes, we are bound to regard these states as interacting rationally; and that what we have yet to explain is a failure of rationality. He concludes that this defines an impossible task, and that even a minor breakdown, as when I give a customer the wrong change, is sufficient to make any kind of intentional explanation inapplicable. Dennett's proposal is then that explanations of shortcomings in rational functioning should only be taken realistically at the properly sub-personal level of cognitive psychology.

The strategy of abandoning intentional explanation is also endorsed by those who claim that the task of explanation undertaken by psychoanalytic theory awaits advances in neurophysiology;

a view which adheres to the strict letter of Freud's original 'Project for a scientific psychology', and is obliged to regard all his subsequent work as a failure to remain loyal to that original statement of intent.[76]

These three options are not exhaustive. A path can be steered between desperate perseverance in belief and desire explanation, and the outright abandonment of any form of intentional explanation.

It may be conceded to Dennett that, if cognitive psychology were complete, we might turn directly to such a science in cases of breakdown. But this alone would do nothing to show that there is not *also*, in each case, an intentional explanation to be made out and taken realistically.[77] And unless this assumption is knocked out, we are licensed to press for a new form of intentional explanation at the personal level. This can be achieved by an *extension of ordinary psychology*, grounded on the supposition that there exist *kinds of mental state that do not interact rationally* – 'irrational' mental states – which are the suitable causes of irrational phenomena.[78]

It is important that psychoanalytic theory's pursuit of this strategy should avoid arbitrariness. So it must be explained why selected parts of the ordinary intentional apparatus are retained and others rejected. The theory should modify ordinary intentional explanation in accordance with our general knowledge of persons as human organisms, and it should yield a unified theory of non-rational psychological processes. Psychoanalytic theory meets these constraints: the weight that Freud gives to biological facts, and facts about infantile development, obviously helps to meet the first condition; and with regard to the second, it is a strength of Freud's theory that it spans jokes, parapraxes, aspects of social behaviour, and artistic practice, as well as neurosis. A further important constraint is that the theory should be *phenomenologically attested*: it must be internally recognisable and 'resonate with experience' in the right way.

The method of theorising suitably 'irrational' kinds of cause of irrational phenomena is not, then, an invitation to facile fabrication, and nor is it, like sub-systemic theory, necessarily embroiled in difficulties of analyticity. More precisely formulated constraints, along with suggestions about how psychoanalytic theory meets them, will come up en route, and chapters 7 and 8 will review the extent to which all of this has been achieved.

Such a strategy is to be found in Richard Wollheim's writings.[79] Central to Wollheim's understanding of psychoanalysis is an extended concept of the imagination: states of imagination have intentional content but are not subject to the requirements of rationality that govern belief, desire and preference. Placing non-rational states with a distinctive nomology at the outset breaks the cycle of having to invoke endlessly further propositional attitudes to explain how those that have been attributed can yield irrational results.

4.11 PSYCHOANALYTIC TACTICS

I now want to make explicit some of the fundamental principles constitutive of psychoanalytic theory, and indicate the kind of explanatory tactics which they facilitate.

I The alternative to Goldman's assumption is to hold that the real sorts to which psychoanalytic motives belong are specified uniquely in psychoanalytic theory: they are *wishes* and *phantasies*. These are not to be thought of as sub-classes of non-psychoanalytic states – they are not species of desires or beliefs, or combinations of such – for their associated way of mental processing differs fundamentally from that of propositional attitudes. The concepts of a kind of mental state, and of a way of mental processing, are conceptually complementary: a kind of mental state is explained with reference to a characteristic nomology.

This tactic can be thought of as offering an alternative way of understanding Freud's argument for the unconscious (in 2.2): after an initial attribution of propositional attitudes has failed to yield a coherent picture, we reapply *in part* our principles of explanation, but this time adduce the existence of a second *kind* of mental state, instead of a Second *Mind*.

II The second principle has already been introduced in the contexts of repression and conflict, and will be returned to several times in later chapters. It is the distinction between propositional and pre-propositional states. The point of making this distinction is that the pre-propositional realm may be thought of as not bound by what governs belief and desire; it is postulated precisely in order to make sense of irrational features of belief and desire that can not be accounted for in their own terms.

III The third principle rests on a distinction suggested, first, by Freud's talk of drives and theory of instincts;[80] and, second, by his distinction of sexual desires with *objects* (such as persons, fetishes, acts) from sexual instincts with *aims* (characterised in terms of bodily zones, and the dimension of activity/passivity).[81] It is the distinction between propositional desires, and what may be called *motivational states*. Three features distinguish propositional desires from motivational states: they combine directly with beliefs to constitute reasons for action; there is subjective awareness of them under a description; and they have a direct, creative relation to choice.[82] Propositional desires are generated out of motivational states with the aid of beliefs about the world, yielding specifications of the desire's object, and fixing the description under which the agent is aware of her desire. As beliefs about alternative means of satisfying desires, and about relations of co-satisfiability with other desires, enter into mental processing, points of choice are created and preferences formed, leading eventually to intentions.

In Freud's terminology, motivational states have aims but not objects, and propositional desires have objects but not aims. An aim is not a propositional specification of a state of affairs. The concept of a motivational state is therefore not to be confused with that of a very general desire:[83] motivational states are states that *cause* people to have desires.[84] This causal relation is necessarily an unconscious one, in the descriptive sense: nothing, for example, corresponds to the description, 'consciousness of lack of H_2O *as causing* thirst'; consciousness begins with thirst, as the given which makes drinking desirable. Similarly, there is no such thing as consciousness of sexual libido *as causing* sexual desires. It is in obvious ways important for psychoanalytic theory that the process whereby motivational states yield propositional desires should be screened from consciousness: crucially, it will be seen in 5.1, it allows wishes to appear on the scene as alternative effects of motivational states. The distinction of desires from motivational states is then highly important in preventing psychoanalytic explanation from surreptitiously lapsing back into the form of belief and desire explanation from which it seeks to distance itself.

IV The distinction of desires from motivational states also contributes to defining a sense in which psychoanalytic explanation, by citing something desire-like,[85] can show behaviour to be *purposive*, without attributing a *reason for action*.[86] This possibility, which may sound curious initially, is however not open to refutation a priori.[87] Its cogency depends upon the detailed treatment, which is still to come, of theoretical concepts such as wish-fulfilment.

The fourth principle consists, then, in psychoanalytic theory's continued employment of the broad concept of a desire's pursuing its satisfaction, whilst severing its relations with the more specific concept of something's being done for the reason that it satisfies a desire. What is this broader concept? It involves the idea of a causal relation between mental elements turning on a connection of content, which is weaker than that of a reason to the action that it causes, but stronger than an arbitrary, 'brute', sub-rational psychological association (something best explained at the sub-personal level): a relation which is due to desire's *giving expression to its intrinsic tendency to cause the realisation of its conditions of satisfaction*. This tendency is distinct from, and broader than, desire's tendency to combine with beliefs to form reasons for action. Psychoanalytic explanation is, then, a 'rationalising' form of explanation in a loose sense, in that it focuses on connections of content propelled by desire. The purposiveness of the unconscious – its productive dynamism – consists in its being effective in ways that derive from wish-fulfilment; this amounts to something more specific than its just having effects tout court, and, indeed, than its just having effects that are simply expressive of it.[88]

This allows much more to count as an effect of desire than is envisaged in ordinary psychology. This extension is however not damagingly open-ended, for, as 5.8 will indicate, the necessary conditions for symbol-formation place natural limits on the versatility of desire.

V The final principle concerns the convergence of psychoanalytic psychology with what Dennett calls 'design level' speculation, that is, speculation which concerns the person's functional construction.[89] Most of Freud's concepts come tethered to an 'economic' description, which refers back to the functional, neurological model of the 'Project'.[90] The importance of economic description for Freudian theory is variable, and no general rules determine the importance of design level speculation to the exposition of any given psychoanalytic concept. This issue will resurface later, and it will be claimed that economic description is important for the understanding of wish-fulfilment – again, because it helps to make an alternative to rational functioning intelligible, by highlighting the role of quantitative properties of the mental – in a way that it has not been for that of repression. So the convergence with design level speculation is only partial – psychoanalytic theory is far from being a non-intentional, design level theory – but it too distances psychoanalytic from ordinary psychology to some degree.

There are two ways of viewing design level description: as *supplementing*, or (per Dennett) as *supplanting*, intentional explanation. The reason for taking the former view of psychoanalytic theory's engagements with design level description – and therefore denying that, for example, to call an idea repressed is just to report a properly sub-personal state, with the implication of a corresponding lacuna at the level of intentional characterisation – is that continuity must be preserved between the various parts of psychoanalytic causal stories. The necessity of continuity derives directly from the requirement (in 4.3) that the Ratman should be able to see his symptoms in a light that integrates them into the rest of his mental life. It can not be that the Ratman is, at the same, personal level, fifty per cent intentional and fifty per cent non-intentional: no one thing could be heterogeneous in that way! So, if any intentional characterisation is to be understood realistically, there is strong metaphysical pressure for a complete intentional characterisation of the person.[91] Design level description in psychoanalytic contexts ought then to be viewed as parasitic on, and not as supplanting, intentional description.[92]

Explanation in terms of wish and phantasy will be presented now in two stages. First, the concept of a wish founds the idea of a mode of mental functioning marked off from that in which rational desires engage: chapter 5 will show how the mechanism of wish-fulfilment takes the central burden of explanation. Second, in chapter 6 the concept of phantasy will be elaborated in order to account for the rich range of phenomena not sufficiently explained by wish-fulfilment. The original account of wish-fulfilment is Freud's, but its elaboration into phantasy is, largely, Klein's. Following this route, we will arrive at a positive characterisation of the unconscious.

The overall structure of the account of the unconscious towards which we are working looks like this:

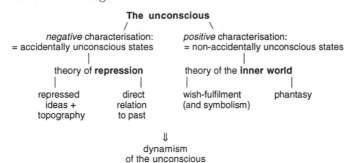

CHAPTER 5

Wish

At the freezing-point of the will [...] To wish is a sign of recovery or mending.

Nietzsche

From experience – The irrationality of a thing is no argument against its existence, rather a condition of it.

Nietzsche

5.1 THE CREATION OF WISHES

Two kinds of phenomena exemplify wish-fulfilment in its purest and most rudimentary form: infantile hallucination, and dreaming.

Freud supposes that the frustration suffered by the infant when it is deprived of nourishment, causes it to hallucinate (by drawing on a memory of) the breast, or experience of sucking, bringing it temporary relief.[1] Wish-fulfilment in dreams is best illustrated where there is no interference from censorship, as in Anna Freud's straightforwardly appetitive dream of wild strawberries, and Freud's self-induced 'thirst' dreams, where his eating anchovies before going to sleep made him dream of drinking.[2]

The representations of the infant and the dreamer are caused by *wishes*. Wishes are conative states whose causes, in these instances, are simple universal biological requirements, the most basic instinctual demands. Other motivational states with a more psychologically complex, less plainly biological character can play the same role. In wish-fulfilment, content is straightforwardly transposed from a wish into a representation of the wish as fulfilled.

The most basic condition in which wishes are created is when action is not possible, as in infancy or sleep; wishes then issue directly from motivational states. Another is when progress toward action is impeded, by either an external or a psychological obstacle; wishes then come about through what Freud calls the regression of a desire.[3]

120

Freud also describes wish-fulfilment in economic terms.[4] Instinctual demands create a level of energy (excitation) in the psychic apparatus that, by virtue of the operation of a simple law of tension-reduction, calls for discharge. The psychic apparatus may be said to have two goals: providing the organism with what it needs, and relieving itself of tension (just as the heart may be said to have two goals, providing the body with oxygenated blood, and expelling incoming fluid). If it achieves the latter, it will also accomplish the former. Standardly this involves action. There is, however, a way of achieving the more immediate goal of tension-reduction that shortcuts the task of altering the objective conditions of the organism. When for some reason action is not possible (when for example the motor system is disconnected, as in sleep), or the object of need is unavailable, an alternative to action is explored: energy is redirected (it 'regresses') to the perceptual-memory system, where it activates a memory-trace ('mnemic symbol') of a previous experience of satisfaction of the same kind as would be required to fulfil the current instinctual demand. The activation ('cathexis') of the memory-trace results in a hallucinatory experience, accompanied by discharge of the surplus energy. This discharge is given experientially to the subject as an experience of satisfaction.[5]

With regard to the use of the concept of energy in this context, several things should be noted. First, when the nervous system is said to 'reroute energy', its operation is not being conceived intentionally; a nervous system does not represent its own homeostasis as a condition of the organism's well-being, and it is consequently not being asked to play a sub-systemic role. Second, economic characterisation is applied to wish-fulfilment only on the basis of prior intentional description: here as elsewhere, the fact that economic conjectures can only be made on the basis of, and understood with reference to, facts about wants and thoughts, means that (as argued in 4.11) psychoanalytic theory's convergence on the design level does not result in intentional psychology's being eliminated. Third, Freud's economic conception of the psychic apparatus is evidently continuous with ordinary psychology's idea that mental states have force (desires are entrenched by habit, enfeebled by neglect, owe their victory to the suddenness of their appearance, etc.).[6] Fourth, the economic description of wish-fulfilment is congruent with a well-known feature of human behaviour, the tendency to prefer short-term relief over long-term satisfaction.

The value of economic description consists in its enabling us to see why, at a level where unassisted intentional explanation would leave a hiatus, matters should be arranged in such a way that, although real satisfaction is not brought about, there can still be an experience of satisfaction.

5.2 FEATURES OF WISH-FULFILMENT

Wish-fulfilment has several features that distinguish it from rational satisfaction.

One, it involves sensory experience in some medium.[7] The rational satisfaction of desire (with the exception of desires for sensory experience), by contrast, does not involve essentially anything sensory.

Two, the concluding experience in wish-fulfilment is a 'blanket' experience of sensational satisfaction,[8] which, although it is brought about by an item with content (the 'mnemic symbol'), is not subordinated to, or constituted by, a judgement. The rational satisfaction of desire, by contrast, is so constituted, and need not involve a specific feeling of satisfaction. Rational satisfaction therefore involves propositional content, and wish-fulfilment only pre-propositional content.

Three, although neither wish-fulfilling hallucinating nor dreaming consists in an act of memory, the dimension of past experience is essential to wish-fulfilment in a way that it is not to rational satisfaction.[9] In wish-fulfilment, the subject goes back to an earlier experience, rather than bringing earlier experience to bear on the present; wish-fulfilment's relation to past experience is the reverse of that in which past experience informs rational action through learning.

Four, Freud insisted that it is a necessary fact about wish-fulfilment that its conditions, when these are fully spelled out, include instinctual demands. He held to this view in the face of evidence superficially to the contrary, supplied by interpretations that discover in wishes greater sophistication of content than is involved in biological need, which might have been taken to suggest some other role for dreams than responding to instinctual demands.

For example, Freud's dream of Irma's injection involves a wish that concerns Freud's patient Irma, and his medical colleague Otto: a wish 'that I was not responsible for the persistence of Irma's pains, but that Otto was'.[10] Such a desire exhibits moral sensitivity, and is therefore at a remove from naked instinctual demands; it is properly located in the preconscious, rather than the unconscious.[11] In order for the creation of this dream to remain a process of wish-fulfilment, a more complex story must therefore be told. Freud does this by regarding instinctual demands as necessary for the process, and preconscious desires and thoughts ('day-residues') as giving the dream its specific form and content.[12] The role of preconscious desires and thoughts is conditional upon their *subserving* the instinctual demand.[13]

This point is important because it indicates that Freud did not envisage wish-fulfilment as a mode of satisfaction available to propositional desires. Propositional desires can exploit wish-fulfilment only indirectly. On Freud's picture, this occurs in the following way. Every propositional desire stands in a relation of 'derivation' to a state of instinctual demand, and by way of 'regressing'[14] to that demand, a desire can result in a wish, susceptible to satisfaction by wish-fulfilment. For example, Freud's displeasure at what he supposes to be Otto's critical view of his unsuccessful treatment of Irma, and his self-reproach in this connection, yield propositional desires deriving from an instinctual state of aggression: when these desires regress, the instinctual state takes over their content, and instigates a process of wish-fulfilment.

Derivation and regression are concepts that presuppose two specific psychoanalytic hypotheses. The first of these is that mental states can be graded in terms of maturity or infantility, and ordered on an axis reflecting universal developmental stages of the mind. These stages are never permanently overcome: elements of the mind may return to a developmental stage from which the mind as a whole has moved on. This makes it possible for a mental state to change in ways that lose or gain for it characteristics of maturity or infantility.

The second hypothesis is a modification of the ordinary criteria for the individuation of mental states. When desiring gives way to wishing, a desire does not just cause, but becomes, a wish. Psychoanalytic theory thereby introduces the important concept of a mental state's *having a history*, and accordingly individuates mental states more broadly than in ordinary psychology:[15] where ordinary psychology would speak of two distinct mental states, psychoanalysis speaks of one (the state that was a propositional desire endures as a wish).

Five, wish-fulfilment allows for a frequent concurrence of 'contradictory' meanings in the objects of psychoanalytic interpretation – in sharp contrast with the univocity of sense that we mostly uncover in the interpretation of speech and rational behaviour. This, a feature noted in 4.6 with regard to Dora, can now be explained. There are very few different kinds of motivational state in comparison with the number of propositional desires derivable from them, and an instinctual demand may simultaneously motivate several desires or wishes: Dora's sexual instinct embraces several objects, and several relations of desiring or wishing to each of those objects. In the absence of a sifting mechanism that would put a requirement of co-satisfiability on the product of wish-fulfilment, different and contrasting instinctual demands may exploit the same wish-fulfilling processes. This results in what Freud calls 'over-determination'.[16]

In conclusion, we see that wishes are a sort of hybrid: they have the *force* of pre-propositional states of instinctual demand, whilst being able to draw on the *complexity of content* of propositional states. Through the assumption that propositional desires are causally dependent on motivational states, and that these consist in biological need or other kinds of instinctual demand, psychoanalytic interpretation is given a definite direction: however sophisticated the content of a propositional attitude, the extended possibilities of interconnection between mental states discovered in psychoanalytic interpretation mean that it is related, at least potentially, to an instinctual condition. This brings the entire extent of the mind within the orbit of bodily determination: even the most 'angelic' mental states are haunted by instinctual conditions.[17]

5.3 THE CONCEPTUAL STRUCTURE OF WISH-FULFILMENT

The next step is to show how the conceptual structure of wish-fulfilment differentiates it from rational satisfaction.

In order to go into this, a rudimentary model of rational satisfaction is needed. The rational satisfaction of thirst, for example, involves a sequence of the following kind:[18]

(1)   a *motivational state* (a biological need for intake of water) initiates the sequence;

(2)   a *desire* (to drink) follows, its content informed by beliefs about the world;

(3) the desire produces a *trying*, to perform an action of a kind to satisfy the desire (to drink).

With the performance of the action come:

(4) *fulfilment* of the motivational state (intake of water),
(4′) *satisfaction* of the desire (water is drunk).

There is consequently a subjective event that may be formulated as:

(5*) the *experiential registration of satisfaction*, which puts the feeling of need in abeyance, and terminates the subject's action-disposition to fulfil the goal set by its motivational state.[19]

Now, in wish-fulfilment – as when Freud's dream of drinking water 'allays' his anchovy-induced thirst – the rational sequence is modified by the absence of (4) and (4′). And yet (5*) occurs, despite the fact that the goal set by the motivational state has not really been achieved. The problem is to explain how (4) and (4′) can be absent, and the sequence still yield (5*).

In rational satisfaction, two beliefs are involved. The first is inserted in the sequence before the experiential registration of satisfaction in (5*), and helps to cause it:

(5) the *belief* that the relevant action has been performed.

The second follows the experiential registration of satisfaction in (5*):

(5′) the *belief* that the desire is satisfied.

What may be supposed is that, in wish-fulfilment, a sensory experience takes over the causal role of these beliefs: the role of (5) and (5′) is played *directly* by the wish-fulfilling representation. The simplest assumption is that, in wish-fulfilment, the experiential registration in (5*) is a direct effect of a sensory experience, and that, once it has been produced, the cessation of trying and temporary abeyance of the action-disposition follow, as in the rational sequence. This is *all* that needs to be assumed under the conditions of primitive wish-fulfilment, such as infantile mentality, or sleep, where there is insulation from belief: it is not a priori that belief is a condition for the cessation of (2), and there is no independent reason – given that there are no further effects to be explained that would provide evidence for the presence of (5) or (5′) – for introducing belief into the process.

There is consequently a logical difference between wish-fulfilment and rational satisfaction. The formula that Freud uses, when looked at closely, lays careful emphasis on the differentiation of wish-fulfilment from rational satisfaction: a dream is said not to satisfy, but to *represent the fulfilment* of a wish.[20]

When a desire is rationally satisfied, a distinction can be drawn between its conditions of satisfaction, and the action which brings these about. The operation of a wish has a different structure: it causes only one thing, a *representation* of its object. Wish-fulfilment can not therefore be analysed into conditions of satisfaction, and cause of those conditions. In terms of the distinction made earlier with regard to the emotions (in 4.5), wishes may be thought of as having particulars, but not states of affairs, as their formal objects. Conversely, in rational satisfaction there is no analogue of the wish-fulfilling representation: actions are not representations. So whereas in rational satisfaction there are two logically distinct components, in wish-fulfilment there is only one. The two components in rational satisfaction are only causally related: actions do not represent conditions of satisfaction. In wish-fulfilment, the causal relation doubles with a relation of representation.[21]

One helpful way of marking the difference of structure is to employ a reflexive description of wish-fulfilment. We can say that, whereas in rational action, persons satisfy their desires, in wish-fulfilment, wishes *misrepresent themselves* as fulfilled.[22]

It follows that the psychoanalytic concept of wish is not the same as, however closely it may be related to, the concept expressed by ordinary use of the term. The colloquial sense in which a wished-for state of affairs may, with good fortune, *really* come about, is not the sense in which a psychoanalytic wish may receive wish-fulfilment.[23] Psychoanalytic wishes are necessarily engaged in the process of wish-fulfilment, a psychological cycle which leads directly to the formation of an immediately satisfying mental representation of the wish's object; which is not true of ordinary, conscious wishes.[24]

5.4 EXPRESSION

There are ways, well recognised in ordinary psychology, in which relief from frustration can be got, without action being properly undertaken: namely, when we *give expression* to frustration, as in emotional behaviour. Expression might therefore seem to provide a relation weaker than fulfilment, which can nevertheless account for the effects of wishes. So, it might be thought that Freud was mistaken in seeing a stronger relation of fulfilment between the wish and the representation formed at its behest, and held that there is licence for an inference to 'dreaming *gives expression* to wishes', but not to 'dreaming *fulfils* wishes'.[25]

What this proposal hangs on is whether or not expression can yield the same depth of explanation as wish-fulfilment. It is, I think, fairly clear that it can not, for the reason that expression is such a broad notion that virtually *any* effect of a mental state may be described as an expression of it:[26] utterances may be said to express beliefs, and rational actions to express desires. The concept of expression does not denote a species of motive, nor does it circumscribe a single kind of mental process.

On the Freudian view, expression is not, in a substantial sense, a basic kind of mental process. Of course, the plasticity of the ordinary concept of expression means that wish-fulfilment can be described as a form of expression of desire; and there is no harm in the loose and abstract assumption – which simply gestures at the momentum or autonomy of mental life – that mental states, over and above their instrumental role in rational satisfaction, tend prima facie to have some effects rather than none, and to have effects that manifest, in appropriate ways, their kind and content. But the direction of explanation goes from the more specific to the more general concept: the formula (in 4.11), that in psychoanalytic contexts desires give expression to their intrinsic tendency to cause the realisation of their conditions of satisfaction, makes conation the basic and explanatory concept. The assumption that satisfying desire is the business of those mental processes that are developmentally prior accords with the fact that we start off as creatures with biological needs, and only later become artists. Also, it opens up the possibility that some forms of expression in human life, such as artistic activity, may be explained as developments, albeit highly sophisticated ones, out of wish-fulfilment.

5.5 WISH-FULFILMENT AND THE REALITY PRINCIPLE

We can now consider what happens to wish-fulfilment when the infant's mind develops in such a way as to take proper account of reality.

In its most primitive condition, the infant's mind does not register the 'psychological mode' of mental states.[27] That is, if a given representation plays a desire-like role, the mental apparatus does not record this fact; at the most primitive stage, there is nothing to 'read' mental content for its direction of fit. Progress is made when the mind gains the capacity to distinguish veridical from non-veridical representations: it can then engage in monitoring its own content, and distinguish those of its representations that fit the world (beliefs) from those that the world is to fit (desires). For this, sensitivity to reality is necessary. The mind is now 'auto-literate'.

Will the effect of this change – in Freud's terms, the first incursion of the Reality Principle – be to put an end to wish-fulfilment? Only if the mind suddenly becomes both wholly responsive only to reality, and omnipotent with regard to itself! Such an assumption – which can not be established a priori – risks confusing the mind's capacity to read its contents, with its distinct and later capacity, to implement the results of such reading. Instead, it may be assumed that the mechanism of wish-fulfilment persists after the first incursion of the Reality Principle, and does so without intrinsic change.

But, since the direction of fit of mental states is now registered, the new complexity in the psychological environment of wish-fulfilment will alter the relation of wish-fulfilment to the psychic apparatus. If wish-fulfilment is now to make changes in the network of propositional attitudes – rather than just carry on in a 'subterranean' fashion, making no difference to the subject's conscious experience and action-dispositions – then a more extended sequence than the one described above in 5.3 is necessary. A simple extension of that model is made by supposing that (5'), the belief that desire is satisfied, occurs as an *effect* of (5*), the experiential registration of satisfaction. So, as a result of the success of the wish-fulfilling representation in causing an experiential registration of satisfaction and allaying the feeling of need, the propositional network mistakes wish-fulfilment for real satisfaction. This mistake may be regarded as a direct, unmotivated move from (5*) to (5'); it does not require the subject to make the more drastic mistake which would be involved if it had actually to believe the wish-fulfilling experience to be a real experience.

This shows one way in which wish-fulfilment may remain efficacious after the advent of the Reality Principle. Other, more complex processes along these lines will be introduced later, in the contexts of symbolism and phantasy.

Freud's language of Pleasure and Reality Principles involves no less than four sets of distinctions: between (i) those conditions of mind in which the veridicality of representations can be tested, and those in which it can not; (ii) those conditions that predate, and those that postdate, awareness of the direction of fit of mental content; (iii) mental processing which is pleasure-directed, and processing which is not; and (iv) mental processing which is truth-directed, and processing which is not. These distinctions interlock in obvious ways. The upshot is a division of the mind into roughly two zones, each characterised by a different nomology. This way of looking at Freud's concept of the Pleasure Principle avoids the danger of misconstruing it as a *desire* for pleasure, that might contingently engage in combat with the desire for truth; and it enables us to identify the fact that awareness of direction of fit is not essential for mental functioning as one of the conditions of possibility of wish-fulfilment.

5.6 WOLLHEIM'S ACCOUNT: IMAGINATION

I will now consider an alternative account of wish-fulfilment, and attempt to coordinate wish-fulfilment with the concept of imagination. Imagination, like expression, is a concept close to the heart of psychoanalytic explanation.

Wollheim takes the case of imagining oneself to be involved in some sexual activity, and deriving pleasure from what one imagines. This he terms 'effective imagining': it is effective in gratifying or providing 'pseudo-satisfaction' for a desire. Imagining is said to occur under, and to be regulated by, the concept of the imagination; the concept of imagination is constitutive of imagining. Effective imagining involves its being for one 'as if' what one imagines were the case. For this, Wollheim makes it a condition that one *believe* that things are so. To explain how such belief can come about, Wollheim introduces the following 'favourable conditions':

(i) the subject must be 'imaginatively engrossed';[28]
(ii) the concept of imagination must become 'suppressed';
(iii) this suppression occurs through the intervention of the Omnipotence Belief, a belief to the effect that the mind is 'omnipotent' or, rather less strongly, that thoughts are 'possessed of exaggerated efficacy'.[29]

A comment is required regarding the Omnipotence Belief. An explanation is indeed required for the transition from imagination to gratification, since this is not a necessary part of imaginative sequences. But if the Omnipotence Belief were, literally, a *belief* about the mind, and its role that of being brought to bear *in order* to facilitate gratification, then a variant of the Censor Criticism would have application to the suppression of the concept of imagination: the problem would arise of explaining the person's rational, self-deceptive use of an inherently irrational belief (leading us perhaps to postulate a sub-system as the agent controlling its intervention). So as not to return us to the difficulties of sub-systemic theory, the Omnipotence Belief must have a different nature: it must be something other than an instrumental belief, and its intervention caused by something more basic than propositional desire.[30]

Wollheim's account should, in sum, not be understood in intellectualist terms. This also indicates what view of the imagination is required for Wollheim's account. The work of imagination should not be viewed as a matter of intentional design, a sort of inner engineering, for that would oblige imagining always to begin with an intention which its content could never outstrip. Imagination that gratified desire would then involve self-deceptive intent.[31] Rather, the role of the concept of imagination, like that of the Omnipotence Belief, must be direct and independent from belief (like the role of concepts in enabling perceptual recognition).

The important respect in which Wollheim's account differs from that presented in this chapter is that Wollheim makes belief necessary for wish-fulfilment. This may be regarded as due to a difference in domain of application. The austere account of wish-fulfilment given earlier applies to the primitive psychological circumstances of dream and infantile hallucination. We will, however, also want to see wish-fulfilment operate in other contexts, where conditions are less favourable for it. One such was described in the previous section, where awareness of reality begins to impinge. A more strongly adverse circumstance is where wish-fulfilment proceeds in opposition to belief. This new condition presents itself as soon as the range of explananda is enlarged to include everything from conscious fantasising to the embodiment of a wish in overt behaviour. It is, then, the question of gratification in the face of *resistance* to the Pleasure Principle that we may take Wollheim's account to be concerned with, and which makes Wollheim's richer apparatus appropriate. I will return to this in 6.7.

Generally, what this discussion shows is that there are two ways of connecting psychoanalytic theory with the concept of imagination. The one, which is Wollheim's, is to begin with the ordinary, non-psychoanalytic concept of imagination, as a process operating within a mental system obedient to the Reality Principle, and treat imagination as a distinct psychological mode. The other, which acknowledges the broad sense in which psychoanalytic states are states of imagining (symmetrically with the earlier remarks on expression), starts with the psychoanalytic concept of a process operating in advance of the Reality Principle, and views the ordinary concept of imagination as evolved out of that primitive form of mental activity. The difference between these approaches is not substantial.[32]

Further questions about psychoanalysis and the imagination concern the analysis of specific psychoanalytic concepts in terms of concepts used to analyse the structure of imaginative products in general, such as the concepts of internal analogues of dramatist, hero and audience; for which I refer to other writings of Wollheim's.[33]

5.7 SYMBOLISM I: DISGUISING DESIRE

The theory of wish-fulfilment so far grants wishes only the power to recover representations of objects from memory. The next ingredient to be added, with a view to accounting for symbolic content of the kind found in dreams, is censorship.[34] Here the dream's content is influenced by *inhibition*. This introduces something new, a registration of relations of conflict between desires.[35] The content of the dream then embodies the dreamer's wish, *and* her opposition to it.

Censorship is served by processes such as displacement, whereby intensity and apparent importance are detached from a significant idea and passed along, by associative paths, to an insignificant idea. Displacement, along with condensation and the other aspects of primary process constitutive of unconscious processing, are formal, 'syntactically characterisable' operations.[36] They account for the dream-work's success in disguising desire, in the negative sense of making the content of wishes inaccessible. But, by the same token, they can not account for disguise in the positive sense: that is, the creation of symbols, bearers of symbolic *meaning*. Psychoanalytic theory however abounds with descriptions of things as symbols in this sense, including not only the mental content of dream and psychosis, but also the bodily states of hysterics, and external objects such as sexual fetishes and toys in children's play. There are, more precisely, two relations to be distinguished in the class of psychoanalytic symbols: an *intra*-psychic relation (between one mental content and another), and an *extra*-psychic relation (between a mental content and an external object). The second relation is involved whenever symbolism figures in overt behaviour, and it is dependent on the first, since the symbolic value of an external object or action for a subject must first be negotiated via its being constituted in his thought as symbolically meaningful. I will concentrate here on the first, intra-psychic relation, and in 6.8 consider how symbolic value comes to be mapped onto external objects.

What distinguishes a psychoanalytic symbol is the supposition that, in the course of pursuing its satisfaction, desire assumes a disguise, this being the form in which it appears in conscious thought; and that this occurs through one thing's taking on the significance of another, this latter being unconscious. Such a process evidently amounts to a great deal more than simple wish-fulfilment. We therefore need to say how it is that desires are 'plastic' and able to mutate by changing their object.[37] This is necessary for making sense of the practice in psychoanalytic interpretation of reconstructing aetiologies of desires, designed to search out their original objects.

A good way of bringing out what is involved conceptually in this part of psychoanalytic theory is to look, once again, at Sartre's criticisms. Sartre writes:

psychoanalytic interpretation conceives the conscious phenomenon as the symbolic realization of a desire repressed by the censor. Note that, for consciousness, the desire is *not implicated in its symbolic realisation* [...] if we had any consciousness, even *only implicit*, of the real desire, we should be cheating, and that is not what the psychoanalyst means [...] for the psychoanalyst this symbolic character [an 'internal analogy'] is obviously not external to the [conscious, symbolic] fact itself, but is *constitutive* of it [...] But this needs to be rightly understood: if symbolization is constitutive it is legitimate to see an immanent bond of *comprehension* between the symbolization and the symbol [...] the relation between symbol, symbolized and symbolization is an intra-structural bond of consciousness.[38]

This argument is a specific application of Sartre's general claim that '[b]y rejecting the conscious unity of the psyche, Freud is obliged to imply everywhere a magic unity linking distant phenomena'.[39] It is that psychoanalysis' conceptualisation of symbolism, once spelled out, requires partitive modelling, and that this, once again, makes nonsense of the relation of symbolisation,[40] since the symbol is located in one part of the mind (consciousness), where it is efficacious but not understood, and the mental content which comprises its meaning in another part of the mind (the unconscious): the two are consequently related in ways that preclude an understanding of their connection, making the overall picture unintelligible. So, for Sartre, we are driven back to a non-partitive understanding of symbolisation, as a mode of expression constituted by an *intention*, that operates through *knowledge* of symbolic meaning. The symbol and its meaning coexist in the mind without partition, and are grasped as united in the same way as expressions in natural languages and their meanings. Which is tantamount to saying that symbolisation is a form of 'cheating', for the role of symbols is then the same as that of promoted beliefs in self-deceptive stratagems.[41] This, as Sartre observes, 'is not what the psychoanalyst means'.[42]

The two, vying models can be represented like this:[43]

5.8 SYMBOLISM II: THE BOND OF COMPREHENSION

It is not hard to see what steps must be taken to prevent the psychoanalytic concept of symbolism from reducing to an aggravatedly problematic form of self-deception. What is needed is an account of the symbolic relation that accounts for gratification, whilst doing justice to the role of disguise.[44] The key lies in playing down the assimilation of psychoanalytic symbolic meaning to the kind of meaning that we find in natural language, for it is this assumption that provides Sartre's argument with its force. I will set out the proposed reconstruction in four parts.

One: It is crucial to note that symbolisation occurs in a *context of desire*. Sartre assumes that the symbol, S, takes the place of the original object of desire, X, through a judgement (of 'internal analogy'), which *gives reason* for S to be substituted for X. The sequence would then be:

desire for X → (inhibition) → judgement of analogy → substitution of S for X → desire for S.

This model is appropriate to rational symbolic substitutions, as when, for example, a message is put into code, or where, given a belief that waving a white flag means 'I surrender', it is rational to let my desire to surrender cause me to desire to wave a white flag. Such substitutions occur in *cognitive* contexts, and are effects of practical reasoning.

By extending the account of wish-fulfilment, we get a different story:

desire for X → (inhibition) → wish for X → X/S association → wish for S.

Here the substitution of S for X occurs at the point where wishes are created, i.e. on the border of the propositional and the pre-propositional. So the process in which a dream-thought is formed, for example, does not consist in 'coding' one propositional thought into another, and the relevant symbolic substitution does not require an act of thought.

Two: Replacing the cognitive context by one of desire obliges us to add other elements to motivate the substitution of S for X, in compensation for the rational motive that has been removed. These consist in certain dispositions attaching to desire. A desire held in check will be disposed to do *something* – almost anything – rather than remain idle. Freud's economic theory, and the relation of desire to instinctual demand, mean that a desire's force does not consist in, although it may be reflected by, the strength of a person's preference, understood as his assignment of value to the desire's satisfaction. This creates a gap, and a relation of partial independence, between a desire's force, and its intentionality: desires have force *whether or not* they have appropriate objects. Now it is clearly economically 'preferable' for a desire to have some object rather than none, because the expenditure of energy by the mental apparatus in active pursuit of an object, whatever its suitability, will at least reduce the organism's level of tension, even if no objective change in the conditions stimulating its instinct is thereby brought about. Because there is a motive for desire to find some object rather than none, a motive that need not be negotiated by a preference, desire is plastic or 'object-hungry'.[45]

(Psychoanalytic theory therefore endorses a limited sense in which the point of desire is simply the expending of force, or exercise of will; but it stops short of the fully 'pessimistic', Schopenhauerian view according to which the explanation for people's having reasons at all lies in a state of blind conatus that is ultimately *antithetical* to the very having of reasons!)

Three: The original mechanism of linkage of S and X does not require conscious recognition of similarity. Freud's emphasis was often on linguistic connections,[46] the arbitrariness of which brings symbol-formation into line with jokes and parapraxes. But even where there is an objective similarity between S and X (e.g. between towers and phalluses), knowledge of which can be presumed in the preconscious, it does not follow that the substitution is a rational act on the model of the conscious creation of a metaphor: recognitions of similarity can enter obliquely and non-rationally into mental processing (as when a detail of appearance causes a stranger in the crowd to be momentarily mistaken for a friend).[47]

Whatever establishes the initial linkage, the relation requires reinforcement, and this is effected by a *sharing of phenomenology* between S and X. An analogy with art shows what is meant. Finding a pictorial or linguistic expression for a mental state involves creating something external to 'match' it, and this relation can not be fully captured or engineered by beliefs about properties shared by mental states and the objects matched up with them.[48] Similarly, through the force of desire's interest in satisfaction, the subjective representation of the object S adopted as a symbol is worked on so as increasingly to assume the phenomenology of the original object of desire, thereby strengthening S's capacity to draw on the motivation rightfully due to the usurped object, such that S and X, initially paired only mechanically, come to be related in such a way that *S provides a path to the phenomenology of X*.[49]

Four: An explicit reply is still owed to Sartre's insistence that there is a sustained relation of *meaning* between X and S to be accounted for. Such a relation might seem to be evidenced by the fact that the substitution of S for X does not occur only in single events of wish-fulfilment, but recurs in, for example, cycles of dreams, thus apparently established in a private 'lexicon'.[50]

The recurrence of a symbol is however insufficient for *rules of meaning*, as opposed to merely expressively cemented constant conjunctions. The absence, or attenuation, in the unconscious of the usual apparatus of monitoring and feedback allows the desire for X to go through the same cycle of processing with S, after the initial substitution, as it would have done with X: this negative condition does the work that would have been performed by a positive representation of their association. Desires do not verify that the 'right' symbol has been used on any given occasion, and interpretations of dreams do not reveal mistakes in the use of symbols. Items can fail in the service of symbolism, only in the sense of being causally inadequate vehicles of gratification. Psychoanalysis may talk of a 'language' of dreams, but this does not stretch to attributing to the dreamer's *Ucs.* a Gricean disposition to communicate with *Cs.* or the analyst; as Freud says, '[a] dream does not want to say anything to anyone. It is not a vehicle for communication.'[51]

In sum, dispositions attaching to desire serve to create symbolism in the place of other, properly meaning-based processes.[52] Symbolic disguise does not require that symbols be interpreted as such by the subject, or that the unconscious form an independent *subject* of understanding; 'unconscious meaning' is not *known* by its subject. There is, nevertheless, a good sense in which some sort of bond of comprehension follows from the forging of shared phenomenology between X and S – just as an individual may be said to 'comprehend' their twitching, of which they are apparently oblivious, as expressing their nervousness. But such attenuated consciousness or comprehension clearly does not create a paradox.

The psychoanalytic model of symbolism is cogent and non-partitive.[53]

5.9 SYMBOLISM III: FREUD AND JUNG

The general tenor of Freudian interpretation of symbols is brought out sharply through its contrast with that of Jung.[54] Jung requires a much stronger sense in which there is such a thing as *symbolic thinking*. This is quite different from the model of disguise: Jung envisages symbolism as providing a unique means of thinking about certain kinds of objects that can not be grasped in discursive, non-symbolic thought. These are, for Jung, quasi-Platonic entities, subjectively identified as 'archetypes'. Such a theory, with its conception of the unconscious as a semi-independent cognising subject distinguished by its heterogeneity from ordinary cognition, will locate the origin of irrationality in faults in symbolic thinking (discord between archetypes), or maladjustment in the relations of symbolic to non-symbolic thought (failure in the process of 'individuation'). The presence of symbolism in behaviour and experience does not, in Jungian interpretation, require conation: when symbols figure in contexts of desire they do so derivatively, transplanted from their primary, cognitive context.

The direction of interpretation in Freudian analysis is, by contrast, fundamentally towards experience of particulars rather than conception of universals, the grounds determining symbolic substitution lying as far as possible within the orbit of individual experience.[55] The existence of an innate symbolising function is explicitly rejected by Freud: 'there is no necessity to assume that any peculiar symbolizing activity of the mind is operating in the dream-work'.[56] Put another way, for Freud, the creation of symbols is not itself a goal of the mind's. Given the universal character of the relevant basic levels of experience, Freud acknowledges the consequence: 'in contrast to the multiplicity of the representations in the dream, the interpretations of the symbols are very monotonous, and this displeases everyone who hears of it; but what is there that we can do about it?'[57]

5.10 CAUSE AND MEANING

The discussion of symbolism points to an issue regarding the philosophical commitments of psychoanalytic explanation that is very abstract, and has been viewed as highly important. This concerns the relation of cause and meaning in psychoanalytic explanation. My suggestion is that the right view to take of this issue is fairly straightforward, and that, in spite of all the attention which it has received,[58] it is not of fundamental importance for the philosophy of psychoanalysis.

Opposition to causal concepts in psychoanalytic explanation may take one of two, opposed forms. First, there is the thesis that psychoanalytic explanations are ill-formulated in causal terms and should be reformulated in acausal, purely semantic terms. Second, there is the thesis that psychoanalytic explanation is dependent on causal notions, for which reason it is false or unintelligible. Sartre is one who holds the second thesis;[59] adherents of the hermeneutic school of Freudian interpretation,[60] the first.

Now, what should be plain from the foregoing discussion of symbolism is that psychoanalytic explanation involves *both* causal relations *and* relations of meaning, and that the analysis of symbolism depends upon their *mutual inextricability*. This makes it a mistake to ask whether psychoanalysis is a form of exclusively either causal or noncausal explanation. I will spell this out further.

Psychoanalysis can not be a form of explanation that operates by appealing only to the bare notion of causation, since, as is also the case in ordinary psychology, psychological relations can not be understood in terms of the bare, general concept of causation. What is required, for both ordinary and psychoanalytic psychology, is an account of the specific nature of psychological causation, and this demands an analysis of the efficacy of psychological properties, these being of a very special kind, and profoundly dependent on semantic characterisations. The distinctive features of psychological causation – such as its coincidence with relations of understanding, justification or expression – may then be regarded as building up our picture of what causation amounts to in psychological contexts. This is the case even when psychoanalytic explanation refers to economic properties of the mental. For these reasons, psychoanalytic theory fits neatly with Davidson's compatibilist view of psychological explanation as a species of causal explanation.[61]

If psychoanalytic theory is thus committed to the explanatoriness of semantic properties of mental states, should it be viewed as operating with these alone, and altogether dispensing with the concept of causation? That is the hermeneutic claim. The first thing to note is that, for the reasons just given, psychoanalysis does not lend any particular support to the hermeneutic view of explanation in the human sciences; so, if it can be shown to be true, its truth must be established independently. Suppose however that, contrary to Davidsonian compatibilism, the hermeneutic thesis that relations of meaning preclude causal relations is correct. What follows? Only, that the task is then set of reconstructing, in terms congenial to hermeneutic theory, the distinction between rational and non-rational mental relations; an alternative way of expressing the distinction between causal explanation in terms of reasons for action, and causal explanation involving only the notion of a weaker connection of content, will have to be found. Consequently, everything that is said in this enquiry in terms of a distinction between causes that are, and are not, reasons, is open to being re-expressed in alternative, hermeneutic, acausal terms.[62]

In conclusion, the only issue specifically pertinent to the philosophy of psychoanalysis buried in the debate about meaning and cause is just that of whether there can be relations of meaning that are not rational, of the sort that psychoanalysis requires. That possibility is of course just what these chapters are investigating.[63]

CHAPTER 6

Phantasy and Kleinian explanation

Wer saß nicht bang vor seines Herzens Vorhang?

Rilke

I am content to follow to its source
Every event in action or in thought

Yeats

6.1 THE CONCEPT OF PHANTASY

The last two chapters have introduced the basic psychoanalytic strategy of explanation, and its associated concepts of the unconscious and wish-fulfilment. But the phenomena that can so far be explained, in terms of desire's plasticity and susceptibility to non-rational satisfaction, are circumscribed in being only *intra*-psychic. This means that psychoanalytic explanation does not yet stretch to irrational phenomena constituted by overt, public behaviour. So, if the psychoanalytic unconscious is to be a source of motivation which can penetrate and ramify in the daylit world of the Ratman – into his spheres of belief and intentional action – more needs to be added.

We said that the Ratman's sadistic rat-fantasy embodies, and is explained by, a wish, which is a certain kind of effect of a motivational state: one that fails to combine with belief, is not the object of awareness, does not involve choice, and is distinguished from the motivational state that causes it by having not just an aim, but an object, here the Ratman's father. When the Ratman cowers before Freud, however, what we have is a more complex phenomenon: a piece of overt, public behaviour, something that consequently engages the Ratman's powers of belief and intentional action. This is the new problem of explanation.

We want to say that, in cowering, the Ratman behaves *as if* Freud were his father, about to beat him; that he 'seems to suppose' or 'seems to think' that this is so. But, as noted earlier (in 4.2), no

140

familiar term captures all of the features of envisagements like the Ratman's: he does not simply desire, or believe, or pretend, that Freud is his father (the 'pretence' can not be dropped). Nor does he merely imagine this to be the case; although imagining has the right kind of neutrality with regard to belief and desire, it equally lacks the belief-like features of the Ratman's envisagement (his fear, and behaviour as if it were so). The concept needed to categorise the Ratman's envisagement will share some features with these ordinary kinds of mental state, but it will not be reducible to any one, or combination, of them.

What we may say – introducing a new theoretical concept – is that the Ratman *phantasises* that Freud is his father, about to beat him. As Freud puts it:

> With the introduction of the reality principle one species of thought-activity was split off; it was kept free from reality-testing and remained subordinated to the pleasure principle alone. This activity is *phantasying*[1]

> The strangest characteristic of unconscious (repressed) processes [...] is due to their entire disregard of reality-testing; they equate thought with external actuality, and wishes with their fulfilment[2]

The psychoanalytic concept of phantasy is that of a non-accidentally inaccessible state, in which the world is represented in conformity with the demands of motivational states, and which receives expression in behaviour. It is derived by intersecting general considerations of strategy (those spelled out in 4.10–4.11) with clinical observation of cases such as the Ratman's.

But, for all that it 'fits the bill' superbly, the concept of phantasy is as yet barely explanatory: for all that has been said of it so far is that it differs from wish-fulfilment in having the power to manifest itself in intentional action. Phantasy will become explanatory once it has been filled out, located in a broader theoretical context, its developmental continuity with wish-fulfilment demonstrated, and its causal origins plausibly established. These are the goals of the present chapter.

It should be noted that, although the concept of phantasy has been introduced with reference to a specific set of effects, those which it is called upon to explain, this much does not bind us to any particular view of its content. Although the content of the Ratman's phantasy must be such as to *lead* him to think and feel and behave as if Freud were his father, about to beat him, this does not commit us to identifying the content of his phantasy with that particular proposition, i.e. with the content 'Freud is my father, about to beat me.' The content of phantasy – *what* exactly the Ratman is phantasising – is so far left open.

Determining the content of phantasy is consequently a further matter, which involves discovering how and why phantasies are formed. Evidence is provided here by dream, free association, the pretheoretical phenomenon of conscious fantasy,[3] and other domains of mentality and behaviour, such as children's play. These are selected because there is independent reason for thinking that they tap and manifest unconscious material. Hypotheses about the content of phantasy are arrived at through intersecting clinical material derived from each of these 'roads to the unconscious'.[4] On the Kleinian account, which I shall follow, the clinical evidence shows the content of phantasy to consist principally of infantile corporeal conceptions, that is, conceptions of persons represented in exaggeratedly physical terms, and phantasised body-parts such as the breast and reproductive organs, endowed with crude, experiential qualities of goodness and badness.

6.2 THE GENESIS AND NATURE OF PHANTASY

Two accounts may be given of the genesis of phantasy.

The first is Susan Isaacs':

A study of the conclusions arising from the analysis of young children leads to the view that phantasies are the primary content of unconscious mental processes [...] this 'mental expression' of instinct *is* unconscious phantasy. Phantasy is (in the first instance) the mental corollary, the psychic representative, of instinct. There is no impulse, no instinctual urge or response which is not experienced as unconscious phantasy.[5]

For Isaacs, phantasies are immediate effects of motivational states, and they occur whenever instincts are activated. They are formed at the earliest points in development, as mental but predominantly sensory correlates of physical processes such as feeding or excreting, and have minimal representational content. On this account, the first appearance of phantasy is pre-purposive: initially, phantasy just registers an impulse's existence. However, by giving impulses a representational shape the way is prepared for phantasy to become purposive: later it may take on roles related to the satisfaction of desire. All that is needed, conceptually, for Isaacs' account is the assumption that the mind experiences itself, and that it does this in a sense that amounts – although it is different from, and much cruder than propositional self-knowledge – to its *self-representation.*[6]

On the second account of their genesis, phantasies are *arrested wish-fulfilments*. The cycle of wish-fulfilment ends with the formation of a representation, an experience of satisfaction, the cessation of wishing, and temporary abeyance of awareness of the instinctual demand. Phantasy is formed if this process is checked just before its consummation at the point (5^*) (in 5.3): if no experiential registration of satisfaction gives the signal needed to discontinue the cycle of processing, the motivational state will continue to feed the wishfully formed representation. Interruption of the cycle of wish-fulfilment converts the wish-fulfilling representation into phantasy, a permanent mental residue which continues to derive force from a motivational state. This interruption may be assumed to occur when the psychic apparatus seeks to implement the Reality Principle, i.e. to impose a condition of veridicality on its representations.

Whereas Isaacs' account locates the origin of phantasy in something loosely belief-like, the alternative reconstruction locates it in something desire-like. The latter has the advantage of providing a more obviously unified theory of psychoanalytic mental processes, but here, as on other occasions in this chapter, I will not choose between the two accounts,[7] this being unnecessary for the end of showing the cogency of psychoanalytic concepts. The two accounts in any case agree on the three basic respects in which phantasy differs from, and represents a developmental advance, over wish-fulfilment, which are as follows.

First, through the medium of phantasy, motivational states are brought into relation with one another, enabling them to interact in new and complex ways. With the formation of permanent representational structures, phantasies form sequences, along which the products of past phantasies are relayed:

As with the external facts of behaviour, so with the development of phantasy, we have to regard each manifestation at any given time and in any given situation as a member of a developing series whose rudimentary beginnings can be traced backwards and whose further, more mature, forms can be followed forward.[8]

Development implies that sequences of phantasy are not arbitrary, and that their content carries over from one stage to the next. This points in the direction of the Kleinian concept of an *inner world*, a permanent structure of phantastic representation with a synchronic and diachronic organisation. Synchronically, the inner world is occupied by a multitude of distinct *internal objects*.[9] Diachronically, it has the form of a *narrative*, a concept that plays a fundamental role in psychoanalytic theory.[10]

The central species of phantasy in Kleinian theory are – in a highly simplified form – the following, which begin to illustrate the variety of functions that phantasy performs.[11] The first properly articulated phantasy, motivated by defence against anxiety about deprivation, is introjection of the nourishing breast (its being taken inside the body), by means of a phantasy of incorporation (of devouring the breast).[12] Granted the initial creation of internal objects, every fresh input of instinctual material demands new adjustments in phantasy. Once installed in the inner world – as a 'part-object'[13] – the breast is attacked when the infant's hunger converts to aggression, and suffers destruction, upon which the (destroyed) breast is represented as bad or poisoned, and consequently as retaliating. A highly important species of early phantasy is formed in response to the problem of ambivalent feelings towards the breast: it is split into good and bad, numerically distinct, internal objects, each of which can thereupon be treated differently (the one cherished, the other attacked). The next section will describe the full context and significance of this process of splitting. Another crucial species of phantasy is that in which a painful part of the mind is projected out of it, and relocated inside another person (projection and projective identification).[14] These universal infantile phantasies determine the basic structure of the inner world. From this starting-point, phantasy is increasingly moulded by experience of reality, following a specific developmental route, which will be described in the next section.

Second, the kind of process that phantasy exemplifies differs conceptually from wish-fulfilment, in that phantasising involves forming one representation on the basis of the content of another, in a sense that constitutes, in a broad sense, *thinking*, as wish-fulfilment does not.

Third, phantastic representation is impinged upon by, and receptive to, events involving objects in the external world, in ways which presuppose intentional relations to those objects. This can be seen if wish-fulfilment of the breast, as a response to hunger, is compared with the phantasy of taking the breast inside one, as a response to the threat of its absence. In order for the mechanism of wish-fulfilment to be activated, it is necessary only for a desire to be created by a material lack in the mind, brought about directly by circumstances in the external world (the mother's absence), without these necessarily being represented by the infant. By contrast, the phantasy of incorporation is initiated by a representation of the breast in terms of its *significance* (as good/bad, full/empty),[15] and in rudimentary modal terms (as potentially absent, or 'unreliable'); which amounts to something closer to a judgement.

It should be noted that, although wish-fulfilment provides the working materials for phantasy, it can not account for what is done with them; this being what is most distinctive about phantasy. The concept of phantasy comes with a package of associated dispositions and processes, and can not be reduced to wish-fulfilment. In particular, phantasy brings with it the concept of psychic *defence*, which is an independent motivational ingredient. Defence may be defined as an operation on mental content that represents the cause of anxiety in such a way as to reduce or eliminate anxiety; which makes the concept of defence broader than that of repression.[16] Operating a defence does not reduce to phantasising, any more than an action reduces to the manner of its execution, or a motive to the action that it generates. Phantasy is, then, a thought-activity with infantile origins, taking place with reference to an inner world, predominantly concerned with psychic defence, which in the course of development becomes sensitive, in restricted ways, to belief about how things are.

6.3 KLEIN'S DEVELOPMENTAL THEORY: POSITIONS AND ENVY

This section is an exegetical digression from the argument of the chapter; the aim is to give a better impression of the nature of Kleinian explanation, by looking at Klein's developmental account of the role of phantasy,[17] and its significance for the understanding of irrational phenomena.

In a Kleinian interpretation, the Ratman's hatred has the property of *pre-ambivalence*: it is formed at a stage where the infant's overall mental structure constitutes what Klein calls the *paranoid-schizoid position*.[18] Mental structure at this earliest point involves only episodic awareness, marked by a rough distinction of self and other, but not by stable representations of reidentifiable individuals. At this stage, and whenever in adult life there is reversion to it in phantasy, the units of thought are primitive notions of good and bad, experienced as mutually exclusive and antagonistic qualities. This means that if a single object is experienced on one occasion as good (satisfying or benevolent) and on another as bad (frustrating or hostile), not one but two representations of the object are formed, as of (so we would say, from the outside) two numerically distinct objects. The attitudes borne towards the object in each representation are of an all-out character: phantasies of expulsion are directed towards the bad object, and of incorporation towards the good object.

Later in development, at the threshold of what Klein calls the *depressive position*, the infant's episodic ontology yields to a grasp of reidentifiable objects. In the transition to this position, the dangers of ambivalence emerge. A serious risk is involved in ambivalence: if the good object is not segregated from badness, and comes to be represented as also bad, it will be destroyed in the course of aggressive attacks in phantasy. The possibility of losing the good object, on whose existence the ego's own survival is felt to depend, motivates the prevention of ambivalence. This is achieved through *splitting*: that is, by severely partitioning good and bad representations of objects in such a way that they are taken to be representations of numerically distinct individuals. The infant's limited capacity for propositional representation means that contrary emotional states focused on a single individual can not be propositionally refined, as they can for the adult; which makes splitting the only effective tactic available to the infant in dealing with the dangers of ambivalence.

This account of infantile development bears on the process of psychoanalysis in the following way. The central task for the Ratman, who is still dominated by paranoid-schizoid forms of representation,[19] is to work through the depressive position: to combine good and bad representations of his parental figure, and appreciate that the good object is the very same object as the bad object that has been attacked, and has survived attack. The hatred that the Ratman bears towards his father can be modified in psychoanalysis by becoming progressively detached from phantasy, and reattached to judgement; allaying his anxiety, and thereby reducing his disposition to resort to drastic phantastic solutions.

The Kleinian account of the Ratman's unconscious hatred therefore analyses it in terms of mental structures with characteristic nomologies. Klein's theory of envy and gratitude deepens this picture. Envy is for Klein the Ur-phenomenon determining motivation from the outset of life. Overcoming envy, and the defences mounted against it, is necessary for phantasy to stop distorting propositional thought; it is an empirical condition for rationality, a proper grasp of reality, and satisfactory relations with other people.

Klein characterises envy as 'the angry feeling that another person possesses and enjoys something desirable – the envious impulse being to take it away or to spoil it'.[20] Klein then turns to 'the earliest exclusive relation with the mother', and contrasts the phantasy associated with greed, of 'completely scooping out, sucking dry, and devouring the breast', with the more complex phantasy, bound up with projection rather than introjection, which marks envy:

envy not only seeks to rob in this way, but also to put badness, primarily bad excrements and bad parts of the self, into the mother, and first of all into her breast, in order to spoil and destroy her. In the deepest sense this means destroying her creativeness. This process [...] I have elsewhere defined as a destructive aspect of projective identification starting from the beginning of life.

This phantasy may be understood in the following way. Envy originates in the paranoid-schizoid position. The first general law governing the formation of phantasy directs it towards producing an ideal situation, in which the distribution of badness and goodness on the 'map' of self and world is such that all goodness is coincident with the ego and all badness external to it. This 'a priori' of phantasy is the rule which fundamentally determines when configurations of psychological states call for phantastic solutions.

When to this matrix we add the operation of the life (preservative) and death (destructive) instincts, which are assumed to be either innate or formed directly out of bodily experience,[21] envy occurs for the first time. The recognition that some goodness is external to the ego means that the world fails to accord with the internal map of an ideal world, and this triggers the operation of the death instinct, which 'solves' the problem of external goodness by 'destroying' it.[22]

This process is reinforced by another factor, the infant's response to its condition of utter dependence on the mother:

The infant's feelings seem to be that when the breast deprives him, it becomes bad because it keeps the milk, love, and care associated with the good breast all to itself. He hates and envies what he feels to be the mean and grudging breast.[23]

This further motivates the pseudo-solution of envy: by denying that there *is* any goodness external to the ego, the relation of dependence is 'eliminated'.

Klein goes on to explore the typical effects and developmental course of envy. Envious attacks on the good breast lead to anxiety when the object of attack assumes, in retaliation, a persecutory aspect.[24] In this way, envy becomes a direct precipitant of anxiety, and must itself be defended against. Klein lists several modes of defence, including idealisation, flight from the mother to other people, devaluation of self or object, greedy internalisation of the breast, and arousal of envy in others.[25] All of which, while the paranoid-schizoid position is still dominant, lead unsuccessfully to increased feelings of persecution, and consequently to repeated attacks on the envy-engendering object.[26]

The depressive position involves, essentially, a secure internalisation of a good object. This counts as a successful solution in phantasy. A second emotion-kind, gratitude, marks that achievement, and defines a regulative ideal for mental life:

A full gratification at the breast means that the infant feels he has received from his loved object a unique gift which he wants to keep. This is the basis of gratitude. Gratitude is closely linked with the trust in good figures. This includes first of all the ability to accept and assimilate the loved primal object (not only as a source of food) without greed and envy interfering too much [...] in a good relation to the internal and external object, the wish to preserve and spare it predominates.[27]

For the Ratman to undo his hatred involves him experiencing gratitude, and this is a crucial component of the condition of integration which Klein conceives as the goal of psychoanalysis.[28] To achieve this, the Ratman must appreciate the contribution made by his own envy to the force of his bad representation,[29] thereby reducing its intensity, and enhancing his sense of security in his good internal object.[30]

6.4 PHANTASTIC SOLUTIONS

This section attempts to define more precisely the sense in which phantasy, motivated by psychic defence, provides solutions.

The fact that phantasy in some sense looks towards the world, operating with some reference to the network of belief which falls under the Reality Principle, and that phantasies form series, each inheriting the successes and inadequacies of its predecessor, gains for it the advantage of sensitivity to a greater range of problems than wish-fulfilment. Its disadvantage is that these can not be solved with the facility of wish-fulfilment.

Phantastic solutions are intermediate between those provided by wish-fulfilment, and those provided by rational action. The mode of solution in phantasy is obviously not properly intelligible as a strategy. It has as much in common with the way in which a painting may be said to solve problems of composition, as it does with the solutions of practical reason: just as a group portrait may be said to solve the problem of arranging harmoniously multiple figures on a picture-plane, so phantasy 'solves' problems of ambivalence by splitting objects.

Of what kind are the problems which it is the purpose of phantasy to solve? Initially, it is helpful to characterise phantasies as *imaginary solutions to imaginary problems*. To describe the problems of phantasy as imaginary does not just mean that, in order to identify an infant's phantasies, it is necessary to take its point of view, but also that it is necessary to identify a problem expressed in phantastic terms in order to see how an attribution of phantasy is explanatory. For example, the coexistence of the life and death instincts directed towards the mother in the infant's mind does not *itself* constitute a problem, for the mother is not *really* physically endangered; but it does yield a problem requiring phantastic solution if instinctual conflict takes the phantastic form of *imperilling an internal object with phantasies of destruction* – an imaginary problem.

This is, however, only half the story, for there is also a sense in which phantastic problems are real. Imaginary internal objects have real *psychological grounds*: a real piece of the infant's mind corresponds to each of its internal objects. The infant's imaginary relations to its internal objects gain their significance from corresponding real relations to the objects' psychological grounds. Because phantasy represents the infant's mind to itself, it provides the infant with a way of negotiating its relations to its own psychological states.

The reappearance of the concept of imagination in this context raises the question of how phantasy and imagination are related. Like the products of wish-fulfilment, phantasy may be correctly subsumed under the concept of imagination, broadly understood.[31] This, however, contributes little to its explanation: phantasy is not explained as a modified form of ordinary imagining. Phantasy is, for instance, not differentiated just by its unconsciousness, since there are or could be unconscious imaginings that lack the other, essential features of phantasy. Its differentiation hinges on the feature noted above, the fact that phantasy is locked into the psychological reality which it represents. To imagine an object, in the ordinary sense, is not to come necessarily into an intentional relation with a psychological entity: to imagine visually doing something to someone is not in any sense to do anything *to a mental image*, or anything else in one's mind. Whereas, precisely such a formula is true of phantasy: when the infant phantasises, this activity involves it in doing something to its mind. It is true of phantasy, as it is not of imagination, that the content of phantasy bears causally on the mind and activity of phantasising itself. There is, of course, in the ordinary case of imagination, feedback from the content to the activity of imagining (*what* I imagine may upset, halt, or accelerate the activity), but this occurs by virtue of the subject's *understanding* of what he imagines; whereas, in the case of phantasy, the causal relation is direct: the psychological grounds of phantastic figures are directly affected by what is done to their phantastic representatives. It is just such a power that Hanna Segal refers to in talking about 'evacuating dreaming', a special form of dream that functions as a phantasy: 'evacuating dream actually successfully evacuates something'.[32]

Phantasy therefore turns back on itself, as imagination does not (such a connection would in the case of ordinary imagination be 'magical'). Phantasy owes its special power to its derivation from wish-fulfilment, and to the systematic and sustained causal reliance of the elements that comprise the inner world on the parts of the mind that it maps, such that the former derive their existence and specific features from the latter; making the inner world unlike a child's world of play, an imaginative construction which it may revisit daily, but which nevertheless lacks phantasy's built-in direct causal relation to the mind.

There are two further, connected points. One, phantastic problems differ from merely imagined problems in not ceasing to exist when not consciously thought of. Two, the distinction between phantasising and imagining shows why it is not possible to gain access to, or make changes in, the inner world simply by imagining under appropriate descriptions the objects contained therein: I can not introspect or come into acquaintance with my inner world simply by forming mental images of it as I believe it to be.

It is a consequence of the distinctive nature of phantastic problems, that phantastic solutions can not rival those by practical reasoning, and vice versa. The two spheres are in this respect discrete. No practical reasoning is capable of addressing problems in the form in which they appear in the inner world (except, of course, highly indirectly, by such means as deciding to enter into psychoanalysis). And, conversely, if a conflict is susceptible to solution by phantasy, it is to that extent removed from the sphere of practical reasoning; wishes, and not desires, form its 'premises'. So, in order for the Assumption of Alternatives to have application to phantastic problems, these would first of all have to be dissolved into real problems.

It is important to make clear why psychoanalytic explanation, in according phantasy the role of solving problems, with the acknowledgement that – due to phantasy's sensitivity to the network of belief – these may include problems concerning real, external objects, nevertheless does not relapse into a form of belief-desire-and-preference psychology. The crucial point is that, whatever its influence on behaviour, things are never represented phantastically one way rather than another *in order to bring about* a change in belief or course of action. Some psychoanalytic interpretations do characterise phantasies as pseudo-solutions to problems apprehended in the real world, in such a way that they may appear to be 'means of escape from external reality'.[33] For example, Freud says that the male child on first witnessing the female genitals suffers traumatic castration-anxiety, and may in defence create a substitutive phantastic object; this, the fetish, solves (what the child believes to be) the real problem of castration.[34] Saying that the child 'solves' such a problem in phantasy seems to imply a preference spanning the divide between real and phantastic mental functioning; as if the latter were *chosen* in preference to the former. But such an 'extra-systemic' point of preference is precisely what there can not be, if the attribution of phantasy is to avoid encountering a modified form of Sartre's objection. So, for there to be a solving in phantasy rather than in reality, it must be that the insoluble real problem is already represented in phantasy: phantasy can provide the male child with a means of addressing the problem of castration only because that problem is already recognised in some set of phantastic terms in the inner world.

This requires us to assume a constant conversion of ordinary propositional thought into phantastic representation, which goes on even when the world does not present the subject with problems. The pre-existence of the phantasy structure, and its operation through economic cues such as anxiety, trauma or intolerable emotion, are essential for explanation in terms of phantasy to avoid the paradoxes which would be involved in the idea of transfiguring, via a preference for phantasy over reality, real into imaginary problems.

Phantasy is not the same as wish-fulfilment, but it plays a broadly wish-fulfilling role, as if it were a circuitous form of wish-fulfilment, detoured to 'agree' with reality in the sense of achieving a minimal coordination with the claims of the Reality Principle. The Reality Principle causes phantastic solutions by impinging once – to register the impossibility of a real solution – and by not impinging again to block, or render psychologically ineffective, the resulting phantastic solution. All this can be summarised by saying that, whereas wish-fulfilment solves *economic* problems, or the merely economic effects of psychological problems, phantasy solves *psychological* problems, with the aid of economic cues.

At this point, and with these contrasts in mind, it becomes appropriate to reconceptualise, in a way that will help to clarify, the relation of wish to phantasy.[35] Their relation is closely analogous to the relation of desire to action: just as desires are the rationalising causes of actions, wishes may be understood as the 'rationalising' causes of phantasies.[36] Just as, in explaining an action Φ, the first move is to a desire analytically related to it (the act-desire to Φ), and subsequent inferences are to deeper and less specific desires which are not so related (the desire that p, which causes the act-desire to Φ), so with wishes and phantasies: lying behind, and causing, each phantasy is a structure of wishes, to which the phantasy stands in the same sort of relation as an action. Furthermore, the phantastic representation caused by each wish serves as an ideational frame, or 'scene-setter', for the formulation of more specific wishes: because the Ratman wishes to be punished, Freud is phantasised as administering a beating; and because Freud is phantasised as his father, there is a wish for Freud's annihilation, and so on. This parallels the dialectical relation of belief and desire in rational action. Interpreting a phantasy therefore consists in relating its various elements to one another in such a way as to reveal a synthetic structure, retracing the original process of bricolage that went into its construction, and representing it as a roughly coherent 'doing'.

The conception of phantasy that we have arrived at can now be illustrated by a re-analysis of the Ratman's 'great obsessive fear':[37]

The outcome of the process is represented on the upper tier by the Ratman's fantasy, the sequence of conscious thoughts that he first reports to Freud. Phantasy appears in two forms, related to one another in a way analogous to the relation of belief to thought. On the lower tier, phantasy assumes a *dispositional* form, involving the inner world; on the middle tier, it assumes an *occurrent* form. The latter draws off, and then returns to modify, the former: when the Ratman, having told his story to Freud (and in doing so re-assailing his good internal object), cowers before Freud, he does this because the damage he has done to the internal object at the level of dispositional phantasy causes an occurrent (retributive and self-punitive) phantasy of being beaten, by Freud-his-father.[38]

6.5 THE CONTENT OF PHANTASY: PROPOSITIONAL VERSUS PRE-PROPOSITIONAL

Is phantasy a propositional attitude, or is it, like wish-fulfilment and repressed ideas, pre-propositional? Phantasy bears the hallmark of propositionality, the conformity of attributions of phantasy to the canonical 'X Ø's that p' form ('the Ratman phantasises *that* his father is about to beat him'). This is a strong and simple reason for treating phantasy as a propositional attitude. But it is not conclusive. If phantasy is treated as a propositional attitude, we forsake the theoretically appealing connection between psychoanalytic mental states, and pre-propositional content. So we should pause to consider the possibility that the linguistic criterion does not provide a sufficient condition for propositionality. I will argue first against the propositionality of phantasy, and then in favour of its pre-propositionality, suggesting a particular analogy for the content of phantasy, which will be exploited in the rest of this chapter. The topic will be treated again in 7.2.

First, although the Ratman's conscious fear of Freud involves and creates propositional attitudes in him, it lacks grounds: the Ratman does not know why he fears Freud. This is not because phantasy happens to give bad reasons for belief, but rather because phantasy is incapable of giving reasons for believing at all. This suggests that the relation between the content of phantasy and that of belief is not one of inter-propositional entailment, but of some other kind.

Second, the 'propositions' that are putatively the objects of phantasies – 'Freud is my father, about to beat me' – subsist in a judgemental limbo, unconnected to other propositions, neither directly tied to the world in the way that beliefs are, nor indirectly in the way that desires are, by way of being the natural and logical companions of beliefs. Since phantastic content is not fixed in a pattern of propositions to the same extent as ordinary psychological content, general considerations about meaning inveigh against the claim that it is propositional.[39] To conceive phantasy as a propositional attitude would be as strained as conceiving dream-thoughts as momentary 'episodes of believing'.

Third, phantasy violates the connection of propositionality with rationality which is made by the notion of direction of fit: presupposed by the idea of a mental state's being an attitude towards a proposition, is a contrast between the world's merely impinging on a subject (as it does in sensation), and the subject's grasping that things are so and so, which requires them to represent how they stand in relation to the world.[40] This last condition is necessarily violated by phantasy.

Fourth, this last point can be re-expressed in terms of the features of psychological processing characteristic of phantasy. Phantasy does not involve linguistic tokens as bearers of truth and falsity, does not respond to representations as evidence, registers the environment under only a few selected and crude 'descriptions', lacks the kind of self-revision that would show sensitivity to memory, responds only to motivation, and so forth – causal features, in sum, that set phantastic representation apart from truth-directedness and hence apart from propositionality.

Fifth, the explanations advanced by psychoanalytic theory for the incoherence and indeterminacy of unconscious content discourage a view of it as propositional. There is, first, the pre-verbal nature of unconscious content, a feature which it shares with the mental content of infants and animals, and indicates that the important factor of language in fixing propositional content is missing. Second, unconscious processing is constituted by primary process, which does not conform to the rules of inference.

The sixth reason derives from the ideal status of internal objects. Phantasies are not *about things* in the same sense as beliefs are about things, such aboutness being necessary for propositionality. Ordinarily, a thought can be contrasted with its object.[41] But this distinction can not be pressed in the case of phantasy, where there is nothing to choose between talking of X's-phantasy-of-O and of O-as-in-X's-phantasy: little distinction can be drawn between a subject's having a relation to an object in phantasy, and her having a relation to the phantasy; between a subject's reaction to her superego, and her reaction to a thought about her superego. Phantasy, unlike belief, does not articulate its distinctness from its object. Only when additional and extrinsic considerations are added – viz, the interpretation of phantasies as causal vehicles and representatives of their psychological grounds – can something like the thought/object distinction get a proper grip on phantasy. The situation is similar to that of pictorial representation: objects of pictorial representation too can only be individuated in a relatively diminished sense, fundamentally by way of being demonstratively identified in the painting's pictorial space.

These are powerful reasons for denying that phantasy is a propositional attitude. The possibility that phantasy is instead pre-propositional is best introduced by indicating loosely analogous contexts. In some of these, pre-propositional mental states help to generate propositional attitudes. The concept of a representation or mode of presentation, as a constituent of thoughts, has already been referred to in 1.3. Gareth Evans employs the notion of non-conceptual content in analysing spatial thought,[42] and it needs to be assumed that in perception a level of representation below belief provides the basis for perceptual judgements.[43] Stephen Stich gives, as an example of what he calls 'sub-doxastic' states, subliminal recognition of pupil-dilation, a factor in sexual attraction.[44] Mental images provide a context where propositional attitudes may be generated, through being 'read off' from, pre-propositional content.[45] The 'body-image' is a level of awareness of the position and movement of one's limbs.[46] Such pre-propositional content is content whose description requires concepts which its subject need not possess, or exercise, in order to have those contents.[47] In other contexts, pre-propositional states help to facilitate action: the background of Rylean 'know-how' or practical competence,[48] and the sensorimotor 'schemata' described by Piaget.[49] Indeed, O'Shaughnessy identifies a non-conceptual form of agency.[50]

It is, of course, significant that nearly all of these contexts lie on the border of the propositional with the sensory and bodily, and are therefore causally proximate to the source of phantasy. The case of mental images suggests a specific and helpful analogy for the content of phantasy, already hinted at above. Phantasy may be likened to *pictorial representation*: for the question of how best to conceive the content of phantasy is very close to the question of what view to take of the content of pictorial representations. The suggestion is that we should think of phantasy as an Inner Picture; somewhat as if phantasies were unconscious mental images.

Freud's well-known 'characteristics of the unconscious' may fruitfully be compared to central features of pictorial representation.[51] Pictorial representations, like the states of *Ucs.*, are 'exempt from mutual contradiction' (there is no clear pictorial equivalent of negation); they manifest 'condensation' and 'displacement' (even perspectival realism is imperfectly mimetic, and dependent on representational codes); are 'timeless' (pictorial representation does not exploit the medium of time); and do not 'pay regard to reality' (pictorial representations do not generally present themselves assertorically, as being either true or false). So it may be said, rather than that the unconscious has a 'logic' of its own (a tempting but ultimately opaque formulation),[52] that it shares some of the constitutive features of pictorial representation.

In conclusion, at the very least, phantasy should be classed as only *quasi*-propositional, and safely marked off from the network of propositional attitudes governed by a direction of fit with the world; with the observation that the phenomenon of pre-propositional content is a general one to which other contexts already commit us. An objection to the claim that phantasy is pre-propositional will be considered, and rejected, in 7.2.

6.6 THE INFLUENCE OF PHANTASY I: STRATEGY, RESISTANCE AND THE GOALS OF PSYCHOANALYSIS

This section and the next are concerned with the question: How does phantasy succeed in affecting the network of propositional attitudes? Part of the task of making the influence of phantasy intelligible is in fact negative: connections must be laid down in such a way as to *eliminate strategy* from the workings of the unconscious. We can begin by returning to resistance, a cornerstone in Sartre's case against psychoanalysis set out in 2.5–2.6.

Freud describes some typical features of resistance: the analysand's 'associations fail or depart widely from the topic that is being dealt with', whilst he 'is only aware that his associations have become more difficult'; suffering 'distressing feeling when he approaches the topic', the analysand 'pleads a failure of memory'.[53] A typical instance of resistance is where a single event, such as an emission of anxiety, simultaneously causes two further events, an extra-psychic conversational digression (the external manifestation of resistance), and an intra-psychic failure of recollection (an increase in repression). These two effect-events clearly reinforce one another, and answer to the same disposition (opposition to the making-conscious of the memory). The mental events composing resistance do indeed have the *function* of blocking the inferences which the analysand ought to make, but they are not *themselves* rational operations. Resistance is, consequently, directed to intra-psychic, not extra-psychic, ends; it is consequently not – pace Sartre's interpretation of the phenomenon (in 2.5) – an intentional attempt to thwart the analyst's attempts at interpretation.

We can, therefore, reject Sartre's view that the pairing of repression with resistance implies their rational coordination as a form of self-deceptive burial and promotion. Rather, it consists in their being two identifications of a *single complex dispositional state*: 'resistance' picks out the same state as repression, in terms of a specific range of its effects. So the first move to make, with regard to any phenomenon supposedly exhibiting unconscious rationality, is to pare down the description of it until we have something that can operate without intention, and to reject – as 'intellectualist' error – any more complex description.

However, this leaves something out: justice has still to be done to the fact that resistance takes such forms as considering abandoning treatment at the precise point where a breakthrough is about to be made, the analysand typically fabricating 'good reasons' for doing so. How is such, evidently intentional, behaviour to be accommodated? The picture needs to be filled out by regarding subjects as *self-deceived with regard to their unconscious motivation*. At a certain point in analysis, the analysand's access to his own mental states has the following structure: he has *enough* knowledge of the danger constituted by his unconscious motive to know that he has an interest in *not* knowing further about it. Without his knowing the identity of his unconscious motive, the limited information, 'there is something it is desirable for me not to think', gives the analysand reason to self-deceive; and so he self-deceptively promotes beliefs that will enable him to quit analysis on terms that will bury his awareness that it is succeeding, painfully, in identifying the cause of his neurosis. The transference has a similar structure: the Ratman knows only that he *must* at all costs think of Freud as great and powerful, without knowing why he must think this; only later will he locate the source of that imperative in his defence against a murderous wish.

Structures combining ignorance and knowledge in these ways pervade psychoanalytic explanation. A new and important concept is needed to account for them. Explaining the full effects of unconscious motivation may require the attribution of selected beliefs, viewed as direct effects of phantasy, which express its content loosely, in terms that fall short of providing the subject with the full story of her motivation. Her exact degree of consciousness of the nature of her motivation is a variable matter. These incomplete and unspecific beliefs, the most basic propositional effects of phantasy, may be called *propositional reflections* of phantasy. Propositional reflections get consciousness to 'do things for' the unconscious, so to speak, without bringing in strategy. To admit such states as mediating phantasy's effect on the propositional network is harmless, from the point of view of deflecting Sartre's criticism, once the non-rational states of wish and phantasy have been made fundamental. So, it may now be allowed that the Ratman, although he does not believe but rather phantasises that Freud is his tyrannical father, nevertheless believes Freud to be 'something like' his father, and that he has reason to fear Freud in ways that are 'father-related'. The crucial point, by now secure, is that propositional reflections are overlaid on, and not at the *core* of psychoanalytic explanation. Their importance will be stressed later, with reference to the preconscious, where they are located, in 7.3.

We should now turn to the question: What is psychoanalytic treatment able to achieve?[54]

The first and most obvious goal of psychoanalysis is to create self-knowledge: the Ratman comes to believe that he hates his father in connection with his own sexual desires. This does not of course mean that the Ratman knew all along that he hated his father; analysis has created a propositional belief where there had previously been none. The analyst's differential probing, in combination with his own redirected attention, refines the Ratman's propositional grasp of his unconscious motivation at each point where the analyst's interpretation is correct. When, for example, Freud indicates to the Ratman that he had omitted his father from the original report of the fantasy, the Ratman is forced to recognise the anxiety he associates with this figure; subsequent probing isolates the particular respects in which this occurs, and the process continues until a reasonably precise and subsisting belief about his feelings for his father has been formed.

So far, the analysand is portrayed as just a passive learner. But psychoanalysis is also supposed to change persons in non-cognitive respects, i.e. cure them! Now, if we are right in thinking that unconscious processes are not governed by preferences, then a puzzle surrounds Freud's claim that knowledge can indeed make a difference to their operation (in a way that it can not to, for example, the processes of one's internal organs): how can any power in fact accrue to psychoanalysis? It is after all one criterion of a motive's being genuinely psychoanalytic that the mere revelation of its existence to the analysand should not suffice to bring about its extinction or inertness.

But acknowledgement of unconscious motivation on the part of the subject *need* not be impotent.[55] To assume this would be to withdraw to an epiphenomenalist view of conscious, self-attributive belief, a view which ordinary psychology does not endorse. Even if unconscious processes do not originate in preferences, there is no reason why they, like other psychological processes, should not be susceptible to modification in the light of consciousness of them. Psychoanalysis involves, after all, what Freud calls working-through (*Durcharbeiten*),[56] a pattern of repeated and sustained realisations, and other changes in the quality of experience, such as the undoing of 'derealisations' (the motivated misrepresentation of external things as unreal).[57] Incorporated in working-through is a fundamental change in one's relation to unconscious wishing and phantasising, described by Freud as the renunciation of a source of gratification and its replacement by remembering, identified by him as a condition of the success of psychoanalytic work.[58]

On an optimistic estimate, then, the upshot of psychoanalysis will be, first, that some of the motivation that would have leaked into wish and phantasy, and thereby into the formation of symptoms, is reappropriated so as to yield a propositional outcome; and, second, that some of what can not be thus reclaimed is at least stripped of some of its influence, by becoming merely repressed, that is, excluded from awareness but worked over in dream, or processed in other ways compatible with the prevention of symptoms.[59]

There is a further, richer way of conceiving the goal of psychoanalysis: as the 'acknowledgement of psychic reality'.[60] One aspect of the acknowledgement of psychic reality is a qualification to the inaccessibility of phantasy: a sense, albeit attenuated, can be found in which phantasy may become introspectable,[61] not in the way that one has immediate access to one's beliefs, but in the sense that even the most complex and least immediately self-ascribable of a person's behavioural dispositions may gain for him an internal phenomenological recognisability.

Since resistance can be analysed non-strategically, it may be claimed that other candidates for signifying unconscious rationality, such as jokes, parapraxes and the psychopathology of everyday life, can be analysed in similar terms; they will be considered in 7.3. The non-strategic character of behaviour which 'enacts' phantasy will be considered in 6.9. The notion of internal recognition of phantasy will be reviewed in 8.2. In 6.8 and 7.6, the concepts of sublimation and integration will be added to the account of what psychoanalytic treatment may bring about; and in 7.1 a discussion of the inner world will amplify the account of what acknowledgement of psychic reality consists in.

6.7 THE INFLUENCE OF PHANTASY II: THE PICTORIAL ANALOGY, DOMINATION AND THE OMNIPOTENCE BELIEF

A positive account of how phantasy achieves its influence is now needed.

A rudimentary level of phantastic influence consists in its power to cast situations and objects in certain emotional 'lights'. This happens when situations and objects 'tally' with a phantasy of the subject's in such a way as to take on an appropriate emotional quality. These affective effects of phantasy are direct, unstructured and shallow.

The harder question concerns forms of influence where the content of phantasy carries over to propositional mental states (as in the creation of propositional reflections), and where phantasy motivates the propositional network. My suggestion here is that the question: How does phantasy exercise an influence on conscious thought and action? is best considered in terms of its analogy with the question: How does pictorial representation yield experiences of representational effect in the spectator? The appeal of the analogy should be clear. Likening the relation between phantastic and propositional thought to that between images and discursive descriptions invites us to think of the influence of phantasy as *un*like that of deceiver-to-deceived (the interpersonal, sub-systemic, Second Mind model); and it encourages us to think that irrational beliefs and desires may be the effects of elements that are not themselves beliefs or desires.

The characteristic mode in which pictorial representation operates on the spectator is – on an intuitive analysis of the phenomenon[62] – by *setting conditions as for perceptual belief*. Put another way, pictorial representation fixes conditions which are isomorphic with the perceptual conditions that are standardly sufficient for the belief that p to be formed from the perception that p; pictorial representation offers a visual experience as-of-p. So, pursuing the analogy, it may be ventured that phantasy sets inner conditions for belief and desire of a kind isomorphic with those set by ordinary awareness of the world.

The important difference between the two cases is, of course, that the effect of pictorial representational in a spectator does not consist in belief, whereas lasting changes in belief and desire are just what phantastic influence must explain. It might therefore be objected that the pictorial analogy gives out too soon for it to help with the awkward question of how phantastic influence may stretch to belief, desire and even intentional action. Looking into the analogy more deeply, however, the difference will be turned to account, and made to yield a full explanation of phantastic influence.

The reason, or one of the principal reasons, why spectators do not take beliefs away from pictures is that these are always set in, and against, a world (the room in which they are hung), relative to which they are seen to provide only 'as-if' perceptual conditions. Similarly, after-images are given in a context of veridical consciousness, against which they appear unreal. But an unconscious mental image would be in the same position as dream-imagery: it would lack such contrastive grounds. So nothing in the way that an Inner Picture is given will display it as unreal, in a way that would disqualify it from having a role in forming belief and desire.

If no obstacle to phantastic influence stems from the side of the Inner Picture itself, what is there to oppose its influence on the side of the propositional network that receives its impress? How much is needed to account for the influence of the Inner Picture depends upon how vulnerable the propositional network is thought to be. Here two views are possible. One is that influence must be Difficult, because the network of propositional attitudes is insulated, in the sense that it admits as influence only what it considers to be rational, and congruous with its own truth-directed ways of functioning. (Just as a court of law decides what does and does not count as evidence.) On this view, in order for a person to be influenced by a phantasy, it is necessary for her to be in some sense persuaded: at some point, false belief about the credentials of the Inner Picture – about its claims to reality – must enter.

The other view is that unconscious influence need only be very Easy: we can not defend ourselves against influences of which we have no knowledge, unconscious processes are by definition not objects of rational assessment, and no other countervailing conditions prevent phantasy from generating belief and desire directly.[63] (Just as the proceedings in a court of law may be affected, unawares, by the temperature in the court-room.)

We have, I think, intuitions supporting each of these views. They also correspond to two opposing ways of understanding the representational effect of painting: as requiring, or as dispensing with, illusion.[64] The view of phantastic influence as Easy corresponds to the view of pictorial representation as dispensing with illusion: it points out that no beliefs span the propositional/pre-propositional divide (influence occurs behind the back of belief and desire), and that the representations formed by wish-fulfilment come without a tag indicating their status (so their origin does not need not be forgotten). It therefore compares phantastic influence with the kind of error that I might make if I walked into a room where, unbeknownst to me, a dramatic rehearsal was taking place, and naturally but mistakenly supposed the actors' utterances to be sincere, and their gestures to disclose real passions. To take their behaviour in this way is to come to have beliefs that, of course, *entail* that I believe what I witness not to be a drama: but I do not have to pass through that particular thought at any stage.

The view that influence is Difficult, by contrast, corresponds to the view of pictorial representation as requiring illusion: it calls for a hypothesis about what may sometimes facilitate it. This may be found in a conceptual item held over from the analysis of wish-fulfilment in 5.6: the Omnipotence Belief. This, we said, is not an instrumental belief, and nor should it be identified with any particular species of phantasy (e.g. manic phantasy). A more appropriate term of comparison for the Omnipotence Belief that has been suggested is the body-image.[65] The Omnipotence Belief constitutes a pre-propositional *mode* of self-representation – rather than a specific representation – in which the relations of self to world are distorted in such a way as to validate phantastic representations. There are several ways in which this 'belief' could be propositionally specified: as a belief about one's thoughts, or one's power, or magical causality, or the relations of inner to outer. It does not matter greatly if theory leaves its specification indeterminate.[66] It may be that what decides between the various propositional specifications of the Omnipotence Belief is the evidence of phenomenology: the right formulation will be experienced as matching psychological reality in the right way (as the notion of omnipotence did for the Ratman[67]).

On the view of phantastic influence as Difficult, it will be said that the Omnipotence Belief's operation is non-intentionally cued whenever phantasy takes an occurrent form, and that it installs the illusion that facilitates error on the part of the propositional network. It is as if the wall that provides the background to a painting were to disappear suddenly, leaving the painting's powers of illusion un-checked: when the Omnipotence Belief comes into play, the impression ascends that the mind *makes* the world take the form that it is envisaged as having in phantasy, or more simply, that the mind's contents 'are' the world.

I have talked so far as if there were but one kind and degree of phantastic influence. But of course distinctions are needed here, and these are pertinent to the question of how unconscious motivation bears on human freedom and responsibility.[68] I will mention two important distinctions.

Intuitively, we want to distinguish cases where phantasy merely *inclines* a person to a certain set of attitudes and course of action, from cases where its power eliminates choice (as in, for example, the Ratman's inability to settle the matter of his debt), which may be called *domination* by phantasy. What are the psychological grounds of this distinction? The answer is surely that it consists straightforwardly in the *strength* of phantastic influence. This may be measured by the quantity and depth of the propositional material necessary for countering phantastic influence: a phantasy has force to the extent that it can prevail in opposition to the propositional reserves with which the agent identifies, and which are central to his conscious personality.

The second distinction is between ordinary domination by phantasy, as just described, and the special form of domination which some of the Ratman's behaviour exhibits, and which we – with Freud – refer to as *compulsion*. What differentiates compulsive from ordinary domination is in the first instance something phenomenological. Compulsion consists in a certain kind of impotence of reflective thought *vis-à-vis* the formation of intentions: not only do episodes of reflective thought cease to be causally efficacious, they also cease to represent themselves as such, and represent themselves instead as epiphenomenal, in such a way that one knows that one's thoughts can not make any difference to what one will actually do. This distinguishes compulsion sharply from akrasia, where reflective thought continues to represent itself as potent.[69]

What explains such a condition? How can the Ratman's momentarily formed intentions gain the upper hand over the rest of his propositional network? The solution must lie in some factor capable of reversing the usual balance of psychological forces. One suggestion is as follows.

A model of ordinary, 'free' desire is the following: desire is free if I *desire to desire it*, or would so desire if I reflected appropriately (it being assumed that such second-order desires are sensitive to rational deliberation). Whatever the adequacy of this, Harry Frankfurt's well-known formula,[70] as an analysis of human freedom in general, the idea provides a helpful way of thinking about freedom of desire, which I will spell out.

There is a class of desires with regard to which no question of second-order desire standardly arises, or at least does not do so in the ordinary way: namely, those desires that stem directly from current bodily needs. With regard to such need-generated desires, there is (exceptional conditions to one side) no choice but to follow suit and desire in accordance with them. The higher echelons of rational deliberation are short cut: one has to desire, and desire to desire, the satisfaction of a current bodily need. Now, the concept of regression provides us with the idea that desires may change their place in psychological chronology. So, if we allow that, by regressing, a desire may acquire the characteristic appearance of persons' earliest desires, which stem from needs, it becomes possible to see that a propositional desire may be *misrepresented* as issuing from a bodily need, and thereby take over the psychological force of such a need. With regard to such 'physically subsumed' desires,[71] no question of second-order desire arises (or, again, it does not do so in the ordinary way). Compulsion is then explained as a condition in which a desire's exaggerated force derives from its being unconsciously misrepresented as issuing from a current bodily need.

The rough model of how psychoanalytic causation bears on freedom is, in sum, as follows. Freedom is lost when desire is not free. The specifically psychoanalytic cause of loss of freedom of desire is domination by phantasy. Compulsion is a special form of domination, and is explained by the misrepresentation of desires as issuing from current bodily needs.

These ideas can now be brought together with the earlier remarks on the question of how phantastic influence is achieved. On the view that influence is Difficult, the Omnipotence Belief is a prerequisite of all phantastic influence, implicated in the very nature of phantasy,[72] and domination by phantasy is determined by other variables, such as psychological force. By contrast, the view that influence is Easy holds that the Omnipotence Belief is unnecessary for phantastic influence itself, and only needs to be adduced to explain domination by phantasy. Leaving these two views as they stand, the conclusion is that, on either assumption about the vulnerability of the propositional network, for each of which I said we have supporting intuitions, the influence of phantasy is non-strategically accountable.

6.8 THE INFLUENCE OF PHANTASY III: EXTERNAL REALITY, UNCONSCIOUS SEEING-AS AND SUBLIMATION

The next question (left over from 5.7-5.8) is: How does phantasy latch onto situations and objects in the external world in such a way as to turn these into symbols? When the influence of phantasy extends this far, a further relation – between a real object, correctly grasped as external, and an unconscious thought – is added to the primary intra-psychic relation between unconscious and conscious mental contents. Again the goal is to describe this relation so that it amounts to something less than an extravagant, false belief.

Children's play, which is for Klein a key source of information about unconscious phantasy, provides an appropriate starting point. Play requires *coordinative representation* of S, the external symbolic object, and X, its unconscious symbolised meaning, in a way that dream does not: because the physical landscape of play, unlike that of dream, is constrained by the laws of nature, the child must *make* S follow a route appropriate to X, in order for its play systematically to express its phantasy.

Klein's play technique begins with her suggesting an ordinary meaning for an object: 'I took a big train and put it beside a smaller one and called them "Daddy-train" and "Dick-train".' At this level thought is mapped onto external objects through pretence: Dick simply pretends that he is one train and his father another. Psychoanalytic symbolism only begins later, once the unconscious has become engaged. In the context of child analysis, this engagement is initiated by the analyst; outside that context, the unconscious engages spontaneously. Klein says that Dick's interest in trains and stations 'had a common source [...] the penetration of the penis into the mother's body [...] he picked up the train I called "Dick" and made it roll to the window and said "Station". I explained: "The station is mummy; Dick is going into mummy."'[73] There is now a second level at which thought is mapped onto external objects: the train, S, is a symbol for Dick's penis; a thought of the train 'doubles with' a thought of his penis. This is the level at which external objects are psychoanalytic symbols.

We now need to account for the way in which S and X come together for Dick. A model with which to analyse the coordinative bridge Dick forms between S and X is provided by the perceptual-pictorial phenomenon of *seeing-as*.

When one object is seen-as another, the two are coordinated without being identified. For example, in Reynold's portrait *Mrs Hale as 'Euphrosyne'*, the spectator sees both Mrs Hale and Euphrosyne in the same parts of the picture, enjoying the same relations to other parts of the picture; but they do not think that Mrs Hale *is* Euphrosyne. Similarly, Dick's thoughts of the Dick-train and of his penis converge on the same object, but not through a belief in their identity: the formation of the thought of the train as his penis consists in a sheer, sub-rational superimposition of imagery, rather than a classificatory judgement.

The world's being unconsciously seen-as it is pictured in phantasy creates further possibilities. These concern the ways in which propositional and phantastic thought may organise one another.

Propositional and phantastic thought work towards complementary ends, but according to different laws. External objects are the objects of propositional desires, and, at the same time, map on to phantastic representations, which help to explain those desires. The fact that both desires and phantasies belong to one and the same mind, and that desires derive from, and are continually modified by, phantasies, guarantees that the two act in convergent directions. Conscious desires and unconscious phantasies are not like two sets of desires belonging to different persons (in which case there would be no reason why they should not go their own separate ways). The structure of unconscious seeing-as allows propositional thought to subserve phantastic ends: external objects can be thought of consciously, in their full reality, and simultaneously bear the significance of internal objects. The converse structure is one in which the intimate interaction and natural convergence of propositional thought and phantasy make it possible for thoughts of limitless conceptual sophistication to move according to laws that are not rational, and hence display the character of phantastic thinking.

These structures can be set out more formally. First: propositional thought may 'transmit' its sophistication to phantasy. This provides a further key to a non-strategic view of the unconscious. Given a structure in which an external object S is seen-as an internal object X, it follows that an unconsciously motivated propositional operation $\emptyset$ performed on S will also serve to reorganise phantasies of X. This goes towards explaining how the unconscious can appear, falsely, to be rational, as it often does in resistance: if $\emptyset$ is an *intelligent* operation on S, and S is seen-as X, then an appearance of intelligent operation on X will result. So, phantasising may *seem* to involve intelligent strategic manoeuvres, although in fact it will be guiding a person's relations to the world systematically but non-strategically, and without their having any representation of this process.

Second, the process also runs in the opposite direction: phantasy may 'transmit' its crudity to propositional thought. A *primitive,* unintelligent phantastic operation Ψ performed on X, will, if S is subsumed under X, carry in its wake blocks of S-related propositional material. This explains for example the Ratman's constitutional conflictual structures, referred to in 4.6: anything believed by the Ratman to be 'the order of a male authority' will be subjected to a sequence of alternating operations of absolute acceptance and rejection. So intelligent conscious thought may be made to follow routes so strikingly crude and unintelligent as seemingly to contradict its own rational nature.

An important specific form of unconscious seeing-as should next be singled out. *Sublimation* is the more complex relation of person to symbolic object which is correlated with the acknowledgement of psychic reality. Segal gives, as an example of the sublimation of a masturbatory phantasy, a man's dream of playing a violin duet with his lover.[74] This she juxtaposes with the case of a schizophrenic who can no longer play the violin in the presence of others, for the reason that, for him, to do so would be to masturbate in public. The dreamer, unlike the schizophrenic, has achieved sublimation.

What distinguishes sublimation is a negative belief, expressing the Reality Principle, to the effect that $S \neq X$: a realisation that S is only a symbol. When the unconscious seeing of S-as-X is brought up against an appreciation of their real non-identity, that structure is not abolished, but rather robbed of its irrational coercive power; bringing unconscious seeing-as closer to ordinary perceptual seeing-as, in which there is no confusion of identity. Sublimation therefore forges a modified bond of comprehension, of a kind which lays the basis for artistic activity.

The corrective belief constitutive of sublimation need not, of course, take an explicit form; it is implicitly present whenever the subject is aware that the symbolisation is, as Segal puts it, 'created by the ego' whenever S is no longer 'felt to *be*' X, but is instead 'felt to *represent*' X.[75] This comes about through the evolution of a sense of agency, and thereby a realisation of authorship, with respect to the association of S and X. Sublimation therefore involves, in the first instance, not gaining a new piece of self-knowledge, but a phenomenological change, and an accompanying attitude toward S. When this attitude is sufficiently well entrenched, it will prevent phantasy from becoming dominant.

An important consequence of all this is that we must abandon the earlier perspective in which unconscious influence is adduced only when 'gaps' are detected in conscious phenomena. Rather, the influence of phantasy is *constitutive*, to some degree, of normal, ordinary mental life. It follows that, rather than regarding the influence of phantasy as intrinsically malign, we should instead see the important normative distinction as holding between classes of phantasy (distinguished by their relation to developmental positions), and kinds of relation to phantasy (domination versus sublimation). The outright elimination of phantastic influence is neither possible nor desirable, and, on the Kleinian account, benign phantastic influence, which is consistent with rationality, issues from phantasy characteristic of the depressive position, a point to which 7.1 will return.

6.9 THE INFLUENCE OF PHANTASY IV: ACTING-OUT

According to Pears, Freud's case-material shows that belief is sometimes the *goal* of unconscious activity. Pears takes Freud's case of a woman who performs several times a day an elaborate obsessional ritual, which consists of running into a room, taking up a particular position beside a table on which there lies a stained table-cloth, and then ringing the bell for her maid. The woman was unable to provide any explanation for her behaviour until, through analysis, she made a connection with her husband's impotence on their wedding night: he had attempted to disguise this from the hotel's maid by pouring red ink onto their nuptial bedsheet. The woman's aim, says Pears, is 'to stimulate the opposite belief in her unconscious mind', that her husband had been potent.[76]

If Pears is right, then there exist unconscious desires to have (unconscious) beliefs. Pears says that the unconscious creates beliefs by exploiting a psychological law concerning the 'recoil' effect of action on belief: if A behaves as if p, A will tend to believe that p.[77] So, on Pears' account, the psychological sequence in such cases is clearly instrumental:

$$\text{desire for p} \rightarrow \text{desire to believe that p} \rightarrow \text{action as-if-p} \rightarrow$$
$$\text{'recoil' effect} \rightarrow \text{belief that p.}$$

Contradicting this analysis is a non-strategic alternative, suggested by Freud's statement that the woman's obsessional action 'represented [her] wish, in the manner of a dream, as fulfilled in a present-day action':[78]

desire for p → wish + phantasy that p → acting-out of phantasy that p.

Pears' instrumental analysis – in terms of 'intending to be seen in this place by the maid in order to make myself believe with her aid that my husband was potent' – is ousted here by one with a different form, in terms of acting-out. The analysis in terms of acting-out has several components, which are not assembled to form a practical syllogism or strategy. There is, first, a phantastic modification, motivated by a wish, of the woman's painful nuptial memory; second, a relation of unconscious seeing-as between the maid, and a phantasised witness of her identification with her husband's sexual potency;[79] and, third, an intention directed towards a real person, the woman's present maid, to get her into the room.[80]

Obviously, such a non-strategic analysis will not be found intelligible if it is assumed that intentional doings can be accounted for only when viewed instrumentally,[81] since the final term in the non-strategic sequence does not lead to anything further. But the exclusivity of an instrumentalist perspective on action is precisely the assumption that the concept of acting-out is meant to challenge. And it does so with a powerful warrant from ordinary psychology: *expressive behaviour*, as ordinarily conceived, involves, in most of its forms, intentional action, but is nevertheless non-instrumental. Numerous concrete forms of behaviour can be cited in illustration: classic expressions of emotion such as throwing crockery in anger and raising one's hands in desperation, and ludic and sexual behaviour, provide obvious examples. These show – if it needs to be shown – that people are capable of doing things, in full possession of their senses, without having to think of what they are doing as serving some instrumental purpose. There is, in fact, a deeper instrumentalist assumption whose rejection is required by the non-strategic analysis, which is that agents can want to do things only because they want things to *be the case*. Rejecting this assumption makes the route to intentional action open to sources other than the evaluation of and preferences over states of affairs.[82]

The structure of acting-out is continuous with that of wish-fulfilment, described in 5.3. Acting-out can not be decomposed into pseudo-instrumental relations: just as wish-fulfilment lacks conditions of satisfaction in the sense of rational action, so the state of the world projected by a phantasy when it is acted-out is thought of by the subject confusedly, both as if it were actually the case, and as if it were brought about through the phantasy's being acted-out. Which means that we can not properly speak of acting-out, any more than wish-fulfilment, as having conditions of satisfaction.

Why, if not for any intended purpose, does acting-out take place? In other terms, why is phantasy 'done', rather than just thought? It follows from the fact that acting-out is not instrumental, that its purpose or function can only be given in broad, economic terms. Once again, the answer lies in force of desire: it may be supposed that the Inner Picture simply *impresses* itself into the realm of action. Unconscious seeing-as sets up the 'props' for acting-out, and thereby provides a channel leading out into the world, through which the force of desire may find wish-fulfilling expression. So, it is not necessary, in acting-out, for the person to *conceptualise* turning her phantasy into action, or *devise* a way of bringing this about. In fact, the transition from thought to action, from intra- to extra-psychic status, need not be registered by *Ucs.* at all. The distinction between representation and action is in any case obscured at the level of unconscious processing, where (as the pictorial analogy leads us to expect) things and doings are not properly distinguished. Acting-out is in this way continuous with the formation of representations, making it a natural extension of phantasy, one which requires no fundamentally new motivational supplement.

As an auxiliary factor in the explanation of acting-out, pleasure, either conscious or unconscious, has of course a role, in cementing symbolic connections and motivating the repetition of symbolic activity. The pleasure attaching to an action gives reason, independently from belief, for the subject to repeat it.[83] Whilst it is true that the relation of pleasure to its cause, unlike that of pain, is typically intentional (pleasure usually comes with an appreciation of its cause, *as* that which is enjoyed), this is not necessary: the only propositional content that *need* go into a species of pleasure adequate to perpetuate symbolic activity is contained in the diffuse thought that 'desire has been satisfied'; no bond of comprehension is needed for pleasure of an 'animal' kind.[84] The role of pleasure in this context is therefore symmetrical with that of anxiety, the other species of quasi-emotion crucial for psychoanalytic theory, whose propositional content is similarly attenuated (notoriously, anxiety differs from fear in not needing an object).[85]

Freud, at one point, felt obliged to describe the unconscious, in Second Mind vein, as a *distinct subject* of pleasure, holding that there is 'unpleasure for one system and simultaneously satisfaction for the other'.[86] His reasoning, it would seem, is that illicit pleasure caused by the fulfilment of desire through symbolic means can not be felt by the same subject that forces the desire undercover. This partitive consequence can however be avoided, by breaking with the initial condition of belief on pleasure: pleasure about which nothing much is believed, needs no special unconscious interpreter, and can therefore be felt by the usual, unitary subject (with the difference that it is felt unconsciously, an idea that will be defended in 8.1).

To summarise the model of psychoanalytic explanation of irrational phenomena set out here in Part II: from motivational states proceed desire and wish; wish is susceptible to wish-fulfilment; desire may revert to wish, through regression; wish-fulfilment, when inhibited, turns to symbolism; when the Reality Principle impinges so far as to gain ascendancy over wish-fulfilment, phantasy evolves; phantasy extends its influence to the propositional network, and, through unconscious seeing-as, creates dispositions to act-out; which is where psychoanalytic explanation stops, in the immediate background to propositional attitudes, without need of anything further to mediate before ordinary psychology takes over again. In this way, what begins as the operation of a primitive psychological mechanism is able to come into intimate proximity with intentional action.

PART III

Psychoanalytic conception of mind

CHAPTER 7

Metapsychology and psychoanalytic personality

Quite often human beings do things which seem literally unbelievable. But isn't this because we nearly always fail to cast the right sort of psychological light on our spontaneous decisions and examine the mysterious birth of the reasons that made them inevitable? [...] Many would rather refuse to acknowledge an action than trace the bonds and tortuous links which join one element to another, secretly, in the mind.

Balzac

7.1 METAPSYCHOLOGY I: FREUD'S STRUCTURAL THEORY, AND THE CONCEPTS OF EGO AND INNER WORLD

This chapter serves two purposes. First, it examines the metapsychology of Kleinian explanation. Metapsychology – Freud's term for a viewpoint which unifies all aspects of psychoanalytic explanation, 'the consummation of psychoanalytic research'[1] – may be understood as concerned with the conditions of possibility of psychoanalytic explanation. Second, the chapter considers some of the broad consequences of psychoanalytic explanation for our view of human personality. In this section I will consider some important features of Kleinian theory, and indicate how they facilitate revisions of some of Freud's concepts.

Freud's later topography of id, ego, and superego, known as the 'structural theory',[2] which superseded the topography of Cs., Pcs. and Ucs., anticipated and laid the grounds for Kleinian theory. I will try to show how the structural theory can be understood in Kleinian terms.

The structural theory's tripartite picture of ego, id and superego relates these elements to one another somewhat as different stages in mental processing. The id provides an input of motivational material, whose bearing on the propositional network the ego negotiates by

175

means of phantasy, the superego monitoring and directing the operations of the ego in completing this task.[3] Consciousness, on this picture, characterises only part of the ego. Consequently, repression takes place *within* the ego: the unconscious ego represses parts of itself.[4] The id, ego and superego are identified by their relations to one another, and to the person. These relations are in the first instance causal, but, as I will show shortly with reference to the ego, on a Kleinian interpretation they are also representational, and this gives them aspects of interpersonality.

The structural theory breaks definitively with Second Mind conceptualisation of the unconscious. This does not mean, however, that the second topography falsifies the first, for the latter was never, I have argued, committed to Second Mind conceptualisation. The second topography is contained immanently in the first: it provides an explicit expression of facts already recognised on the first topography, and employs mental parts of the same logical kind. The chief difference is that the structural theory reverses the first topography's order of priority, by making the identification of the place of a mental item independent of its descriptively (un)conscious status. The two topographies are therefore not exclusive, and can be superimposed on one another; Freud's later writings in fact use sets of terms drawn from both topographies.[5]

A basic question about psychoanalytic metapsychology is the following: What kind of entity is supposed by speaking of *the* unconscious, as opposed to unconscious mental states? Freud's nominalisation may seem to challenge the ordinary view of mental unity. However, in terms of the criteria set out in 3.8, psychoanalytic theory does not qualify as person-divisive. It is certainly not so committed by Freud's description of psychoanalytic topography as comprising 'agencies' or 'systems',[6] for it has been shown that these terms do not in Freud's usage signify sub-systems, in Pears' sense. Also, it should be noted that conflictual relations do not hold between consciousness and the unconscious intrinsically (consciousness and unconsciousness are not mutually antagonistic properties), but only on account of the particular nature of the contents of *Ucs.*, and their consequent connection with repression.[7] Constitutional conflict is indeed built into the second, as it is not into the first, topography, but, again, this alone does not signify metaphysical person-division, which depends on the further character of the constitutionally conflicting parts. Freud exhibits the parts' functional interdependence, as much as he does their conflict: they relate to one another as different stages in psychological processing, where 'process' is defined with respect to a single organism. It is indeed because this is so – because the parts require one another in order to constitute a human organism, and because a whole human organism is presupposed for their existence[8] – that intrapsychic conflict is inevitable. It is also important that much important psychic conflict on the second topography occurs *within* the ego, indicating that Freud's criteria of individuation for topographic parts are not guided exclusively by facts of conflict. The ego and the id, as parts of the soul, do war, but they are not each of them warring souls.

Psychoanalytic theory is therefore a non-person-divisive theory of the second sort defined in 3.8: although its parts are conceptual innovations – and not just extra faculties or functions – they are consistent with everything involved in individuating persons as substantial unities.[9]

An illustration of the non-partitive character of Freud's later theorising is provided by his revision of the account of resistance in the light of the structural theory: in later discussion, resistance is said to be either the work of the ego, or the id, or the superego.[10] Freud constructs a taxonomy of the causes of lack of progress in analysis, in which mental parts, far from being agents, are heterogeneous groupings of motives and mental structures; they have an important relation to a person's characterised compartments at the propositional level, but are decidedly not sub-systemic.

The evolution of Freud's treatment of defence also shows this. The mechanisms of defence (a concept, it was said earlier, more general than that of repression[11]) that later interest Freud, are clearly independent of partitive conception. For example, disavowal (*Verleugnung*) – a notion which clearly attributes, and assumes, a propositional inconsistency – provides the key to many forms of phantastic solution.[12] Other mechanisms emphasised in later writings, such as undoing, isolation, derealisation and depersonalisation,[13] are defined in largely phenomenological terms, and suggest reflexive, non-sub-systemic forms of mental activity. So it may be said, if we momentarily readopt Sartre's perspective, which identifies the original goal of psychoanalytic explanation with the resolution of propositional inconsistency, that Freud now tolerates, rather than trying to solve, the 'paradox' of self-deception.

The ego is the central character in the structural theory. It has, of all the psychological entities postulated by Freud, the richest range of properties. It is described by Freud as a totality of permanently cathected neurones, which performs reality-testing, has the functions of belief, doubt and perception, renounces instinctual satisfaction, and sends forth experimental cathexes of attention to the external world. The ego is the reservoir of libido, the seat of anxiety, and the source of repression. It is formed through identification, as the 'precipitate of abandoned object-cathexes'. Originating in primary narcissism, the ego is the object of narcissistic libido, and of moral dissatisfaction in melancholia.[14]

In casual uses of the term, the ego may be just an oblique way of referring either to the whole person as contrasted with any of her parts, or to the person envisaged in terms of her propositional network. But the genuine concept of the ego is more theoretically involved. It is founded on two basic classes of attribution: attributions of function, given in terms of psychoanalytic mechanisms, and attributions of phantasy. As an example of the first, the ego emits and registers anxiety-signals, triggered by awareness of external objects or id-material, thereby guiding phantasy in defence.

The complexity of its functions means that the concept of the ego is liable to being stressed in contrasting directions. For Anna Freud, the ego is primarily a subject of defence in relation to external objects.[15] In ego-psychology, the ego's functioning is sharply distinguished from that of the whole person, and is related – by virtue of its constituting a privileged, 'conflict-free' sphere – to themes of adaptation, integration and normal functioning.[16]

The Kleinian conception of the ego is distinguished by the priority it assigns to attributions of phantasy. Segal's report and analysis of a dream serves to spell this out:

The patient, who was a naval officer, dreamt of a pyramid. At the bottom of this pyramid there was a crowd of rough sailors, bearing a heavy gold book on their heads. On this book stood a naval officer of the same rank as himself, and on his shoulders an admiral. The admiral, he said, seemed in his own way, to exercise as great a pressure from above and to be as awe-inspiring as the crowd of sailors who formed the base of the pyramid and pressed up from below. Having told this dream, he said: 'This is myself, this is my world.'

In this lucid dream the subject's

personality-structure is also clearly represented by the three layers, the instincts pushing upwards, the super-ego pressing down from above, and his feeling of his ego being squashed and restricted between the two.[17]

The dream exemplifies a central and pervasive structure of phantasy: the officer *mis*represents himself (a whole person) *as* his ego (an aspect of a whole person). The dream's phenomenology (being crushed, in awe) defines his place, synecdochically, as restricted to the performance of ego-functions; and it correspondingly *mis*represents the id and superego as *not* being himself, and their doings (pressings) as not being his own activities.

Phantasy thus gives rise to a further sense of 'ego', as something which is represented in phantasy, which may be threatened, unstable and so forth, and to which the person typically assimilates himself altogether in unconscious thought. This Kleinian conception enables us to speak of one concept of the ego as constant throughout the various conceptions of Anna Freud, ego-psychology, and others; Kleinian theory may, moreover, claim to subsume these other conceptions. What brings into simultaneous focus the various properties of the ego is the primary, *intentional* sense of the ego as the whole person self-misrepresented, as in the naval officer's dream: the ego is a phantastic self-misrepresentation of the person, one which captures those of his features constituted by the various mechanisms and functions which are stressed in the other, non-Kleinian conceptions of the ego. For this reason, the term's value depends, as Jean Laplanche and J.-B. Pontalis note,[18] precisely upon its *not* being 'disambiguated'. Person and ego therefore coexist in a conceptual framework in which the doings of the ego are a sub-set of those of the person. It follows that making the ego the subject of a psychological verb involves no move in the direction of properly sub-personal psychology.

The ego is a mental part in a new sense, which needs to be explained.

A psychoanalytic interpretation may say, for example, that the ego operates a defence against an attack by the superego. Now, it may be asked if this does not, after all, take us forcibly back to the position occupied by sub-systemic theory, according to which there are mental components which think of, and are pitted against, one another? The ego is however not a sub-system, for several reasons. In the first instance it is not a rational agent, and not constituted by propositional attitudes. But even if phantasy were a propositional attitude – meaning that there are after all thoughts in which one part of the mind represents another propositionally – a fundamental difference remains, regarding order of explanation: whereas one sub-system's thought about another sub-system is, according to the theory, explained by the latter's independent *reality*, this is not the case with phantastic representation, which *creates* its object. In this vein, Wollheim compares internal figures to fictional entities.[19] It should also be observed that, because psychoanalytic theory does not conceive persons as exclusively subjects of propositional attitudes, phantasy-parts are *explicable* by reference to a unitary subject, as sub-systems are not; and that whereas sub-systems are adduced only in response to irrationality, phantasy-parts are *constitutive* of ordinary personality.

A complication to the fiction analogy for internal objects, which shows the delicate handling they require, is that, as argued in 6.4, there is a sense in which an internal object such as the superego really does exist, over and above its being an intentional object of phantasy. Internal objects supervene on sets of facts about the content and activity of phantasy, but also have *real grounds*, as fictional characters ordinarily do not. To each internal figure, a stretch of causally efficacious psychological reality (e.g. a force repressing a desire) corresponds, and this piece of psychological reality is in some sense the object of thought when a phantasy is entertained (e.g. when that force is personified as an admiral). The content of phantasies reflects true causal propositions about these objects, reflected in their phenomenology: Segal's dreamer is 'right' that *whatever it is* that demands of him rigid conformity to rules has some of the properties, e.g. of being immoderate and unyielding, that it is experienced as having in the dream. Also, an internal figure may be organised, loosely, around a real individual, making its status comparable to that of a historical figure who has passed into mythology.[20]

Phantasy-parts such as the ego and super-ego therefore remain distinguished from sub-systems, in that (a) they are subject to a sustained relation of creation by a single mind (like the voices I represent when I imagine a conversation), as sub-systems are not, and (b) the pieces of psychological reality which they embody are not rational agents. When the ego represents itself as a middle-ranking naval captain, it *portrays* itself as a 'centre of rational agency', opposed to other such centres, but it is in reality no such thing: the ego is 'wrong' to think of itself as a homunculus. Psychoanalytic theory never 'concurs' with the ego on this point: it affirms the existence of internal figures, in the sense appropriate to fictional entities (and with the extra dimension noted above), but not the reality of their homunculoid properties – which is why it never crosses the line into making the ego a sub-system.[21] The idea that phantasy creates its object may then be restated more precisely: phantasy creates the principal *aspects* of its objects in terms of which it represents them. Whereas sub-systemic theory *succumbs* to the phantastic division of the person into homunculi, psychoanalytic theory stands on the border of that picture, but holds back from assenting to it.

Wollheim articulates this key element in the background to the Kleinian concepts of ego, internal figure and inner world:

the [psychoanalytic] theory not only provides a model of the mind and its workings, but also coincides with, or reproduces, the kind of picture or representation that we consciously or unconsciously make to ourselves of our mental processes.[22]

One important component of this picture is of the mind as a *place*, the pseudo-spatial site of the inner world, occupied by internal objects.[23]

It will help at this point to recapitulate the conceptual rationale for internal objects and the inner world.[24] The objects of the thoughts attributed by psychoanalytic explanation can not be real, external objects, because their incoherence and so forth signifies that the requisite cognitive sensitivity of thinker to world is missing. These thoughts *can* however be understood as directed towards imaginary objects.[25] Purposes of explanation require these imaginary thoughts to be related to the external world, via the processes of symbol-formation,[26] but this does not mean that their objects must be the same as those of belief and other propositional attitudes.[27] The closest internal objects come to real objects – such as those on which they are originally modelled – is through the relation, as Wollheim puts it,[28] of being their *counterparts*. Despite this divergence of objects, purposes of explanation also prevent the content of phantasy from floating free from that of propositional thought: internal objects are, after all, posited in order to provide something psychic to underpin, and explain, features of conscious mental life, often because they enable several real persons to be seen as sharing the role of 'bearer' of the same internal object. The rationale for the inner world lies in the depth and holism of interpretation which it facilitates. The hypothesis of internal objects therefore answers to conceptual motivation, and it coheres with what the clinical evidence inclines us independently to believe, namely that the subject of phantasy conceives herself as physically inhabited by different personalities. This conception allows a causal story about how internal objects come into existence, in terms of incorporative phantasy, to be told.

A comment is due on the specific description of internal objects as constituting an inner *world*. In part, this just records the persisting and reidentifiable character of internal objects, the fact that they bear intentional and affective relations towards one another, composing a drama, housed in the subject's body. But the notion has a further aspect, which concerns the *realism* of the subject's relation to his inner world. As Donald Meltzer puts it, 'in all of Melanie Klein's work [...] the internal world of objects is experienced in an absolutely concrete sense in the unconscious'.[29] This does not mean that the inner world is *believed to be* a world; no beliefs at all are held about it. Experience of the inner world is nevertheless realistic, like perceptual experience, and unlike experience of fantasies and mental images. This self-standing feature of phantasy may be explained by the inner world's being indeed representative of something beyond itself, namely the real psychological grounds of internal objects; and, complementarily, by the fact that phantasy is imbued with a phenomenology, including a projected spatiality (like that of paintings).

The idea of an inner world therefore goes beyond that of a set of thoughts with associated emotional values, and talk of internal objects is not just shorthand for talk about types of thoughts about external objects. Doing justice to the intentionality of the subject's relations in phantasy requires it to be modelled in such terms, rather than, as a competing and reductive formulation has it, in terms of patterns and modifications in representations of the self and the real world.[30]

The inner world's realism provides the key to the 'acknowledgement of psychic reality', described (in 6.6) as the Kleinian conception of the goal of psychoanalysis. Psychic reality is not demolished through its being acknowledged; if unconscious motivation were transmuted by its recognition, this would be a reason for regarding the unconscious as just composed of nascent, or deeply buried, beliefs and desires. Rather, like a visual illusion, psychic reality persists even when it has been recognised as such.[31]

The attitude towards one's unconscious motivation which psycho-analysis seeks to promote is therefore complex and distinctive. When the analysand sets himself in opposition to a psychoanalytic motive of his, he does not do so in the spirit of the akrates who resists his inferior desire. Rather, the analysand will regard his unconscious motive as deriving from an inaccessible state which can not be revised by a 'change of mind', fundamentally because it does not have the necessary relation to reality; he will grasp the impossibility of assimilating his relation to his phantasies to his relation to his beliefs. In Kleinian theory, the unconscious remains, unalterably, a body of states whose relation to the propositional network falls within certain fixed parameters: the two are never wholly discrete, but equally the unconscious can never be properly integrated into the propositional network. It should be noted that, because this set-up is constitutionally determined, and unanalysable at the level of personal psychology, Sartre's objection that psychoanalytic explanation requires the unconscious and consciousness to form a 'magic unity',[32] is defused: there is no more of a conceptual problem about interaction between the unconscious and the propositional network than there is about the relation between ratiocination and memory; the un-conscious 'communicates' with consciousness in no stronger a sense than the intellect communicates with memory in using its materials.[33]

For Freud, the basic tension is between the mind's subjection to the Pleasure Principle, and its awareness of reality; in effect, an opposition of imagination to reality. With Klein, the emphasis is shifted: because phantasy is constitutive of ordinary mental life, all of the mind's relations to reality are guided to some degree by imaginative influences.[34] However, not all such influences are of equal value. The contrast between the paranoid-schizoid, and depressive, positions is between an imaginative endowment of reality that dissolves or distorts its true features, and one that preserves these, whilst adding to them. Consequently, Kleinian theory establishes a conceptual connection between different kinds of phantastic content and the (un)desirability of phantastic influence. This connection turns on the relation of phantasy to the propositional network. Phantasy that is paranoid-schizoid necessarily intensifies mental conflict, deforms the content of propositional attitudes, and exerts influence only by domination.[35] Depressive phantasy gears the propositional network towards integration, and a realistic appreciation of other people's complexity. For this reason, some psychoanalytic categories, such as perversion,[36] have direct normative implications. So for Klein, the analysand's task is to bring about, through working-through, a substitution of propitious for malign unconscious motivation, rather than a wholesale elimination of unconscious motivation. The inescapability of phantastic influence may well be, from the point of view of commonsense, a somewhat 'dispossessed' condition, but, as observed in 6.6, it does not entail the propriety of fatalism with regard to unconscious motivation. Kleinian theory means that we live in the permanent shadow of imagination, and its ethic is a kind of harmony with and within imagination, rather than an aspiration to stripping away its contributions: psychoanalytic therapy readjusts imagination's relation to the world, rather than providing a solvent for it.

To conclude this section, I will mention two important respects in which Kleinian theory simplifies psychoanalytic theory, and unifies its account of mental processes.

First, the persisting and reidentifiable character of internal objects yields a picture of the mind diametrically opposed to that of the mind as a Heraclitean flux:[37] the individuation of internal objects 'anchors' psychoanalytic states, by providing them with a source of identity across time. This helps to rationalise the concepts of repressed ideas, and of psychological states as having histories.

Second, Kleinian theory enables the residual weaknesses of the theory of repression (described in the conclusion of 4.7) to be eliminated. Kleinian remodelling yields an alternative explanation of how repression achieves its effects: repression is an accompanying *aspect of phantastic processes*. On this account, what happens in many if not all of the cases taken to exemplify repression in Freud's interpretations, is that the object is unconsciously re-represented by the subject, in a way that eliminates its anxiety-provoking features. The reduction of anxiety is then due to the formation of a phantastic representation of the object, rather than the unconsciousness per se of an idea of it; the divergence of 'ideas' of a single object, central to the theory of repression, is reconstrued as an effect of different ways of processing.[38]

The concept of topography, or mental place, continues to be employed in Kleinian theory, but because mental place is now directly correlated with a kind of mental process, of which it is a function, it ceases to be an independent variable, and the explanatory burden of the concept of mental place is brought down to the same level as it has in ordinary psychology. In this way, it ceases to be a brute fact that unconsciousness reduces anxiety: an intervening term, phantastic representation, explains that connection. This also shows how Kleinian theory is able to explain the existence of *non-accidentally* inaccessible mental states: the unconsciousness of phantasy, in the adult, is a necessary developmental result of its differentiation from propositional mental functioning.

Because repression, in Freud's sense, is now constitutively built into phantasy, and no longer a self-standing process, the term tends to gain a new meaning in Kleinian writing: it comes to refer to a particular *outcome*, namely successfully preventing phantasy from becoming dominant, in such a way that unconscious motivation is instead sublimated, and worked over in dream.

7.2 METAPSYCHOLOGY II: OBJECTIONS AND PHILOSOPHICAL ASSUMPTIONS

This section examines some objections to the metapsychology. This will enable some more of its basic philosophical assumptions – in addition to those already set out in 4.10–4.11 – to be spelled out.

I Although Kleinian metapsychology clearly eradicates Second Mind modelling from psychoanalytic theory, it may be wondered if Sartre's objection can not be restated with reference to the Kleinian concept of a multiplicity of modes of mental functioning. The Censor Criticism might be thought still to have application to the notion of phantastic influence. It was said that phantastic solutions emerge when the Reality Principle retreats. But – the Sartreian objection might run – how is this possible? Solutions can only be undertaken, to the extent that the reality of the problems they address is appreciated. How, then, can contact with reality be lost, as the psychoanalytic story requires, without awareness of the problem itself becoming eclipsed, destroying the motivation for the alleged solution? A plurality of principles of mental functioning is therefore as paradoxical as a dualism of mind and matter: in each case we are required, impossibly, to occupy two mutually exclusive realms at the same time.[39]

What assumptions are made by the reformulated Sartreian objection? It requires the architecture of mental states to be subjected to what might be called a *principle of rational connectedness*, according to which it is impossible for one mental item to have any connection with another item playing a rational role, without its own role being rational; such that, whenever rationality is present at all in the mental system, it will permeate throughout its entire extent.[40] This would indeed entail that the explanation of human action must be exhaustively in terms of reasons for action, and thereby exclude psychoanalytic explanation.

The characteristic pattern of psychoanalytic explanation rejects the principle of rational connectedness. It is one in which, for example, a phantasy causes a desire, which, via the rational formation of an intention, causes acting-out; but where the phantasy is not a reason for acting-out. For example, the Ratman's intention to take a train in order to repay his debt is formed, rationally, out of his desire to obey the Captain; but this desire is formed out of a phantasy of filial obedience, and consequently his intention, although it is ultimately caused by, is not formed out of, his phantasy, by way of the phantasy's being a reason for the intention. Other central examples of non-rational patterning are repression and resistance, where the activation of complex dispositions, which serve as 'points of assembly' for mental processes, takes the place of rational connectedness. By such means, a single cause (e.g. the frustration of a desire) may generate a web of further events that converge on a single result (symbolic satisfaction), without this being a case of a reason for action spreading its force. Such patterns separate intentional explanation from explanation in terms of reasons for action, and assume the existence of psychological structures whose operation departs from the principle of rational connectedness.[41]

Now, two observations should be made. First, in order to show that paradox forms around psychoanalytic causal stories, a principle as strong as that of rational connectedness is needed, but ordinary psychology *itself* requires the principle's abandonment for the explanation of ordinary irrationality, to which ordinary psychology is committed. The view of persons as substantial unities lends no support to the idea that the mind's architecture must conform to the principle of rational connectedness. Its more likely source is in the unity of consciousness (as in Sartre's philosophy).[42] But, if this is so, it is plain that the principle rests on a misinference from the character of consciousness, the way that the mind is subjectively given, to the nature of the mind as a whole.[43]

Second, the fact that human action is *primarily* explicable in terms of reasons for action does not make this the *only* form of psychological explanation of persons. It is legitimate to hold apart intentional and rational-choice explanation, so long as it is explained *why* persons fail to act on their best beliefs and desires, the 'sub-optimality' of unconscious 'preference'. And this demand was met in Part II, which set out in detail what Ernest Jones described as Freud's fundamental discovery,[44] the distinction of different kinds or principles of mental process. Further relevant philosophical assumptions underpinning psychoanalytic explanation will be given below. In sum, any redeployment of Sartre's argument against the revised metapsychology will simply beg the question by assuming rational connectedness, and thereby clash with ordinary psychology.

But, it may still be objected, psychoanalytic explanation in terms of chains of effects stemming from unsatisfied desire creates an impression of incompleteness: Why *should* all these processes co-occur? It might be objected that, if the principle of rational connectedness is rejected, the convergence of mental processes becomes a sheer miracle.[45]

If an explanation is to be given for there being, as the psychoanalytic picture claims, complex dispositions which 'manage' psychological causation, it can only take the form of *functional explanation*. Such explanation has the following form: Were it not the case that psychoanalytic dispositions tended to bring about a state of affairs G, where G counts as a goal for the organism, they would not exist; the fact that they bring about G explains their existence. Once again, economic description is essential to enlarging our conception of what may count as a goal for the mental, by allowing non-rational satisfaction to be seen as functionally desirable: the benefit that makes an irrational upshot count as a goal is tension-reduction. What gives psychoanalytic theory the right to turn at this point to functional explanation is, of course, its pre-established association with biology, the natural home of functional explanation.[46]

Still, it may be wondered if the psychoanalytic picture does not somehow, incredibly, assimilate one whole portion of the human being, Centaur-like, to an *animal*, or even to something fit to be thought of as a *hydraulic machine*, with respect to which the concept of purpose has only tenuous application? To dispel this impression – that the psychoanalytic causal picture eliminates purpose – it should be pointed out that the psychoanalytic picture provides for at least what may be called *purposiveness*, if not specific purposes, in the perspective of the person subject to unconscious motivation. The person engaged in symbolic satisfaction will not, on the account given in 6.9, experience himself as 'driven by brute force'. He can come to find behaviour in conformity to phantasy purposive without his judging at any point that he has a reason for action: pleasure is an effect of wish-fulfilment; symbolic substitution has a phenomenological depth; and unconscious processes have propositional reflections. These features, in combination, make it subjectively purposive for a person to confirm the symbolic connections set up by his unconscious, and to act-out, even though the concept of acting for a reason has reached a vanishing-point.

II We want to maintain a contrast between what goes on in the Freudian unconscious, and the properly sub-personal processing of information. But how can this be done convincingly, if both are equally remote from the person's consciousness and will? If, on the other hand, psychoanalytic processes are put on a par with the actions of persons, they risk being assimilated to all the other things that persons more plainly do,[47] either causing psychoanalytic explanation to slide back into ordinary psychology, or inviting such processes to be considered the covert actions of a Second Mind.

Psychoanalytic theory therefore needs a way of classifying conceptually such events as wish-fulfilment, repression and the activation of unconscious dispositions, that will represent these as more than properly sub-personal mechanisms. Psychoanalytic explanation may be kept in harmony with the logic of ordinary psychology through a modification of our view of agency. This can be done by acknowledging not just one category of agency – action, as opposed to mere happening – but two.[48] The second form of agency, to be contrasted with action, may be called *activity*.

The distinction of kinds of agency may be elucidated in terms of the concept of a rational motivational structure. Where mental causation amounts to action, a rational motivational structure is involved.[49] A rational motivational structure is constituted by, and implements, such a priori principles governing practical reason as 'form reasons for action by combining desires with appropriate means-ends beliefs', and it processes mental content in ways defined by the concept of a reason: it constructs reasons by pairing beliefs and desires, and spreads the force of reasons, deriving more specific from more general desires, guided by belief. So, whereas mental action involves a rational motivational structure, mental activity is independent of it.

The idea that there is a form of agency distinct from action coheres with the fact that ordinary psychology already employs distinctions, of an entirely unmysterious kind, regarding the agency-status of psychological events: compare hearing, as inactive, with listening, which is active.[50] Agency can not be restricted in such a way that all that is not more or less deliberate in mental life (an essential portion) is relegated to the status of mere happening, since there are, as O'Shaughnessy has stressed, well recognised physical and public cases for which a category of activity, distinct from action, is needed: what he calls 'sub-intentional' acts, like tongue-moving and finger-drumming.[51] What gives mental activity its right to be classed alongside action as a species of agency is the univocity of will in both contexts: action and activity are equally exercises of the will.

In this way, what distinguishes psychoanalytic from ordinary psychology is captured not by a contrast of personal with sub-personal, but by a distinction between *kinds* of mental agency. The psychoanalytic processes hitherto referred to as mechanisms should now be redescribed as mental activities.

III Psychoanalytic theory employs a *mixed discourse*, in which the mental is assigned heterogeneous properties.[52] Sartre's, and many other forms of objection to psychoanalytic explanation, operate on the basis of a monism of psychological properties: it is objected, for example, that mental conflict is necessarily impervious to phantastic solution, on the grounds that mental conflict can be *nothing but* consciousness of propositional inconsistency. Psychoanalytic explanation, by contrast, holds that the several kinds of property of mental states interact so as to obstruct or intensify one another's causal role. Chief among these are of course economic properties, topographic properties (the language of mental distance), and (as 8.2 will emphasise) phenomenological properties. Their interaction composes a mental architecture which does not involve the principle of rational connectedness across its full extent, and lacks transparency.

IV The idea that psychoanalytic states are pre-propositional played an important role in Part II. However, the reasons advanced for denying that phantasy is a propositional attitude may also seem to support scepticism about phantastic content itself. Phantasy falls midway between infantile experience and adult belief,[53] and attempts to spell out its content may seem self-defeating. The Omnipotence

Belief, and the phantastic representation of the mind as a place,[54] illustrate this: it may seem that, as soon as an attempt is made to specify their content, we have something too outlandish to be sensibly attributed.

This problem arises even if the general notion of pre-propositionality is granted, for phantastic content differs in an important respect from pre-propositional content in other contexts. Perceptual content is pre-propositional, but it is determined, on one side, by its immediate proximity to the world which is causally responsible for it, and on the other to the perceptual beliefs which mirror it. Phantastic content lacks these two 'fixes', just as it lacks the fix provided by language: it does not represent veridically that which causes it, and it is not related rationally to belief through providing evidence for it. Thus Kleinian theory attributes something that is thought-like, but no more determinate in its content than confused experience, and this may seem paradoxical.

The force of this objection fades, however, as soon as it is remembered, first, that the difficulty we face in specifying phantastic content receives a perfectly adequate developmental *explanation* in psychoanalytic theory; and, second, that attributions such as the Omnipotence Belief emerge from the edifice of clinical interpretation as uniquely successful ways of bringing interpretative order to these. So, although truth-directedness does not fix phantastic content, other constraints remain adequately in play.

A more radical objection may, however, come from philosophical quarters: neo-Kantians may deny the very possibility of pre-propositional content, on grounds having to do with a priori requirements for mental content.[55] Without entering into the arguments for such requirements, we can go on to indicate how the neo-Kantian objection may be met.

It will always be possible to get away with the weak claim that pre-propositional states are states defined by *causal powers*, to produce certain contents in the mind, or, more obliquely, to affect the mind in ways that allow for their being reconstructed in terms of certain contents. That would do for the purpose of showing the coherence of psychoanalytic theory. This retreat is however unnecessary. Psychoanalytic pre-propositional content is attributed on the basis that the mind to which it belongs is a representational system whose existence and functioning involves essentially the conceptualisation of content and formation of propositional attitudes; pre-propositional content is only claimed to form a limited *part* of such a system. Kantian constraints can be met by the system *as a whole*, and need not be met by each content individually. Introduced as members of a system that necessarily conceptualises its central class of contents, pre-propositional contents avoid violating Kantian constraints.[56]

Again, the pictorial analogy helps: just as what a picture represents can call for conceptually complex description, without this implying that pictorial representation is discursive, psychoanalytic content can be amenable to conceptually rich specification, without being propositional.

7.3 METAPSYCHOLOGY III: PRECONSCIOUS STRATEGY AND PROPOSITIONAL REFLECTIONS

Neurosis, understood in terms of phantasy, explains why the Ratman has the desires and intentions that he does. Now, it is a condition of something's being strategic, that it contribute to some further end.[57] Neurosis, however, is fundamental in explaining the Ratman, in the sense that it serves no deeper end. To think of neurosis as strategic would consequently be to attribute a strategy without an accompanying rationalising context.

Denying strategy to the unconscious does not, however, commit us to a simple or monopolistic picture, in which the unconscious is supposed by exclusively non-rational means, without any kind of propositional intermediary, to provide a sufficient explanation for *all* of the explananda within Freud's clinical and investigative scope. There are, within the orbit of a case history, many strategy-suggestive phenomena, some of which are genuinely strategic.[58] The crucial point is that these do not stand at the core of psychoanalytic irrational phenomena; they are not located at the basic level of causal determination. This section will attempt to lay to rest any remaining doubts on this score, by examining putative instances of unconscious rationality in Freud's case histories.[59]

Here are the instances, and Freud's interpretations of them. A girl who is aware of her mother's adultery makes herself 'unable, owing to anxiety, to go out in the street or to stay at home by herself'; she 'had made herself ill in order to keep her mother prisoner'.[60] Dora's illness is similarly designed to interrupt her father's adulterous liaison,[61] and Little Hans' phobia of horses is calculated so that he will find himself kept at home with his mother.[62] By engaging in an elaborate bedtime ritual, a girl attempts to prevent, 'by magic', her parents from having sexual intercourse, and thereby producing a younger sibling who would rival their affections for her.[63] The Wolfman's constipation is self-induced, in order to satisfy his homosexual desire to be administered enemas.[64] Freud attempts to smash 'accidentally' an inkstand on his desk, in order that his sister should give him a more desirable one.[65] As putative indicators of the unconscious' powers of rationality, there are dreams in which arithmetical calculations are performed;[66] others which become more opaque in response to the success of the analyst's interpretations;[67] and still others which are in complicity with the analyst, whom they are designed to 'oblige'.[68]

Do these show the unconscious at work in designing means to ends, and Freud as promoting a conception of it as doing so? Without going into each instance in detail, Freud's overall perspective on such cases can be indicated. The first set of examples concerns what Freud calls the analysand's 'gain from illness'. Freud distinguishes sharply the 'internal' and 'external' aims of illness. The gain from illness is an external aim. External aims 'support the patient in being ill', and 'are probably to be found in all developed cases'. They of course exhibit instrumentality. External aims help to establish a particular symptom in everyday life, but they do not account for the 'formation of symptoms', which is a result of the illness' internal aim.[69] Gains from illness are therefore ancillary, and their attractiveness insufficient to cause the formation of irrational symptoms, although they may be necessary to explain why a particular symptom is selected and installed. Freud also denies that a coherent strategy coordinates the gains from illness with the losses of neurosis.[70]

In cases such as the Wolfman and the girl's bedtime ritual, an instrumental desire may *seem* to be directly responsible for the existence of a symptom. But what Freud says of the Wolfman is that 'his bowel behaved like a hysterically affected organ'.[71] That is, the physical syndrome is *expressive* of phantasy. If intention is present at all, its role is only the secondary one of fostering the condition, which requires only recognition of the pleasure of acting-out. Similarly, the central examples of bungled actions cited by Freud are all '*sacrificial act*[s]', 'propitiatory sacrifice[s]', with *symbolic* relations to mental processes.[72] The same goes for the girl's bedtime ritual.

Still, what is to be done with the instance of the inkstand? Clearly this is not, as described by Freud, a psychoanalytic irrational phenomenon.[73] So it is accommodated, as an instance of ordinary, self-deceptive irrationality, within the operations of the *preconscious* (*Pcs.*).[74] The preconscious is the site of all the hidden intentions that Freud diagnoses in the *The psychopathology of everyday life*.[75]

Regarding the alleged signs of rationality at the level of dream-formation, Freud says:

> the dream-work does not in fact carry out any calculations at all, whether correctly or incorrectly; it merely throws into the *form* of a calculation numbers which are present in the dream-thoughts [...] the dream-work is treating numbers as a medium for the expression of its purpose in precisely the same way as it treats any other idea[76]

The apparent indicators of instrumentality in dreaming can therefore be written out quite easily: increases in dreams' esotericism are due to a disposition to intensify distortion, in response to the anxiety generated by the analyst's interpretation;[77] and their suggestibility is similarly accounted for by the general dispositions involved in the transference.[78]

What we do not find in Freud's cases and interpretations, then, is a class of phenomena which are *instrumental with respect to unconscious determinants*, or *symbolic and instrumental in the same respect*, or *whose instrumental value is explained by the same thing as explains their symbolic value*.[79] Jokes, for example, on Freud's account, are intentional and instrumental in certain respects – the intention being to amuse, sometimes accompanied by a further, more specific intention (e.g. to insult) – but they are symbolic with respect to the unconscious processes of evasion of inhibition, and economisation of energy, which give them their essential psychological value.[80]

The two basic principles shaping Freud's theorising in these contexts can be spelled out. First, the occurrence of *insulated* rational operations, of *limited* kinds, is consistent with the non-strategic character of the *overall* mental process within which these operations occur. Second, strategic operations may occur as *mediating terms, or sub-components, in the service of non-strategic processes*.[81] So, even if it were a psychological law that whenever people act, they *have* to think of what they are doing as furthering some end, all this would show is that psychoanalytic interpretation should expect a 'cover-story' to be thrown over each instance of unconsciously motivated action. Nothing in Freud's account rules out such preconsciously designed rationalisation.

Evidently crucial for the causal stories just described, is the concept (introduced in 6.6) of propositional reflections of unconscious states, located in the preconscious. The concept of the preconscious itself is quite unmysterious, and corresponds roughly to what ordinary psychology (when not Cartesianised) conceives the mind to be; it is the level of mind manifested in ordinary, wakeful, self-conscious life. It is a condition of the preconscious' being explanatory in the context of psychoanalytic irrationality that it not be regarded as autonomous, else it becomes identical with *Ucs.*, and that its operations be viewed against a causally determining background provided by *Ucs.*: the unconscious causes, non-strategically, the preconscious to perform operations that *Ucs.* does not, and can not, itself perform, and that equally could not be understood to derive from the propositional network alone.

Propositional reflections appear in most full psychoanalytic interpretations, and they do so wherever the person displays, or must be credited with, some sort of dim awareness of her unconscious motivation. Propositional reflections serve two roles: they form a bridge from the Kleinian infantile-corporeal specifications of the content of phantasy, to ordinary conscious thought, which follows its contours; and they resolve the absurdity created by an attribution of knowledge of unconscious motivation, by substituting a *restricted* propositional object of awareness. So, to account for conscious or unconscious pleasure in a symbol S, the subject is credited with enough of a grasp of S's significance, in the form of a propositional attitude of broad scope and indefinite content (to the rough effect that 'S is desirable'), and this substitutes for knowledge of S's meaning. The psychoanalytic model is, in full (revising the earlier diagram in 5.7):

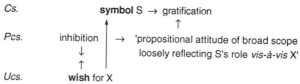

Because the propositional attitude in *Pcs.* is so vague, it does not conflict with the propositional attitude involved in inhibition of the wish for X, permitting the process of symbolising to go through.

The specificity of propositional reflections, and accuracy with which they echo the content of unconscious motivation, are not fixed matters. Whilst the 'table-cloth' woman discussed in 6.9 had little or no understanding of the significance of her behaviour (she could say nothing about it), the Ratman, in acting-out a reparative phantasy of protecting his beloved by removing a stone from the path of her carriage, was aware that this constituted 'protection', and took this to be his intention.[82] His phantasy, unlike hers, was acted out through the medium of an accurate propositional reflection of it.[83]

Two remaining objections that might be advanced are the following. The first concerns evidence. Given that the criteria for applying the strategic/non-strategic distinction provided by surface descriptions of mind and behaviour may be exceedingly fine, and often not enable the degree to which the subject has preconscious awareness of their motivation to be determined with precision, why *bother* to uphold the distinction, rather than let it collapse, and find other ways, with sounder criterial foundations, of capturing the contrasts between cases?

This (weakly verificationist) proposal would mean that there is no deep distinction between psychoanalytic and ordinary explanation. It requires a somewhat abstract reply. It is not true in all contexts that forms of description which are criterially distant from surface phenomena should be exchanged for others that are less distant, for the justifiability of a distinction does not derive from its relation to observational features alone. A framework which incorporates a conceptually deep, but criterially weak, distinction may be preferred to another which employs conceptually shallow, but criterially stronger, distinctions, when there are *theoretically inspired* reasons for doing so. This is the situation whenever abandoning the deep distinction would make the domain of phenomena *unintelligible*. Sartreian paradox (an unconscious that is both rational and irrational) is what we get when the strategic/non-strategic distinction is abandoned. The overarching need for explanation therefore functions argumentatively as a reductio of rejecting the deep distinction. (In fact, the distinctions of psychoanalytic theory *are* adequately underpinned by observable features:[84] for instance, psychoanalytic phenomena never exhibit the demonstrable rational connectedness between mental items argued in 1.3 to mark the threshold of strategicality.)

The second objection concerns the concept of strategicality itself. Could it be that the predicate 'strategic' *does not express a determinate concept*? Given that the concept of aiming, of meaning to do something, is fundamental to ordinary psychology, the objection threatens to lead us out of intentional psychology altogether.[85] But in any case, the possibility of indeterminacy cuts in favour of psychoanalytic theory. For, *if* the ordinary concept of strategy has no content which determines its application one way or another when confronted with some, ambiguous psychoanalytic phenomena, then it should be counted a virtue of psychoanalytic theory that – again, making gains in explanation – it *refines* the ordinary concept, separating out the broader notion of desire's purposiveness, from the narrower notion of a reason for action, and thereby grounding the strategic/non-strategic distinction.

From an exegetical point of view as well, there is no need to leave the issue of Freud's own view of the canonical form of unconscious motivation indeterminate. It has, of course, been agreed that Freud's employment of Second Mind reasoning shows him to have entertained several, philosophically different models of explanation. But the issue need not be left so undeveloped: the evidence is unequivocal that Freud consistently assigned sources of strategy to the preconscious, and sources of non-strategic influence to the unconscious, and that he regarded this distinction as a constitutive cornerstone of psychoanalytic theory. The reconstruction in Part II sought to display and respect his conceptual motivation in this respect.

7.4 PSYCHOANALYTIC EXPLANATION AND ORDINARY IRRATIONALITY

The next question is, What role – if any – do psychoanalytic processes play in the explanation of ordinary irrationality? Two thoughts present themselves. On the one hand, given the distinction of ordinary and psychoanalytic irrational phenomena, it ought to be empirical evidence that decides whether or not, for example, phantasy and self-deception interlock, and if so in what ways. On the other hand, surely something can be said a priori – that is, simply on the basis of the conceptual character of the patterns of explanation involved – about how they may be expected to interrelate.

The first thing to bear in mind is that, as chapter 1 argued, ordinary irrational phenomena have their explanations in ordinary psychology, which psychoanalytic explanation does not either displace, or re-analyse. As noted in 4.7, it would be mistaken to identify the burial of belief in self-deception with repression; nor, as 5.2 implied, can self-deceptive promotion of belief be identified with wish-fulfilment. The next point to be made is the obvious one that, since self-deceptive intent and phantasy operate at different levels, both may be cited, without over-determination, in the overall explanation of a single case. Furthermore, since it is reasonable to suppose that psychoanalytic and ordinary processes do not in general just coexist, but actually complement one another, it is tempting to speculate that there are correspondences between explanation by self-deceptive intent, and explanation by phantasy.[86] There is, for instance, a striking parallelism between the propositional schism brought about in self-deception, and the phantastic manoeuvre that Freud describes as the splitting of the ego, a form of disavowal:

it will be possible for the ego to avoid a rupture in any direction by deforming itself, by submitting to encroachments on its own unity and even perhaps by effecting a cleavage or division of itself.[87]

Perhaps, then, ego-splitting underlies self-deception. On this model, a specific *type* of ordinary irrationality is paired with a specific *type* of psychoanalytic process. Now, it may be that the clinical evidence will support such laws, but it can not be claimed a priori that they *must* exist since, after all, it may equally be the case that the psychoanalytic causes of self-deception are not of any single type.[88]

Even if type-type laws are not to be found, conceptual considerations suggest other, weaker but nevertheless significant roles for psychoanalytic explanation with respect to ordinary irrationality.

The following clinical example and interpretation (by Jekels, quoted in full by Freud) shows a clear conjunction of self-deception with unconscious motivation.[89] A doctor 'had in his possession an earthenware flower vase which, though not valuable, was of great beauty', which 'had been sent to him in the past by a (married) woman patient'. When his treatment of the woman had failed, he had 'restored all the presents to her relatives – except for this far less expensive vase, with which he could not bear to part, ostensibly because it was so beautiful'. Yet he 'was fully aware of the impropriety of his action and only managed to overcome his pangs of conscience by telling himself that the vase was not in fact of any real value, that it was too awkward to pack, etc.' Some months later, worried that visitors would notice the vase, he dropped it clumsily, once into five or six pieces, a second time 'into a thousand splinters, and with that vanished all hope for the vase'.

In ridding him of the embarrassment of his 'embezzlement',

'this parapraxis had the current purpose of assisting the doctor'. But psychoanalysis also discloses a strong symbolic meaning for the vase: it represented the doctor's wife, who had died when young, and remained for him an object of passionate feelings.

The case has the following form. The breaking of the vase is explained locally by a preconscious intention, deriving from a desire to avoid embarrassment in front of his visitors. But this desire is reinforced by anxieties stemming from, and the entire situation within which it operates is structured by, a symbolic equation. So, had there been no symbolisation, there would have been no preconscious motivation for the parapraxis, and the vase would not have been dropped. The same goes for the doctor's self-deception, his 'telling himself that the vase was not in fact of any real value, that it was too awkward to pack, etc.': had no pressure been exerted by the symbolic value of the vase, no self-deceptive intent would have been formed.

This example does not support any type-type psychological law, but it does suggest the following important thought: that psycho-analytic factors supply the missing solution to the Special Problem of ordinary irrationality. This very general claim – which is committed only to there being some psychoanalytic cause, of whatever type, for each instance of ordinary irrationality – there is excellent reason to accept: in the absence of any more suitable candidate, psychoanalytic factors are exactly the right *kind* of thing to play the role of providing a causal background capable of explaining why there is disturbance, and deviation from rationality, in the propositional network. In this spirit, psychoanalytic causes may be said to contribute to the explanation of the involuntary structures responsible for the inertness of the Principle of Continence in akrasia. Similarly, the theory of wish-fulfilment may be taken to contribute to the explanation of wishful thinking, not by way of their being identified, but in the broad sense that wish-fulfilment provides the psychological ma-chinery needed for forming belief-like representations out of wants. If this is so, it may be claimed that explanations of ordinary irrationality are ultimately conditional upon psychoanalytic explanation.

There is a second connection between ordinary irrationality and psychoanalytic explanation which may be claimed a priori. Phantasy provides an obvious way of deepening the characterisation of a person's compartments. There are reasons, deriving from the holism and epistemology of psychoanalytic interpretation, for expecting each of a person's rational goal-structures to be anchored loosely in a complex of phantasy. Could it be that there are *no* connections between people's self-deception, akratic lapses and wishful thinking, and their psychoanalytic processes? The topics of their self-deception, akrasia and so on would then be wholly indifferent to their unconscious preoccupations! This is impossible: not only would it offend against the holism of the mental, which demands that a person's propositional and psychoanalytic concerns be seen as united, but it is also epistemologically impossible: the epistemological supports of psychoanalytic attributions lie partly in ordinary irrationality, since (as shown in 4.4) ordinary irrational phenomena are powerful indicators for unconscious motivation. In the end, then, ordinary irrationality is bound to tie up with psychoanalytic explanation; only the specific forms of this connection are an empirical matter.

7.5 PSYCHOANALYTIC EXPLANATION AND COMMONSENSE: SAVING THE APPEARANCES

A widespread, and to some extent natural, way of understanding the impact of psychoanalytic explanation on commonsense is in terms of a contrast between psychological appearance and reality. Psychoanalytic explanation might be understood as showing that we do not really mean, think or feel, what we seem to mean, think and feel. And this may lead to a sense of paralysis: psychoanalytic explanation may be experienced, nihilistically, as rendering subjective existence impossible, because it requires all conscious phenomena to be seen only as indicative of, or standing proxy for, something else – and thus as empty of intrinsic meaning.[90] Alternatively, scepticism about the coherence of psychoanalysis may issue: for it is a familiar thought that the mental is *constituted*, if only in part, by subjective appearances, and so logically *can not* be illusory, as psychoanalytic explanation is taken to imply.

Here I want to show why the contrast of appearance and reality is misleading in this context, and the alleged nihilistic and sceptical upshots unfounded.

The distinction of appearance and reality in the context of psychology trades off its application in two other contexts. One is the familiar perceptual contrast of a misleading appearance with how things really are – the stick half-immersed in water that looks bent.

The other concerns reductive theoretical explanations of surface phenomena in terms of depth phenomena, or scientifically specified micro-structures, for which Locke's treatment of secondary qualities is often taken to provide a paradigm.

One psychoanalytic context that might seem strongly suggestive of the first sort of appearance/reality distinction is symbolism, because it involves substitution and disguise. There, however, no demotion of the ordinary mental to 'mere appearance' takes place: on the contrary, symbolic interpretations presuppose that *both* terms of the symbolic relation have reality. All that can be meant by the appearance/reality contrast in such contexts is that only one of the terms is consciously apprehended. But this is analogous only to a situation in which an object is presented from a perceptual angle which fails to display all of its features – a situation which is quite unlike that of the 'bent' stick. The same holds for dreams, which are not false appearances in the mind of something of which there exists a *true* appearance. When psychoanalytic interpretation says that one thing 'is in fact' another, this is quite unlike the situation where the meaning of a statement has been misidentified and is corrected, or where self-attributions are retrospectively revised ('what I really had in mind was ... '). The central point is the following: the 'bent' stick contrast of appearance with reality concerns two terms, *both* of which are identified *within* the ordinary, pretheoretical world view; whereas psychoanalytic realities are located *outside* that world view, and so can not impugn the reality of ordinary appearances.[91]

As for the other sort of appearance/reality distinction, theoretical reduction, it should be plain that even when psychoanalytic theory comes closest to suggesting a 'real essence' for mental states, as in Klein's account of envy – which may seem to want to tell us what, despite all appearances, 'really goes on' in envy – this is the wrong way of understanding the upshot of psychoanalytic theory. Lockeian contrasts of nominal and real essence require these to be heterogeneous. But the concepts employed in psychoanalytic understanding of emotion are too close, logically, to those of ordinary psychology, for the relation to be one of real to nominal essence. So when psychoanalytic theory tells us what envy is, it is not the 'is' of theoretical identification (understood according to scientific realism) which is employed.[92]

Of course, psychoanalytic explanation does not necessarily leave *everything* just as it was before. Although, usually, it just supplements ordinary attributions of, for example, intention, it may sometimes incline us to withdraw or replace them. Revision of ordinary psychological attributions is however not a built-in feature of psychoanalytic explanation. As indicated in 6.6, psychoanalytic explanation is in general opposed to the idea that consciousness is epiphenomenal. Nor does psychoanalytic explanation rule out, in any sense, the existence of emergent motivation at the level of consciousness. Psychoanalytic theory therefore does not tell us that we are permanently 'deceived' about ourselves, or that we do not really desire what we think we desire; instead, it contributes to the explanation of *what motivates* our conscious desires. The precise extent of this contribution is an empirical question, not determined by the nature of psychoanalytic theory.[93]

Psychoanalytic theory yields no imperative to redescribe all ordinary experience in a psychoanalytic vocabulary. The upshot of psychoanalytic interpretation of persons should accordingly be likened to the adding of detail and deeper perspective in a growing, palimpsestic, but single picture – rather than a process of stripping-away to reveal a 'true' image.

7.6 PSYCHOANALYTIC STATES: SELFHOOD, OWNERSHIP AND INTEGRATION

This section considers how psychoanalytic conception bears on our ordinary view of persons. How do we stand in relation to our psychoanalytic states, and how does psychoanalytic theory conceive of persons, metaphysically?

The import of the first question can be appreciated by considering Sartre's statement:

By the distinction between the 'id' and the 'ego', Freud has cut the psychic whole into two. I *am* the ego but I *am not* the id. I hold no privileged position in relation to my unconscious psyche. I *am* my own psychic phenomena in so far as I establish them in their conscious reality [...] But I *am* not those psychic facts, in so far as I receive them passively and am obliged to resort to hypotheses about their origin and true meaning [...] I can know myself only through the mediation of the other, which means that I stand in relation to my 'id', in the position of the *Other*.[94]

This is a different charge from the Censor Criticism. Sartre's essential point is clear. Psychoanalytic states are *advanced* as personal or owned by the subject.[95] But the usual, most natural criterion of personal status or ownership is Cartesian: a state is personal, or owned, if it can be self-ascribed on an immediate, incorrigible basis. Another intuitive condition for personal status is simultaneously violated: psychoanalytic states do not fall within the perspective of choice. So it may seem that psychoanalytic theory produces a contradictory relation to the psychological terrain that it describes: it entails that, with respect to the unconscious, I am 'in' my mind, only as, and just as, I am 'in this room'! This explains Sartre's view of psychoanalysis as alienating, and Lacan's view that it exposes our ordinary self-conception as an illusion: 'I am not, wherever I am the playing of my thought.'[96]

Given all this, by virtue of what can psychoanalytic states be deemed personal, rather than part of persons' properly sub-personal constitutions? For this, the liberal, non-Cartesian criterion of personal status described in 2.10 is needed. Although the attribution of psychoanalytic states does presuppose a third-person vantage-point and theoretical understanding, psychoanalytic states have none of the scientific character of cognitive-psychological attributions. Psychoanalytic states extend ordinary psychology, as cognitive-psychological predicates do not, and exploit its broadly rationalising form of explanation; they are postulated in response to needs for explanation created by irrational phenomena at the personal level. Psychoanalytic states participate intimately in the person's mental, particularly emotional life, transmit their content to the propositional network, count as a form of activity, and provide the well-springs of motivation, receiving expression in intentional action. And, as 8.2 will argue, psychoanalytic states have phenomenological properties, and are quasi-manifestable, in the sense that, after a certain point, theory may fall away in their self-ascription – features which restore a loose connection with consciousness.

So, although we are not logically compelled to admit psychoanalytic states into the class of personal states, equally nothing debars us logically from doing so, and the features listed should, in combination, suffice for them to be admitted. Faced with psychoanalytic attributions, it is intuitively sound to extend the category of psychological ownership: even if this does demand a minor modification to the ordinary conception of personality, less distortion results than would be involved in dissociating oneself from one's unconscious by classing it as sub-personal.

The second question, of how psychoanalytic theory conceives persons, has particular importance, in view of the fact that

Continental writings on psychoanalytic theory frequently cast it in the role of a philosophical theory of the self, in the same sense as those provided by Descartes and Kant.[97] I will indicate why, despite psychoanalytic writing's having some features which make it susceptible to being understood in such terms, this is severely mistaken.

When we talk about persons' consciousness of self or selfhood – their 'sense of self' – there is a crucial ambiguity. One thing that could be meant is a person's *logical* grasp (distinguished by its special, immediate, and 'interior' character) of himself as a *subject of predication*. This conception contradicts the Humean conception of persons, but it determines nothing as to what properties are to be ascribed to persons.

The second meaning of selfhood is a sense of oneself *as* integrated, self-controlling and self-determining. This, selfhood as *psychological integration*, presupposes grasping oneself as a logical subject, and involves the ascription of a particular complex property or organisation of properties to the person. Its distinction from the first sense of selfhood is shown by the schizophrenic, who lacks selfhood in the integrative, but certainly not the logical sense. Whereas logical selfhood is all-or-nothing, integrative selfhood comes in degrees.

Now, it is quite true that psychoanalytic theory talks a lot about the self.[98] This is because psychoanalysis is concerned with selfhood as integration, which Klein describes as the goal of analysis.[99] But the degree of integration which psychoanalysis aims to secure is not complete: psychoanalysis is concerned with the radical failures of integration which cause psychoanalytic irrational phenomena, but it may leave untouched numerous failures of integration identified at the level of ordinary psychology. This is because the materials of psychoanalytic explanation are 'coarse', relative to the very much finer distinctions available in propositional thought, which allow for conflicts not expressible in psychoanalytic terms. Psychoanalytic integration concerns, primarily, the vertical relations of propositional to unconscious states, not the horizontal inter-relations of propositional attitudes. From which it follows that psychoanalytic theory does not stretch to satisfying or explaining completely the strong concern for unity described in 3.8. Its account of integration says nothing about the emergence of logical selfhood.

The same goes for the important controversy in psychoanalytic theory as to whether or not the ego exists from the beginning of mental life.[100] This issue may be redolent of philosophising about the self, but it is really just concerned with empirical structural conditions for mental development.

Failure to distinguish the two meanings of selfhood has dire consequences. First, it produces conceptual mayhem, by conflating empirical conditions for psychological integration with logical conditions for self-individuation. Second, it leads directly to Humeanism about the self: for, if logical and integrative selfhood are one and the same, it follows that the existence of a self just *is* the holding of certain integrative relations.

This helps to explain why an association should be thought to hold between psychoanalysis, and a Humean metaphysic of personal identity. Richard Rorty illustrates the tendency to think this. Rorty acknowledges that 'the traditional picture of the human situation has been one in which human beings are not simply networks of beliefs and desires but rather beings which *have* those beliefs and desires'.[101] He claims, however, that Freud, in contradiction to the Kantian picture,

helped de-divinise the self [... and] take seriously the possibility that there is no central faculty, no central self [... Freud] does not see humanity as a natural kind with an intrinsic nature [... he] substitute[s] a tissue of contingent relations, a web which stretches backward and forward through past and future time, for a formed, unified, present, self-contained substance.[102]

Now there are indeed features of psychoanalytic writing, such as the functional character of its developmental stories, that may on casual inspection seem to express a picture of persons as nothing but approximately unified vectors resulting from the interaction of conflicting mental states, but Rorty's metaphysical reading is justified only if psychoanalytic theory is *independently* construed as being in the business of trying to account for logical selfhood – an assumption for which there is no evidence. Of course, if it is assumed in advance that any non-Humean conception of the person is metaphysical and as such objectionable, or that all alternatives to Humean conception are metaphysically extravagant, then there may be reason for harnessing psychoanalytic theory to Humeanism, and using it as an instrument for countering 'divinised' notions of the self. But only if such assumptions are made is there any motivation for seeing psychoanalytic theory as Humean; if instead persons are viewed as natural substances, and this metaphysical category accepted, there will be no temptation to think this.

It may however be objected that the distinction of meanings of selfhood was in the first place made *too* sharply. Are there not connections, so far overlooked, between the two meanings of selfhood?

It is probably true that the distinction between logical and integrative selfhood is not *subjectively* represented in all contexts. That persons sometimes experience logical selfhood as bound up and fused with integrative selfhood is highly plausible: in fearing madness, for example, the prospect of radical non-integration is experienced as a threat to one's very existence (madness means destruction); experientially, but not logically, madness puts at stake the *existence*, and not just the psychological organisation of the logical subject.[103] However, conceding that logical and integrative selfhood may be identified in subjective contexts – where, as it might be put, psychological order is experienced as constituting selfhood – gives no reason for qualifying, or revising, the view that logical and integrative selfhood are objectively distinct. Shortly I will suggest *why* experience should double up the two meanings of selfhood.

A second reason for thinking that the distinction between logical and integrative selfhood may have been overdrawn is that the Lockeian tradition, which is not obviously confused, does after all locate the criterion of personal identity in continuity of memory relations. Such relations would after all seem to concern integration, suggesting that self-individuation and integration are not after all discrete issues. But this point loses its force as soon as it is realised that the Lockeian criterion (as it stands in its original empiricist formulation) does *not* in fact rule out a Humean view of selfhood;[104] and since it therefore does not account for a logical grasp of oneself as a subject, it can not in fact pull together the two meanings of selfhood. In a moment I will indicate how the alleged connection between Lockeian personal identity and integration is superseded by a superior conception of the link between the two meanings of selfhood.

It follows from what has been said so far that psychoanalytic theory *is not* a philosophical theory of the self – nor does it contain the germs of one – and that to think, as does Lacan, that Freud somehow 'undoes' the cogito, is a confusion:[105] psychoanalytic theory on its own can not falsify a philosophical account of the self, any more than it can provide one.[106] The most that psychoanalytic theory can establish is a set of empirical preconditions for persons to form the *concept* of logical selfhood.

Although psychoanalytic theory is thus logically neutral between philosophical theories of the person or self, there are considerations which dictate powerfully a weaker than logical, yet highly plausible association between psychoanalytic theory and a particular philosophical view of persons. Psychoanalytic theory's attachment to positing biological grounds for mental life, such as instinct, which determine the mind's developmental course, and its stress on the intertwining of the mental and physical, brings it into harmony with a view of persons as psycho-physical substances forming a natural kind, the view adopted in 3.8. Logical self-individuation is, on that account, connected with membership of a natural kind whose instances are normally endowed with a certain causal unity, and whose psychological order conforms to laws defining the natural kind. This *does* connect, without confusing, the two meanings of self.

Only a skewed reading of psychoanalytic explanation could take it as having the Humean implication that the only things that exist are acts or events of repressing, phantasising and so on. There is, of course, 'one thing' which remains in question as the subject of repression and phantasy, and that is the person. Unlike sub-systemic theory, psychoanalytic theory is capable of acknowledging, although it does not give a philosophical account of, personal unity, or – if this be the same thing – the reality of the self. It leaves persons, as non-Humean logical subjects, intact; instead of dividing them, it yields explanation through an enlarged conception of the mind's activity and contents. Sub-systemic theory is revealed to be – despite its denial of personal indivisibility, and the transparency of the mental – tacitly Cartesian in its assumption that the *extent* of minds is fixed within the bounds of ordinary, known kinds of mental state. Sub-systemic theory, correctly detecting a limitation in ordinary psychology, attempts to dispel the reflexive strangeness of irrationality by multiplying minds. Psychoanalytic theory achieves this result by representing the mind as encompassing unfamiliar kinds of mental state: by viewing persons as expressing phantasies, it explains, as ordinary psychology can not, the self-contradictions constitutive of irrationality.

CHAPTER 8

Consciousness, theory and epistemology

the mind
Acquired transparence and beheld itself
And beheld the source from which transparence came
Wallace Stevens

as he had no theory, and no coat on, he was
unanimously set at nought.
Dickens

8.1 CONSCIOUSNESS AND UNCONSCIOUS MENTALITY

This chapter begins with a question so central that it may seem as if it ought to have been considered at the outset of this enquiry: Is the concept of unconscious mentality coherent? After all, if unconscious mentality is a contradictory concept, then the whole question of psychoanalytic explanation is dramatically cut short.

There are two views of the relation of consciousness to mentality. The one, which may as well be called Cartesian, says that mentality and consciousness are equivalent; or, in a more extended formulation, that there is no coherent concept of unconscious mentality other than of dispositions to states of consciousness.[1] The other, Noncartesian view – which is clearly required for psychoanalytic theory – is, of course, that there are or could be unconscious mental states; or, that unconscious mentality need not reduce to dispositions to states of consciousness. My suggestion will be that, without going into this (potentially abstruse) issue far enough for it to be completely resolved, it can be concluded that there is no a priori obstacle to an extension of ordinary psychology profoundly dependent on the notion of unconscious mentality, and that such is justified if demanded by considerations of explanation.[2]

207

Why should it be thought that mental states are necessarily conscious? Obviously, because the mental states attributed in ordinary psychology come with consciousness, are 'inseparably intertwined' with our being conscious of them, are themselves precisely ways of being conscious of the world and ourselves.[3] Now, granting all this, we see immediately that the connection between mentality and consciousness is twofold.[4] There is, first, the analysis of mentality itself *as* consciousness:

a mental state directed towards an object x (or state of affairs p) is *consciousness of x* (that p).

Let this be written as consciousness*. And, second, there is a cognitive relation to that very mental state:

consciousness *of* consciousness* of x (that p).

This – which may be written simply as consciousness – corresponds more closely to what ordinary psychology means by 'consciousness'. It is obviously a condition, if not a sufficient one, of self-consciousness.

In these terms, what the Noncartesian holds is that a mental state (consciousness*) may exist without consciousness;[5] and the Cartesian, that a mental state (consciousness*) may not exist without consciousness. Now, on the face of it, all that should be needed for the truth of the Noncartesian view is the bare distinction between mental states (consciousness*) and consciousness: for we do not generally take it that the existence of things depends on consciousness of them – that being what the Cartesian asserts of mental states (consciousness*).

What could block the crucial move of separating mental states (consciousness*) from consciousness? Perhaps the Cartesian may grant the logical distinctness of mental states (consciousness*) from consciousness, and yet assert the metaphysical dependence of the former on the latter.[6]

Denying the independence of mental states (consciousness*) from consciousness is tantamount to adopting a position on the mental equivalent to that which Berkeley adopts on the external world: for if mental states are dependent on consciousness, then they are – by the standard definition of reality – *ideal* rather than real.

Now, of course one wants to recognise, along with Berkeley, all sorts of differences and asymmetries between minds and non-mental entities. But these must surely not have the consequence that minds do not *exist*, or *have reality*, in the same sense as non-mental entities.[7] Yet this is just what *is* said if the independence of mental states (consciousness*) from consciousness is denied.

Suspending this objection (which a complex redefinition of 'real' might, arguably, deflect), the Noncartesian's point becomes the following. The assertion that mental states (consciousness*) depend on consciousness amounts to – at least, in the sense that its motivation does not differ from that for – a kind of phenomenalism about the mental: that is, an identification of each mental state with either actual or possible states of consciousness. Phenomenalising the mind, however, rules out thinking of it as a system of causally inter-related states, which is how ordinary psychology conceives it, and seems, furthermore, to require the highly unexplanatory thought that consciousness is a creator ex nihilo of mental states, an idea that is no less strange in the case of the mental than it is in that of the physical.[8] Note that even Locke's genetic constraint on mentality – that there can be nothing in the mind which is not, or has not previously been in consciousness[9] – which may at first glance seem compatible with realism about mentality, is in fact peculiarly arbitrary: if an originally conscious idea can become unconscious at a later time, why can an idea not be originally unconscious, and later become conscious? The only possible rationale for the temporal asymmetry in Locke's constraint would seem to lie in a view to the effect that the creation of a mental item involves consciousness as a necessary genetic condition. But this notion, of consciousness as a *creative cause*, also contradicts commonsense, and it is very hard to see what sort of defence it could receive. We ordinarily take it that mental states do their work in the mind not just because there is consciousness of them, but that the causal power of mental states is independent of, and may consequently transcend, consciousness of them. All that the Noncartesian view needs, then, is agreement that the explanatory value of the states that ordinary psychology attributes does not derive exclusively from there being consciousness of them.

The discussion therefore leaves an asymmetry between the positions of the Cartesian and the Noncartesian: whereas the Noncartesian's claim requires them only to explicate 'unconscious' as 'not conscious', the Cartesian would need to explicate 'conscious' in fully-fledged metaphysical terms, in order to establish their claim – a heavy burden of proof.[10] There is, it seems, no position to be occupied between outright Noncartesian realism, and idealism about the mind, which appears to lack intelligibility or motivation.[11] Pending an account from the Cartesian as to how minds can really exist, and yet be mind-dependent, or of the motivation for phenomenalising minds, we are condemned by the bare, ordinary notion that minds are real, and that ordinary psychology has causal-explanatory commitments, to recognise enough of a distinction between minds and consciousness to legitimate the idea of unconscious mentality: an unconscious mental state is a mental state (consciousness*) of which there is no consciousness; and such states may be attributed if demanded by considerations of explanation. So, as has been assumed throughout the enquiry, the way has indeed been open all along to explanation in terms of unconscious mentality.

Two things about the argument should be noted. First, it should be observed – since it is now often thought that the mind must be conceived *either* in a Cartesian, *or* a theoretical fashion – that the argument does not assume that ordinary psychology is a form of theoretical explanation, and that asserting the reality of unconscious mentality does not of itself give any reason for embracing that view (the theoretical view will be discussed in 8.3). Second, the argument does not exploit the famous difficulty, perhaps impossibility, of saying what consciousness *is*, in such a way as to cast doubt on the philosophical integrity of the notion. Indeed, an *un*analysed notion of consciousness – namely, consciousness* – was granted at the outset. This point is important because, as 8.2 will show, psychoanalytic explanation is in no sense hostile to Cartesian, in the sense of consciousness-invoking, concepts; in fact, it could not dispense with them.

In the rest of this section I will answer three objections to the Noncartesian view, touching on (without doing justice to the complexity of) Freud's own analyses of consciousness.

(1) Psychoanalytic theory has been thought to lead to, even if it does not assert outright, a general (and incredible) *repudiation* of consciousness.[12] The reasons for this – a more abstract worry than that discussed in 7.5 – are worth going into. Sartre puts the issue in focus:

Either we accept a theory of consciousness as consciousness through and through, in which case we must reject the unconscious; or we start from the contrary idea and, as happens in all the treatises of psychology that I have read or known, consciousness disappears, becomes inexplicable. It becomes a little piece of paper that one occasionally attaches to a phenomenon, sometimes conscious, sometimes unconscious. But this is totally inconceivable[13]

The anxiety expressed here is that, if it is so much as conceded that there *could be* such a thing as a mental state without consciousness, consciousness will be ousted from the mind: for if a mental state can exist in the unconscious *in its entirety*, what can the addition of consciousness then consist in? Nothing at all, it would seem. So, allowing the full reality of unconscious mentality would seem to imply that consciousness is a nothing, at best an epiphenomenon.

Endorsing the idea of unconscious mentality *need* not imply a devaluation of consciousness, or make it only an accidental or epiphenomenal property of the mental.[14] This consequence is blocked, in the present context, by the recognition that psychoanalytic theory allows a wholly acceptable conceptual dependence of unconscious on conscious mentality, in so far as psychoanalytic states are necessarily parts of *the mind*, the concept of which *is* necessarily connected with that of consciousness. Psychoanalytic theory has no need to deny that, if there were no phenomenon of consciousness, or even of self-consciousness, there would be no unconscious, or that – for a wide range of mental states – the feature of consciousness is highly causally significant (indeed, the efficacy of psychoanalytic therapy requires such a supposition[15]).

There is an analogy here with the concepts of purposiveness without reasons for action, and of pre-propositional content. Just as a person, as something that is explicable essentially in terms of reasons for action can, in some respects, be explained in terms that refer to desires but not to reasons for action; and, just as the mind, as something that involves conceptualisation essentially, can tolerate the inclusion of some unconceptualised members; so a mind, as something that involves consciousness essentially, can tolerate the inclusion of some unconscious members.

Behind statements such as Sartre's, another sort of charge seems to lie. It is that consciousness is repudiated implicitly by any theory, such as Freud's, that does not show how mentality can *imply* consciousness. Now, it may be that psychoanalytic theory heightens our awareness of the problem of securing causal value for the mental without making consciousness epiphenomenal, but this amounts to an objection only if psychoanalytic theory is understood as having philosophical ambitions, and lying under philosophical obligations.

And, as argued in 7.6, this is mistaken: psychoanalytic theory is not required to explain the relation between mentality and consciousness, any more than it must explicate the nature of consciousness itself. These problems should be pushed back to philosophy, and psychoanalytic theory released from the burden of them.

Freud was aware of the philosophical perplexities surrounding consciousness, 'a fact without parallel, which defies all explanation or description'.[16] In the 'Project', Freud describes consciousness as a 'mechanism of psychical attention'.[17] In a similar vein, Freud later identifies consciousness as 'a sense-organ for the perception of psychical qualities'.[18] Freud's specific speculations on consciousness include connections with verbal or sensory images, critical levels of intensity, degrees of organisation, and cathexis. The theory of word-presentations, as a condition for preconsciousness, makes an important connection between consciousness and dispositions to overt linguistic behaviour.[19]

What is obvious is that these analyses – however reductively Freud intended them, a matter which is not clear – are *functional*, and that psychoanalytic theory's treatment of consciousness is limited to its formulating a theory of the determinants of consciousness only in so far as this will contribute to a theory of the system Cs.[20] Because psychoanalytic theory's interest in consciousness is circumscribed by the goal of explaining functions such as avowal, defence, and working-through, there is no pressure for the class of determinants of consciousness which it postulates to have a unified, non-disjunctive form, or for Cs. to do more than approximate to our ordinary concept of consciousness, or any philosophical elaboration of it. Consequently, there will be no strict conceptual connection between consciousness as Cs., and consciousness as a special kind of unity or source of the cogito; and this will not be an objection to psychoanalytic theory.

This, at any rate, is how Cs. must look to someone who thinks that consciousness necessarily resists functional characterisation. On another view, there is nothing wrong with regarding Cs. as a continuous extension of the ordinary conception of consciousness. On this view, when consciousness is opposed to another mental system, either Pcs. or Ucs., what happens is that we are made to realise the immanently topographic character of consciousness in ordinary thought: we appreciate that, implicitly, consciousness must have been conceived all along in ordinary psychology, as a set of contents that form a functionally characterisable system, which can be juxtaposed to, and interact with, other mental systems.

(2) Another line of objection to unconscious mentality might be called, after Berkeley, *anti-abstractionism*. It is that the notion of unconscious mentality attempts to abstract from conscious mentality, in a way that amounts to an illegitimate move from what is known, to what can not be known or even conceived.[21]

This objection fails to bear on non-accidentally inaccessible mentality, since the concepts of ordinary psychology already extrapolate or 'abstract' from conscious experience in the relevant sense. But perhaps the idea of non-accidentally inaccessible mentality presents a greater difficulty. Is positing mentality that can not be made conscious like positing a physical object that can not be experienced (which might invite one to think that what is being talked about must be only a theoretical entity[22])?

What needs to be appreciated, in order to see that the intelligibility of non-accidental inaccessibility requires no conceptual innovation, is that the unconsciousness of non-accidentally inaccessible mental states is explained by its fundamental features, the 'special characteristics of the system *Ucs.*', which make them sufficiently different *in internal constitution* from states that can be conscious, so as not to appear in consciousness, except in distorted and indirect forms, and under special conditions (such as dreaming). The bare concept of unconscious mental existence is then the same in ordinary and psychoanalytic psychology; what changes is just its explanation.

(3) The final objection is that any adduction of unconscious mentality as an empirical explanatory hypothesis will be *redundant*, relative to other and preferable empirical hypotheses.[23]

This is familiar territory, and the appropriate response obvious. It can not be shown a priori that better hypotheses must be available: neural states are in no position to take over from mental states,[24] and the reconstruction of psychoanalytic theory in this enquiry has argued that the nature of psychoanalytic explananda guarantees the indispensability of unconscious mentality.

What, in view of all this, are the consequences of psychoanalytic theory for the doctrine of privileged access? The issue is complicated by the variety of the doctrine's formulations. Clearly, psychoanalytic theory contradicts the claim that there is necessarily for any mental state, without any kind of qualification, a conscious self-ascriptive belief about that state. But it does not obstruct the claim that, *if* there is a conscious self-ascriptive belief about a mental state, then that belief will be justified or even incorrigible. The existence of a special kind of epistemic authority over one's own mental states can be accommodated in psychoanalytic theory if (i) the range of such authority is restricted so as to exclude non-accidentally inaccessible kinds of mental state; and, to preserve itself in the face of accidental inaccessibility, (ii) a distinction between normal and abnormal conditions of mental functioning is drawn, abnormal conditions being also excluded from its domain. So the doctrine of privileged access finally survives in that, when mental states are of the right kind, and conditions are normal, the knowledge that there is of them will exhibit a certain kind of immunity to error, or correction by others. The proper metaphysical corollary of this epistemic doctrine, whatever it may be (such as, that conscious mental states are self-presenting, or that they are known by a special organ of inner perception), is therefore also unimpugned. Again, the appropriate appearances are saved.[25]

8.2 PHENOMENOLOGY AND QUASI-MANIFESTATION

Psychoanalytic states have phenomenological properties: they are endowed with hedonic qualities, such as pain, pleasure and anxiety; phantastic content is experienced, as the content of belief is not; and unconscious emotions are felt, as are conscious emotions. Since psychoanalytic states are unconscious, it follows that there must be such a thing as *unconscious phenomenology*. This section will amplify these claims.[26]

In ordinary psychology, fantasies and other imaginative products are coloured by qualitative aspects, imagistic accompaniment, and affect, as beliefs and desires are usually not. Phenomenological properties have, as noted in 7.2, a special connection with irrationality: they may function as a kind of mental grit, clogging the operation of rational processes. These non-propositional features carry over to psychoanalytic wish and phantasy, and their causal value is heightened in the unconscious, where they become crucial determinants of the course of mental processes. This is just what the instinctual, infantile, and physically proximate character of the unconscious leads us to expect. The Inner Picture analogy, in conjunction with the claim that the inner world is experienced realistically, suggests that a kind of spatiality also imbues the experience of phantastic content: the mind is experienced as a place.[27] Phenomenological properties also parallel and reinforce economic properties, such as the intensity of anxiety. The upshot is that phenomenological properties have greater explanatory importance in psychoanalytic than in ordinary psychology.[28]

Unconscious pain illustrates sharply the role of phenomenology in psychoanalytic explanation. The notion goes back as far as Freud's accounts of hysteria: Freud says that Frau Emmy's physically experienced pain functions as a 'somatic symbol' of past mental pain.[29] Mental pain is not originally a psychoanalytic concept. We use the notion whenever we talk about 'painful thoughts', and it comes to the surface when we try to characterise the force of certain emotions and moods (dejection, grief, anguish); it is closely allied, if not identical with anxiety.[30] Kleinian theory elaborates greatly both the specific notion of unconscious pain, and the general notion of thought as capable of subjectively acquiring physical characteristics. This enables the psychoanalyst to interpret unconscious pain as being, for example, manipulated purposefully in phantasy: Donald Meltzer says that in some cases 'there is a certain transportation of mental pain, not simply defence against it. Its location can be shifted, rather than its existence denied.'[31] Also of relevance in illustrating the role of phenomenology, are clinical reports of cases in which psychotic patients self-ascribe *conscious* experiences of thoughts with qualitative and physical properties, such as colour, velocity and spatial orientation.[32] The postulation of unconscious pain in psycho-analytic contexts is enjoined by Occam's razor: it provides the simplest way to account for certain ranges of effects; by comparison with the painfulness of pain, any other story would be highly convoluted.[33]

There is an important sub-class of phenomenological properties, which are acquired by psychoanalytic states through a prior misrepresentation of the nature of those states. We referred in 4.4 to the Ratman's 'sexualised' thinking, and saw above how Meltzer interprets the manipulation of unconscious pain. These ideas converge naturally on a single general thesis, in terms of which they in turn receive elucidation and support. It is argued for by Wollheim under a name taken from a phrase of Freud's: the 'bodily ego'. The thesis says that thought 'represents itself as something corporeal: or, more specifically, either as something that can be brought into the body and made part of it, or as something that starts off as a part of the body and can then be pushed out of it'.[34] The Bodily Ego is a conception of the same order as the Omnipotence Belief, and it is introduced by the same characteristically psychoanalytic form of argument: unconscious mental misrepresentation is adduced as required to account for the efficacy of mental states.

The concept of unconscious phenomenology is, however, likely to meet with objections.

In the first place, it may be alleged that the concept of a painful thought is too perilously close to that of, for example, a 'square' or 'hard' thought, to be understood literally,[35] and that reports of painful thoughts should consequently be paraphrased by judgements about their *objects*. 'The thought of my partner's infidelity hurts me' would then become something like 'my partner's infidelity is terrible'. In this way the thought's 'pain' would be made to reside, as it were, in the message rather than the messenger.

But this proposal is misguided. The phenomenology of painful thought is far closer to that of pain associated with bodily injury than it is to regret, or any properly intentional state: it is the impact of the thought itself which seems to occasion the pain. Furthermore, only the painful nature of thought itself will explain what the mind typically does to painful thoughts. In response to their impact, painful thoughts are 'rejected', by which it is certainly not meant that there is a change in belief, or that a remedial course of action is resolved upon: *something* seems to the subject to be rejected, which is not a proposition, but the thought itself.[36] So, although some responses to painful thought may be compatible with the presumption that pain is only 'relayed' by thought in the way that a skylight 'lets in' the blueness of the sky (the sky is blue, but the skylight remains uncoloured), in others thought resembles a transmitter of heat: it relays the painfulness of states of affairs by itself becoming painful. Then we shoot the messenger and not the message.[37]

Second, the concept of unconscious phenomenology is likely to seem obviously paradoxical. It will be objected that, since pain is necessarily *nothing but* a type of sensation whose entire nature is given in its being consciously felt, it can not – without blatant self-contradiction – be held to exist without consciousness of it.[38]

Of course, a compelling reason for thinking that unconscious pain is possible can not be given to someone for whom reasons for believing in mental pain are restricted to consciously recognised feelings of pain; but what can be done is to show that not only such a kind of reason is relevant. The route out of paradox is to press home the distinction of consciousness* from consciousness, and distinguish two relations in ordinary consciousness of pain. One is the relation of the sensation's impinging on the subject: the pain's *hurting*, or being *felt* (consciousness* of pain). The other is *consciousness of* its impinging or being felt. The quality of pain is essential to both of these relations: quality is what makes the pain impinge in its particular, distinctive way; and it is what is exposed in consciousness of this.[39] The appearance of paradox in unconscious pain is due to the fact that the language of ordinary psychology allows us to speak of both of these relations as relations of consciousness, feeling and experience. But, although they are not distinguished in commonsense, and are consciously given as one, they are nevertheless distinct.

The refinement which psychoanalytic theory requires, and forces recognition of, therefore splits 'consciousness' into two senses: (i) the non-cognitive sense of phenomenological properties of mental states *registering* with the person; and (ii) the cognitive sense associated with, and manifested in, the ability to *self-ascribe* that state. Thus, a wedge is inserted between the statement that pain is 'a type of sensation whose entire nature is given in its being consciously felt', and the statement that pain 'can not be held to exist without consciousness of it': the first is true, but the second false. *What it is* that extends beyond consciousness in the case of unconscious pain is just what it is that is apprehended when pain is consciously given. Thus it would be a mistake to think that the supposition of unconscious pain involves unfelt or unfeelable pain, or an attempt to 'imagine pain that I *do not feel* on the model of the pain which I *do feel*'.[40] Unconscious pain is not a candidate for being predicated of stones.

It is important to note that the *psychoanalytic* concept of unconscious pain does not endorse, or even imply the intelligibility of, such claims as that a neurologist might justifiably attribute pain to someone who flatly denied that they had any such experience. The psychoanalytic attribution of pain, unlike the neurologist's – whose attribution is of a kind which fails to intimate the possibility of pain's ever having a qualitative character – does not tacitly deny its qualitivity, and does not therefore break with the ordinary concept of pain: psychoanalytic attribution takes off from knowledge of pain as it is consciously given, and is constrained by our consciously derived knowledge of its qualitative nature.

Unconscious emotion is a notion that puzzled Freud himself: 'It is surely of the essence of an emotion that we should be aware of it.'[41] Consequently, Freud qualified his attributions of unconscious emotion: separating 'idea' and 'affect', Freud says that whilst in repression the representational component of emotion becomes unconscious, its affective component does not.[42] This would mean that unconscious emotions exist only in the conditional sense that there exist unconscious ideas which, were they to become conscious, would join with certain conscious affects. Thus Freud seems to take a dispositional view of unconscious emotion.

Whether or not the bipartite analysis of emotion – the separation of representational and affective components – that Freud assumes is correct, the dispositional view of unconscious emotion does not fit with Freud's general view of unconscious mental states: it is inconsistent with his stated view that the only feature that a mental state necessarily loses in becoming unconscious is the quality of consciousness;[43] and it jars with the unqualified attributions of unconscious emotion that we find in Freud's clinical descriptions (e.g. of the Ratman's hatred).

The dispositional analysis of unconscious emotion can in any case be avoided, by reapplying the (by now familiar) realist form of analysis. Ordinary psychology does not suppose that causal power attaches to *consciousness* of emotion, but rather that this consciousness is *of* something with causal power. Emotion, and consciousness of emotion, are two different things, related somewhat as a belief is to the episodes of thought which manifest it. The qualitative dimension of emotion, which displays its representational and causal properties, is the phenomenological property which consciousness of emotion apprehends it as having. Unconscious emotions then exist in an integral, rather than truncated form: they are states whose causal power derives from their phenomenology, i.e. which are effective in certain directions *because of how they feel*.

Finally, I want to indicate the existence of another consciousness-invoking phenomenon which appears in psychoanalytic contexts. As noted in 6.6, clinical reports suggest a sense in which psychoanalytic states may come close – over time, and through a process of education in psychoanalytic self-interpretation – to being introspectable.[44] For instance, an analysand trained to interpret herself for her use of projection in psychic defence, may acquire the ability to register its operation directly. In this way, psychoanalytic conceptualisation may become incorporated into phenomenology.[45]

Of course, psychoanalytic states can never become accessible in the same sense as propositional attitudes, but they may nevertheless gain an *internal recognisability*, that approximates to a form of observational knowledge, in being locally independent of inference and the exercise of judgement.[46] The way that psychoanalytic states may appear in consciousness may be called 'quasi-manifestation'.[47] This form of introspectability is mid-way between ordinary consciousness of one's mental states, and madness, the direct invasion of consciousness by unconscious content, as in psychosis. Quasi-manifestation necessarily lacks the sense of agency which usually accompanies mental life, but may nevertheless have a negative connection with the will: quasi-manifestation may facilitate a minimal ability to hinder the influence of phantasy.

The quasi-manifestation of psychoanalytic states requires the subject to have the concept of the relevant kind of psychoanalytic state, and this concept is not basically observational, but initially acquired in the course of learning how to explain irrational phenomena, through adopting a third-personal perspective on oneself.[48] It follows that psychoanalytic states can quasi-manifest themselves only to those who have previously mastered a non-observational conceptual framework. This combination of conditions may sound odd, but the situation is the same in other quarters: a tribesman can not seem to see a solarised photograph, or a non-geologist perceive complex stratigraphic features in a landscape.[49]

Quasi-manifestability means that phenomenological considerations may contribute to legitimating psychoanalytic interpretations: it will be a reason for believing an interpretation, that it succeeds in getting the states that it attributes to quasi-manifest themselves. Analogously, phenomenological considerations may in principle help in adjudicating between competing psychoanalytic theories, according to their power to elicit corroborating phenomenological realisations.[50]

Granting such scope to the first person may seem extravagant or imprudent, given that people have after all claimed to be able to introspect all sorts of things, such as demons and spirits inhabiting their souls. But, so long as we are not Cartesian, we can not claim to know a priori what can *not* be got at through extended introspection;

so we do not know a priori that psychoanalytic states – the reality of which, unlike demons and spirits, is independently sanctioned – can not be got to quasi-manifest themselves. The next section will note a further significance for this point.

8.3 THEORETICALITY AND ATTRIBUTIONISM

What relations hold between psychoanalytic theory, and *general* philosophical views of the nature of psychological explanation? The two positions that will be considered here are, first, the view of psychology as a form of theoretical explanation, and, second, Davidson's attributionism. Each has been advanced as the natural ally of psychoanalytic theory.

Since psychoanalytic states were introduced, in Part II, in terms of a need for explanation, and cut to size accordingly, does this make them somehow *theoretical* in nature? Different things may be meant by 'theoretical'. Psychoanalytic states are certainly theoretical in a *weak* sense, in that psychoanalytic concepts belong to an explanatory framework, and can not be grasped apart from the sets of interrelated causal generalisations in which they are embedded. But theoreticality in this sense applies equally to the primary qualities of physical objects, and most, if not all, of what ordinary psychology attributes.[51] The stronger, challenging conception of theoreticality is that which draws a contrast between properties and entities with a straight-forwardly realistic (e.g. observational) character, and *intrinsically theoretical* properties and entities, which are not open to being fixed epistemically in a direct, non-theoretical way, and in some sense owe their existence to the theory which constructs them. Let properties and entities so conceived, which are strongly theory-dependent, be called theoretical$_i$.[52] Theoreticality$_i$ clearly amounts to more than being introduced by, and responding to, a need for explanation. If psychoanalytic states are theoretical$_i$, then the claim (in 7.6) that they are owned by the person will have to be renounced.

Of course, if ordinary psychology itself were theoretical$_i$, there could hardly be any reason for denying that theoreticality$_i$ carries over to psychoanalytic states. But, leaving aside that possibility, the relevant question is the following: Is there *special*, independent reason for conceiving psychoanalytic states as theoretical$_i$?[53]

It is not hard to see why one might take this view. Sartre – again regarding psychoanalysis as hostile to subjectivity – emphasises how, in order to grasp psychoanalytic states, I

am obliged to resort to hypotheses [...] just as the scholar makes conjectures about the nature and essence of an external phenomenon [...] I apply to my case *from the outside*, abstract schemes and rules already learned. As for the results, whether they are obtained by my efforts alone or with the cooperation of a technician, they will never have the certainty which intuition confers; they will possess simply the always increasing probability of scientific hypotheses. The hypothesis of the Oedipus complex, like the atomic theory, is nothing but an 'experimental idea'[54]

Sartre's message is, in effect, that Freudian theory is paradigmatically theoretical$_i$ because it posits 'unobservables'.[55] In this vein, it has been claimed that psychoanalytic theory makes us realise the theoretical$_i$ nature of all intentional explanation, including ordinary psychology.[56] Furthermore, it may be thought that the epistemological security of psychoanalytic claims recommends viewing the unconscious as a theoretical$_i$ construct: if psychoanalytic states are accorded only theoretical$_i$ status, their existence accordingly becomes harder to dispute. And, above all, theoreticality$_i$ may seem required by the unconsciousness of psychoanalytic states, since theoretical$_i$ states are ones that, logically, *could not* become conscious.[57]

There are, nevertheless, from the standpoint of this enquiry, conclusive reasons for denying that psychoanalytic states are theoretical$_i$. As already observed, the fact that considerations of explanation lead one to accept the existence of psychoanalytic states is not enough to make them theoretical$_i$; and their possession of phenomenological properties and quasi-manifestability, which provides them with a place in the stream of consciousness, shows them not to be theoretical$_i$.[58] The other reasons advanced for characterising psychoanalytic concepts as theoretical$_i$ rest on assumptions rejected here: as argued in 8.1, the possibility of unconscious mentality does not require its theoreticality$_i$; and, as 8.5 will argue, it is wrongheaded, and again unnecessary, to seek to establish the epistemological credentials of psychoanalytic claims at the expense of their full reality.[59]

It may now be noted that the kind of approach to the problem of irrationality that a theoretical$_i$ view of mental states does in fact generate is sub-systemic theory; and that sub-systemic theory seems to show inadequacies endemic to the theoretical$_i$ approach. The point here is that sub-systemic theory is guided by a tacitly functional conception of the mental: it is inspired by the idea that psychological explanation consists in the attribution of states exhaustively defined by their causal roles, unconstrained by any substantial conception of the nature of that to which they are attributed. This underlying commitment to theoreticality$_i$ is what licences the sub-systemic theorist to innovate in the direction of the multiple self, and it explains the theory's lack of any phenomenological realisation.

The second philosophical view of psychological explanation to be considered is Davidson's attributionism.[60] For Davidson, the nature of mental states and psychological explanation is given through a description of the constitutive constraints operating on those who use psychological language, the interpreters of minds: psychological explanation is interpretation governed by the Principle of Charity, which enjoins the attribution of mental states in such a way as to maximise rationality and true belief. Irrationality sets a prima facie challenge to such a view, but Davidson considers that it can be accommodated. Davidson marries psychoanalytic theory to this project. He reads Freud as committed to the partitive theses quoted in 3.1, and says furthermore that Freud 'wanted to extend the range of phenomena subject to reason explanations',[61] thereby associating Freud with his own attributionism. The claims that psychoanalytic explanation relies on partition, and that it offers 'reason explanations', have already been criticised; here I will suggest that, at a deeper level, there is a disharmony between psychoanalytic explanation and Davidson's attributionism.

Davidson thinks mental partition necessary in order to carry forward psychological explanation when it rubs up against the fact of irrationality. It was argued (in 4.10) that this will not suffice for explaining psychoanalytic irrational phenomena, for which psychoanalytic concepts are needed. It might nevertheless be thought that there is a straightforward way of understanding psychoanalytic explanation, in its Kleinian form, in attributionist terms: employing the concept of the unconscious may be seen as expressing a disposition on the part of the interpreter – the psychoanalyst – to engage on a second wave of interpretation after the first has yielded an attribution of irrationality, the interpreter being entitled to avail himself of whatever further concepts (such as wish and phantasy) are necessary to yield a 'thematically coherent' picture of the mind under interpretation.[62]

But, on closer examination, there is a plain hiatus in the argument for this proposal. To what extent can it – and indeed *any* strategy for explaining irrationality, including partition – be driven by Davidson's view of psychological explanation? On the face of it, Davidson's attributionism simply gives no reason to carry on interpreting after irrationality has been located, since for Davidson the total rationale for psychological language is supplied by the concept of rationality (reasons are causes and psychological causes are reasons). Without rationality, there is nothing to hold up psychology. To suggest that psychology can, for Davidson, be adapted to a psychoanalytic form – employing such concepts as wish and phantasy – would seem deeply incoherent.

The point can also be made by reconsidering Davidson's definition of irrationality in terms of causes that are not reasons for what they cause. What entitles Davidson to such a notion? How *can* the interpreter apprehend psychological causes that are not reasons?[63] The notion of cause in this context seems merely to report the existence of a shadow cast over the lighted plain of reason explanation, and attributions of irrationality to mean something merely negative ('reason explanations do not work here, so there must be an explanation for their not doing so – reality must be at variance with them').[64] It would seem that the very formula, 'a psychological cause that is not a reason', has no proper place in Davidson's account of psychology.[65]

On this basis, the importance of partition for Davidson may be rediscerned. Partition may be seen as, fundamentally, a means of explaining how non-rational psychological causes are possible: it attempts to restore these to reason-status by inserting them into a context (a smaller mind) in which they *can* be seen as reasons after all. Thus Davidson's statement, 'Only by partitioning the mind does it seem possible to explain how a thought or impulse can cause another to which it bears no rational relation.'[66] This, however, shows only that partition has importance internally to Davidson's programme, not that it succeeds in providing explanation.

Could one, perhaps, hold onto the broad attributionist thesis that the nature of the mental is given by constitutive constraints on interpretation, but abandon or modify Davidson's commitment to rationality? This would mean introducing some other principle to replace or supplement the Principle of Charity. The problem comes in seeing what this might be. What is essential for attributionism is that the constitutive interpretative constraints that it proposes should be (i) capable of being grasped without any independent, substantial knowledge of the nature of subjects of interpretation (it must not be presupposed that people *really are* such-and-such); and (ii) nevertheless capable of determining psychological interpretation in specific directions. The Principle of Charity certainly meets these conditions, allowing attributionism to account for (at least the core of) ordinary psychology. But is there a constitutive interpretative constraint which will allow attributionism to account analogously for psychoanalytic explanation? A constraint as broad as 'Attribute mental states in such a way as to maximise thematic coherence' will fall foul of (ii). The deeper problem is that psychoanalytic theory clearly draws on sources of psychological knowledge which lack the severely a priori status required by (i). In other terms, there is no constitutive interpretative constraint for psychoanalytic explanation which can be specified apart from the substantial claims made by psychoanalytic theory about the nature of subjects of interpretation. It would seem, then, that attributionism's need for independent and determinate constraints weds it to rationality, and that this forbids it from tolerating, let alone motivating, psychoanalytic theory.

Attributionism reduces irrationality to a sort of negative construction out of rationality and failures of interpretation. Properly, the story stops here, for attributionism: the only conclusions to be drawn from failures of interpretation concern the limits of human rationality, and these can not be understood in terms that will facilitate an inference to a hitherto unrecognised, irrational kind of mental state, as in psychoanalytic theory. Although an attributionist may claim, of successful interpretation, that it in some sense follows the outlines of psychological reality, the same may not be said for failures of interpretation – only if attributionism is overturned can these be taken to indicate the existence of irrational psychological causes.[67]

This means that *what* we do when we carry on interpreting after irrationality has been located, is not something that can be explained in attributionist terms, and that Dennett's response – a blanket rejection of intentional psychology in the face of irrationality[68] – is the more consistent line for an attributionist to take. It follows that psychoanalytic explanation can only be sustained by a stronger degree of realism about psychology than anything acceptable to Davidson. The realist alternative is to regard the relation between psychology and rationality as looser than Davidson makes it. In this, an indispensable role can still be accorded to Charity: it can still be said that psychological states are governed by laws which, by and large, bring them into conformity with the normative canons of rationality; and that the subject under interpretation herself accepts these canons, and is disposed to enforce them on her own mental functioning.[69] This suggests a more traditional, un-Davidsonian picture of the mind as comprehending an opposition of reason to passion.[70]

The joint failure of the theoretical$_i$ view and attributionism to mesh with psychoanalytic explanation, and their contrary association with sub-systemic theory, point to a general conclusion. Both of those positions may be regarded as attempts to abstract from ordinary psychology a pure 'method' of psychological explanation, and they fail because psychological explanation is in fact linked inseparably to its home topic, namely persons.[71] This point first came out when it was argued (in 3.8) that ordinary psychological explanation is committed to a metaphysical, non-Humean conception of persons. Sub-systemic theory attempts to apply psychological explanation independently from this conception of persons, and its ultimately confused character reflects the misguidance of such efforts at abstraction: we are unable to see how the distribution of psychological states attributed by sub-systemic theory could have been generated, since they can not have issued from persons, conceived as substantial unities. Attempts to prescind psychological investigation from its topic leave us in the dark: we no longer understand, for example, whether sub-systems' mental states belong to the person or not. It follows that, in general, attempts to reconstruct philosophically something to be called 'the nature of psychological explanation', identified independently from its topic, as the task of the philosophy of mind is sometimes conceived, are at some level mistaken.

The conclusion is that psychoanalytic theory, which does not seek to separate the topic from the method of psychology, fits best with a plainly realistic view of psychological language; the next section will make a specific suggestion about what this connection consists in.[72] It is in this sense that Freud's statements – that 'in its innermost nature it [the unconscious] is as much unknown to us as the reality of the external world',[73] but that '[t]he further question as to the ultimate nature of this unconscious is no more sensible or profitable than the older one as to the nature of the conscious'[74] – should be understood: psychoanalytic theory rightfully helps itself to the concept of a mental state from ordinary psychology, whose realism it takes over, and consequently gives no support to either the theoretical, or attributionist view of psychological explanation.

8.4 THE LEGITIMATION AND PLACE OF PSYCHOANALYTIC THEORY: EXTENSION AND VINDICATION OF ORDINARY PSYCHOLOGY

The legitimation of psychoanalytic theory has two parts. The first is conceptual: a demonstration of its coherence, and that there are no theoretical obstacles to accepting it. On the account given in this enquiry, fundamentally this involves showing psychoanalytic theory to be an extension of ordinary psychology, one that responds to a valid demand for explanation. The second part of legitimation is empirical: a demonstration that the theory generates appropriate, convincing interpretations of particular cases. Chiefly with reference to the Ratman, I have begun to indicate how psychoanalytic explanation may be seen to succeed on the second, interpretative score; but obviously this is something that only detailed knowledge and study of many cases (optimally, one's own included) can fully convey. This section will expand on the conceptual legitimation of psychoanalytic theory.

This enquiry has argued that the nature of the clinical problems that Freud's theories were trying to solve has been widely misconstrued. On the one hand, it has often not been seen that Freud's theories are directed at problems occurring at the same personal level as ordinary psychology, namely irrational phenomena. And so it has been thought that psychoanalytic theory ought to be reckoned with in terms dictated by the philosophy of science, as if its pretensions were of the same logical sort as those of, for example, behaviourist psychology. On the other hand, there has been recognition of the proper explananda of psychoanalytic theory, but the specific subset of these has been misidentified (as by Sartre). Once the explananda of psychoanalytic theory are properly identified, psychoanalytic theory ceases to look like either bad science or a paradoxical misapplication of ordinary psychology. In order to bring out the conceptual coherence of psychoanalytic theory, this enquiry has stressed Sartre's criticisms, which concern the logical shape of psychoanalytic explanation rather than its epistemology, and represent the most serious line of objection which it has to face.

The central argument has been, in brief, that some irrational phenomena – the recognition of which is inevitable for participants in ordinary psychology – can not be explained by ordinary psychology, yet require explanation in terms congruent with the ordinary conception of persons; which is what psychoanalytic theory supplies. It will help at this point to specify psychoanalytic explananda more precisely.

Is there a single characterisation of the sorts of reason which Freud considered to warrant the adduction of the unconscious? Freud described the unconscious as '*necessary* because the data of consciousness have a very large number of gaps in them'.[75] If these are understood as gaps in self-explanation, which are psychological in nature, occur at the personal level, and yield self-contradiction, Freud's 'gaps' correspond to irrational phenomena. There is also room, however, for gaps (hiatuses, lacunae) of other kinds to occur in consciousness or ordinary psychological explanation. First, gaps may occur at points where psychological explanation is expected, but which do not involve self-contradiction – the familiar 'shortfallings' of ordinary psychology. Second, there are merely nominal gaps in ordinary psychological explanation, such as the impossibility of explaining *how* it is that one ordinarily remembers something, or recognises words and faces – the 'indifferent blanks' of ordinary psychology. These do not worry us, or attract our attention, because they do not betoken a missing piece in the pattern of personal understanding; ordinary psychology regards memory and powers of recognition as a level of given competences.[76] Although irrational phenomena, which provide the primary explananda of psychoanalytic theory, stand apart from both these kinds of gap, there are also, it will emerge shortly, connections to be traced between psychoanalytic theory and gaps of the 'shortfalling' sort.

What motivates the extension of explanation beyond ordinary psychology is the requirement of persons' metaphysical homogeneity, described in 4.11. This requirement could, logically, be rejected. But if this is done, persons either become compounds, unintelligibly related, of intentional and non-intentional materials, or they are restricted to what ordinary psychology can grasp, producing an arbitrary, ragged-edged definition of the boundaries of persons;

which shows, powerfully, that our understanding of persons is not exhausted by what ordinary psychology can explain. Another way of making the point is to say that psychological significance, which irrational phenomena exhibit, can not come from nothing, and must emerge from suitably psychological ingredients.

Of course, nothing purely logical can *compel* recognition of psychoanalytic explananda.[77] But the limited importance of this point needs to be understood. Although irrational phenomena *could* always be redescribed as merely cognitive failings, extensive errors, we prefer, as the categories of ordinary irrationality show, a picture in which persons are capable of irrationality *as well as* error, because this results in better explanation (neurosis does not look like cognitive poverty); and because irrationality is consistent with, and even made likely by, much that we know beforehand about ourselves, concerning mental passivity, the effects of emotion, nature and force of desire, power of imagination, and so on – features lying within the scope of ordinary, but outside that of rational, psychology.

A thin sense may also be conceded in which the appearance of psychological significance which attaches to psychoanalytic explananda could be illusory – entailing that psychoanalytic explanation could be overtaken by organic (neurophysiological) explanation and treatment. But this concession is slight. Psychoanalytic gaps are sharply distinguished from others that clearly do not merit intentional explanation. To the extent that psychoanalytic explanation might find itself ousted by neurophysiology, there can equally be no logical guarantee of the appropriateness of the psychological description of *any* explananda,[78] including those of ordinary psychology. If neurophysiology could explain irrational phenomena without psychological mediation, it would, surely, have to be powerful enough to do the same for the explananda of ordinary psychology. The threat of eliminativism to which this objection therefore points need not be taken up, since, as stated early on in the enquiry, there can be no pretending that psychoanalytic theory is defensible except on the assumption that ordinary psychology is cogent.[79] It is worth noting that those who are not drawn to psychoanalytic theory often also find nothing epistemologically impressive in ordinary psychology.[80]

The impossibility of bludgeoning someone into recognising psychoanalytic explananda, and of ruling out competing non-intentional explanations, by purely deductive means, is therefore not to the point.

Several features of the psychoanalytic extension to ordinary psychology deserve to be highlighted.[81]

(1) Might the psychoanalytic extension be objected to as 'extravagant', outstripping and losing touch with its base (and thereby opening the way to witchcraft and palmistry being considered equally valid extensions)? The psychoanalytic extension of ordinary psychology is at fault only if, in extending, it goes off course.[82] Assuming the argument of Part II to be sound, the onus lies on the objector to show (in the light of a particular set of rules of valid extension) at what points such deviations occur – for psychoanalytic theory would seem to be a continuous development of ordinary psychology. The fundamental idea on which psychoanalytic explanation hinges is that of a connection of content, driven by the operations of desire freed from rational constraints. The assumption of the primacy of conative, over cognitive, causes in psychoanalytic explanation, expressed in the theory of wish-fulfilment, is warranted because, as noted above, we distinguish irrationality from error, and the explanation of ordinary irrationality already makes it extremely plausible to think that irrationality is in general caused by desire.

(2) Does psychoanalytic theory seek to derive a lot more from its evidential materials than ordinary psychology, either by way of theoretical superstructure, or practical powers of personal transformation? Again, appearances of asymmetry on this score are deceptive. First, just as metapsychology is essential for psychoanalytic explanation, ordinary psychology is saturated with theoretical suppositions regarding notions of character, cognitive powers, social, political and cultural factors, and so on, there being no logical difference between these 'unobservables' and those of psychoanalytic theory. Portraying psychoanalytic theory as a 'grand theory' of the mind is likely to mislead: psychoanalysis seeks to account for motivation, but not for memory, perception, cognition and other competences.

Secondly, we want a vast amount of practical guidance from ordinary psychology (everyday life founders without it); and the practical effects psychoanalysis aims at are not proportionately greater. The role of therapeutic outcomes in the legitimation of psychoanalytic theory I will comment on later.

(3) When psychoanalytic explanation is extended into the sphere of ordinary psychology, it is inferred that phantasy plays an essential role in ordinary mental life, on the grounds that this is necessary if

phantasy is to explain irrationality. The general form of explanation exemplified here, whereby a concept C arrived at through considering abnormal cases is given application to normal cases, is legitimate when (i) it is a condition of C's explaining the abnormal that it have application to the normal, (ii) the requirement that the abnormal be made intelligible is generated by our understanding of the normal, and (iii) the initial distinction of normal and abnormal is not thereby eroded. These conditions are met by psychoanalytic explanation.

(4) The psychoanalytic extension is not, as Sartre puts it, 'mere verbal terminology'. The reason why psychoanalytic 'wish' and 'phantasy' are not just technical jargon for 'irrational desire' and 'irrational belief' (these being what the theory is supposed to explain), is that these concepts are incorporated in a body of theoretical propositions, which manifestly outstrip ordinary psychology. What the homogeneity view of psychoanalytic states (described in 4.9) gets right is that such states are intentional, personal and explain through connections of content; it errs in supposing this to make them identical in kind with what ordinary psychology already attributes. In these terms, Part I of the enquiry showed that psychoanalytic theory is *not* cogent when considered as ordinary intentional psychology; and Part II, that it *is* cogent when considered as revised and extended intentional psychology.

The next task, in legitimating psychoanalytic theory, is to fill out the picture of its relations to ordinary psychology.

Fodor speaks of 'vindicating' ordinary psychology, in this way: ordinary psychology can be regarded as a theory composed of certain central assumptions and high-level laws; as long as scientific (cognitive) psychology preserves enough of these, it can fairly be said that ordinary psychology has been shown to be true.

This represents ordinary psychology as an *anticipation* of scientific psychology. There is, however, another sense in which ordinary psychology is open to vindication, which does not rest on this assumption. Ordinary psychology is chequered with 'gaps' of the second kind defined earlier, the 'shortfallings' of ordinary psychology, where psychological explanation is expected yet unavailable, but which do not involve self-contradiction. Alongside these are recurrent patterns in attributions of propositional attitudes (e.g. 'personal idiosyncrasies'), which can be recorded but not explained in ordinary psychological terms. Furthermore, the explanations of rational psychology itself are in most cases open to being deepened: we often have very little idea of why thoughts occur at particular moments, why feelings change, or why certain reasons are sometimes forceful and sometimes unpersuasive. Some of this is, perhaps, best put down to there being a strain of caprice in mental life. But these features crop up against an entrenched background expectation of psychological explanation: thoughts, changes of feeling, and the force of reasons, are the sorts of things which have intentional causes, and if ordinary psychology does not provide these, it will give an impression of deep arbitrariness (why should it only be able to explain an arbitrary sub-set of the kinds of things that it is able to identify as its explananda?).[83] So long as the Complete view of ordinary psychology (in 1.5) is endorsed, an underlying causal order – a deeper, underlying pattern of mental life – must be supposed.

These non-irrational gaps therefore provide psychoanalytic explanation with a new point of entry: they are its *secondary* explananda.[84] By spreading its net – plugging the further gaps in ordinary psychology, and deepening its explanations – psychoanalytic theory will fill in some of the ceteris paribus clauses that riddle ordinary psychology ('get-out' clauses that deflect apparent counter-instances to it), and do so without obliging us to drop to the sub-personal level of cognitive psychology or neurophysiology.

This secondary application of psychoanalytic explanation has further, welcome consequences. First, it eliminates one reason for viewing cognitive psychology as a necessary complement to ordinary psychology. Second, since the incompleteness of ordinary psychology is often taken to show it to be unamenable to realistic understanding,[85] psychoanalytic theory also helps to lift an important barrier to viewing ordinary psychology in realistic terms. Once ordinary psychology is restricted to the propositional network and its conscious accompaniments, it is no longer required to cover the full extent of psychological reality, which it can not succeed in doing, and accordingly ceases to look like a poor approximation to psychological reality (one that is strictly false, or only 'partly true').[86] The relation between ordinary psychology and psychoanalytic theory is therefore a model of reciprocity: psychoanalytic theory repays ordinary psychology for its extension, by assisting in its vindication.

Psychoanalytic theory, in helping to complete ordinary psychology, does not require the nomologicality of the mental. It requires laws only in the same sense, and to the same degree, as ordinary psychology. These will of course include – as any explanatory framework must – certain high-level laws, those which are constitutive of its central concepts. But psycho-physical laws will not be included, and although lower-level laws, e.g. correlating types of aetiology with types of neurosis, or character traits with unconscious structures,[87] are not excluded, they are not of prime importance for psychoanalytic explanation. The role of laws in psychoanalytic explanation may be glossed in terms of moves in explanation. To know a psychoanalytic law L is to know of some mental condition M that, if M occurs, then a certain psychoanalytic explanation E is more likely to be correct for M than certain other candidate explanations. Symbolism illustrates the situation: psychoanalysis identifies the likely meanings of individual symbols, but does not tightly correlate kinds of symbols with particular kinds of unconscious meanings.[88]

This conception of laws (if the name is deserved) as entitlements to deploy explanations, does not necessarily yield impressive predictions: it just says, depending on what happens (what actions are performed), what explanations are most likely to be correct (what the psychoanalytic causes of those actions are most likely to be). Of course, like ordinary psychology, psychoanalytic theory makes predictions, in so far as its holism commits it to a view of future mental states' being such as to cohere with past mental states; and its role in completing the ceteris paribus clauses in ordinary psychology commits it to the claim that it improves psychological predictability *in principle*. But, because a solid epistemological grip on psychoanalytic states can not be obtained independently of knowledge of ordinary mental states, actual gains in predictive power will be marginal; psychoanalytic additions do not meet the conditions of independence that are required for an effective, practical contribution to predictability. So, although psychoanalytic attributions entail predictive statements about future psychoanalytic mental states, they do not do the same for a person's future actions – the determinants of these are too open-ended to allow for prediction. Prediction is, for psychoanalytic theory, a spin-off from explanation, not an independent source of legitimation.

The thought, in 8.3, that psychology, if it is to provide for psychoanalytic states, must be conceived realistically – grounded in substantial claims about how persons really are – may be developed in the following way. The attribution of propositional attitudes is underpinned, and partially determined by, what may be called psychological *schemata*, provided by our unconscious constitutions. Their role may fruitfully be compared to the way in which, in perception, sensory data is structured by a stock of basic patterns. Once a certain minimal level of information about mental states is reached, at some point prior to that at which they configure so as fully to make sense of their subject, a psychological schema is elicited, on account of which other beliefs and desires, of a more explanatory character, are attributed.[89] This is well illustrated by the way in which Klein's theory of envy accords emotions a deep, inter-relating organisation, in contrast with ordinary psychology's tendency to view them on a one-off basis and seek immediate environmental cues for each instance of emotion.

There is, on this hypothesis, a psychological stratum intervening between bare behaviour, and complex attributions of belief and desire.[90] Psychological schemata may be employed, without being known, in the full sense, by the subject: possession of a schema may be taken to consist just in a propensity to interpret others' mental lives in line with it.[91] The hypothesis of such schemata promotes the idea that we stand epistemologically, albeit at a very rudimentary level, in relations of 'pre-ordained harmony' to one another (meaning that we need not strain to *make up* sense for one another's behaviour).[92] As Freud puts it, 'without any special reflection we attribute to everyone else our own constitution [...] this identification is a *sine qua non* of our understanding'.[93]

Psychological schemata allow it to be explained why, with regard to at least some central cases, we attribute the particular beliefs and desires that we do. This gives reason – of a realist kind, independent of interpretative methodology – for taking our actual attributions of belief and desire to be correct. Out of all the possible sets of propositional attitudes, only some form recognisable patterns and will be attributed by us: namely, those through which the right kind of unconscious background shows. In this way, sets of propositional attitudes are held up, not only from the inside by their coherence, but also from the outside, by their constitutional causes. Psychological explanation does not begin or end in a limbo: it is structured from the start by recognition of an unconscious base.

One way of seeing that such schemata are at work in psychological understanding, is to note how it is possible for there to be attributions of propositional attitudes which form extensive and consistent sets (meeting Davidsonian standards), yet fail to deliver intelligibility.

Kafka's worlds show this dramatically: the minds and forms of life of their denizens, despite being described in tightly consistent, even hyper-rational terms, remain profoundly strange. This is quite unlike the way in which other cultures can seem opaque; it is rather a psychological matter, and invites us to think that the intelligibility of a set of propositional attitudes requires a relation to something external to the set: what Kafka's subjects lack for us is a *motivational constitution*. They do not share our constitution, and we can not see what constitution, if any, they do possess.

What role is left, in the legitimation of psychoanalytic theory, for criteria derived from the philosophy of science? It might be thought that meeting scientific criteria should be set down as a *further necessary* condition, on the grounds that physics, which may be said to analogously extend 'folk mechanics', is not thereby exempted from having to undergo corroborative scientific testing.

Of course, the fact that a theory extends commonsense – in the sense of simply sharing its structure of explanation – is not sufficient for its legitimation. As said earlier, legitimation has two parts: construction of the theory (showing its coherence and warrantability qua extension), and its application (showing its truth, with reference to particular cases). If a theory T extends a part of commonsense C, then the kinds of test appropriate to determining whether or not T is a true extension are dictated by the nature of C. The tests appropriate to physics are determined by the nature of folk physics, and those appropriate to psychoanalytic theory by the nature of ordinary psychology; to think that scientific testing of psychoanalytic theory is necessary is to forget that it extends ordinary psychology, not folk physics.

It does not follow, however, that the idea of validating psychoanalytic theory by scientific canons is necessarily mistaken. But it is appropriate only to the same extent as it is appropriate to ordinary psychology. If there are quantitative methods of evaluation congruent with ordinary psychology (as hypotheses about the causes of political behaviour may, arguably, be statistically evaluated), then psychoanalytic explanation is open to them; although it is very hard to see how they could in any way be decisive.[94] And if convergence with cognitive psychology, for example, is a condition on ordinary psychology, it is equally a condition on psychoanalytic theory; there is no reason to deny that, if cognitive psychology can analyse propositional attitudes, analogous connections between psychoanalytic processes and sub-personal processes are there to be discovered. But psychoanalytic states must first earn their place independently from cognitive psychology.

It should, finally, be noted what view of the importance of therapeutic outcomes for the legitimation of psychoanalytic theory follows from this discussion. The requirement that psychoanalysis be seen to effect *cures*, in order to be legitimated, derives from an inappropriate analogy with the increased control over nature facilitated by scientific theories. And, as noted in 6.6, psychoanalytic theory itself gives reason for thinking that cures, in a strong sense, are not possible. Appropriate canons, derived from ordinary psychology, can demand only that psychoanalysis should make *as much* difference to mental life as self-understanding (knowledge of one's character) generally produces, and this is (whilst not nothing) probably not a great deal; as Freud's last paper on the subject acknowledges.[95]

In sum, the legitimation of psychoanalytic theory depends on prediction, success in discovering laws, and the outcomes of psychoanalytic treatment, only to the extent that these requirements have analogues in ordinary psychology.

8.5 THE EPISTEMOLOGY OF PSYCHOANALYTIC CLAIMS

This section responds to the principal epistemological objections levelled against psychoanalytic claims, namely that they are (1) insensitive to experience; (2) undermined by the role of suggestion; (3) discredited by the factionalism and non-convergence of the psychoanalytic movement; and (4) lack the inductive support needed for causal explanation.

(1) The objection of empirical insensitivity comes in several forms. One is that psychoanalytic theory makes itself true by definitional fiat. The objection is that, according to the reconstruction in 4.10–4.11, unless interpretation attributes a wish or phantasy, it fails to qualify as psychoanalytic, and hence fails to concern itself with the phenomena which are the special preserve of psychoanalytic explanation; thereby 'guaranteeing' that the concepts of wish and phantasy have reference. The charge is the familiar one of self-legitimation due to the theory's insulation of its objects in a theoretical language, in such a way as to make its disconfirmation impossible.

Whilst it is true that the connection between psychoanalytic explananda, and the concepts of wish and phantasy, has been made extremely close, it remains possible to identify the explananda independently: clinical observations can be formulated without reference to wish and phantasy, and these concepts reserved for the metapsychology. To challenge psychoanalytic claims at a clinical level, it must simply be shown that the same set of facts, the existence of obsessional structures and so on, can be accounted for in other, superior terms. The metapsychology can also be contested at a philosophical level: if psychoanalytic theory does not in fact extend ordinary psychology, or does so in ways that are inconsistent with its deepest commitments, or if ordinary psychological explanation is in fact too formless for any theory not to be considered an extension of it, then psychoanalytic claims may be rejected.

Although Popper's philosophy of science is not now widely favoured, his well-known criticism of psychoanalysis nevertheless highlights certain central epistemological issues. Popper says that Freud's theories are 'simply non-testable, irrefutable. There was no conceivable human behaviour which could contradict them',[96] and – falsifiability being for Popper the hallmark of science – that they therefore fall into the class of pseudo-scientific theories, which have no relation to reality or experience, and consequently lack truth-value. Popper claims that

those 'clinical observations' which analysts naively believe confirm their theory cannot do this any more than the daily confirmations which astrologers find in their practice. And as for Freud's epic of the Ego, the Super-ego and the Id, no substantially stronger claim to scientific status can be made for it than for Homer's collected stories from Olympus.[97]

Does psychoanalysis in fact fail to be scientific, by Popper's own criterion of falsifiability? It is, of course, psychoanalysis' own claim that empirical sensitivity, a process of constant adjustment to experience, is built into psychoanalytic interpretation. Adolf Grünbaum has, in any case, dealt with this issue in detail, and his discussions support a firmly negative answer.[98] Incontrovertible evidence of Freudian theory's hospitality to falsification includes: Freud's abandonment of the theory of repressed homosexuality as the pathogen for paranoia;[99] his correction to the theory that dream is wish-fulfilment[100] (a theory which, it has also been claimed, recent work in neurophysiology falsifies[101]); his repudiation of his early claims for the curative power of psychoanalysis;[102] the hypothesised links between orality and anality, and character traits of submissiveness and obsessiveness, respectively, which can and have been experimentally tested;[103] the Ratman's refutation of Freud's hypothesis as to the specific sexual aetiology of adult obsessional neurosis;[104] and Freud's abandonment of the seduction theory.[105]

The details of the examples do not matter here; the central point is that psychoanalytic claims are open to falsification. To show that psychoanalytic claims are unfalsifiable would involve demonstrating that the *nature* of psychoanalytic explanation – as opposed to that of other forms of empirical psychology – entails unfalsifiability. This is highly implausible. Even if the general notion of unfalsifiability – supposedly a logical feature of a theory – were not itself doubtful, it would in any case be unclear what the charge could amount to in the context of psychology. The ordinary self-ascriptions of persons are the obvious candidate for a source of falsification for psychological theories, but every interesting psychological hypothesis is bound to attribute to persons states that they can not straightforwardly introspect or avow, and hence to exceed their ordinary self-ascriptions. It follows that psychological theories must in general be constrained in ways other than simply by agreement with persons' ordinary self-ascriptions, and that these further constraints will be determined, to some degree, by the theories themselves. So it is improbable that psychoanalytic claims could be shown to be unfalsifiable, without the same following for the claims of, for example, cognitive psychology.

There are, nevertheless, two respects in which there is some truth in Popper's claim. One is that the core assumption of the existence of a dynamic unconscious is not open to falsification. This, however, is no embarrassment, since, as argued throughout this enquiry, this axiom is sanctioned conceptually.

Second, it is true that psychoanalysts do not, by and large, see any point in subjecting their claims to extra-clinical testing,[106] of the quantitative sort, purportedly approximating to the methods of the physical sciences, employed in many other forms of empirical psychology. Their good reason for viewing extra-clinical testing as unimportant will be spelled out later.

Another sort of charge is suggested by Popper's statements that psychoanalytic theories 'appeared to be able to explain practically everything that happened within the fields to which they referred', and that he 'could not think of any human behaviour which could not be interpreted in terms of either [Freudian or Adlerian] theory'.[107] Here Popper might be understood as objecting that, even if nothing in the nature of psychoanalytic claims makes them unfalsifiable, there are nevertheless certain concepts built into the psychoanalytic apparatus that, because of their epistemological role, do as a matter of fact have that upshot – namely, and perhaps notoriously, the concepts of resistance, reaction-formation and ambivalence. The latter pair might be taken to show that, with regard to any given psychoanalytic interpretation, any set of data D can be taken to support, with equal force, an interpretation E, or an interpretation which is the opposite of E; and that any interpretation can be supported equally well by the set of data D, as it can by a set which contains the negations of the propositions in D.

It is, perhaps, the most popular, widespread criticism of psychoanalysis that its interpretations confront the analysand with a 'Catch-22'. Freud in fact recognised, in the context of resistance, the charge

that in giving interpretations to a patient we treat him upon the famous principle of 'Heads I win, tails you lose.' That is to say, if the patient agrees with us, then the interpretation is right; but if he contradicts us, that is only a sign of his resistance, which again shows that we are right.[108]

The following statement of Freud's may seem to illustrate the alleged, distorted form of reasoning:

[the telling of] an incomplete story under hypnosis produces no therapeutic effect. I accustomed myself to regarding as incomplete any story that brought about no improvement and I gradually came to be able to read from patients' faces whether they might not be concealing an essential part of their confessions.[109]

Here the charge would be that Freud has devised an interpretative rule on the basis of which every uncured hysteric *has to* agree that their confession has been culpably incomplete, for the situation is defined in such a way that no way is left to persuade the analyst of its completeness; thereby 'guaranteeing' Freud's hypothesis of the efficacy of anamnesis.

The proper response to the 'heads-I-win' charge is to indicate that, if it were good, then a major and indispensable portion of our ordinary knowledge of one another's minds would be hopelessly compromised. Freud's interpretative rule does no more, in the first instance, than apply a criterial test for the reality of a mental state;

as do, for example, ordinary judgements of a person's sincerity. Still, it might be argued that a special justification is required for the psychoanalytic criterion, perhaps because the psychoanalyst is thought characteristically to go one step further than the ordinary interpreter, by using the very same datum to support contrary interpretations. But, again, it can be shown that, in so far as this is true, ordinary psychology is no different. Suppose someone is charged with impatience, and his finger-drumming pointed to by way of evidence. The charge is not refuted by saying that finger-drumming can also signify relaxation, nor that impatience can also take the form of iron immobility. The charge of impatience can be maintained consistently with these possibilities, even in the absence of any clear idea of what their realisation would have required. The underlying point is that ordinary psychology regards motivation as highly plastic in its expression: some motivational (especially emotional) conditions, M, are such that when a person is in M, its betrayal is inescapable for them; however they decide to behave – whether they Ø or refrain from Ø-ing – their behaviour will signify M.

This reflects the fact that we do not hold to the existence of lawful correlations of kinds of mental state with kinds of behaviour above a very rudimentary level. When a psychoanalyst says that a particular instance of hesitation signifies resistance, she does not commit herself to saying of *every* instance of hesitation, that it signifies resistance; and her interpretation is not relevantly challenged by the observation that resistance might have taken an opposite form (e.g. an impressive display of confidence). If it is now reflected what revisions to psychological interpretation would be needed to rule out such epistemological structures as bear comparison with heads-I-win situations – effectively, it would take simplistic psychophysical laws, whose impossibility is the downfall of reductive behaviourism – then psychoanalytic interpretation is seen to be directly in line with ordinary realism about psychological states, i.e. our view that their reality transcends our means of detecting conclusively their presence or absence. Epistemological structures resembling heads-I-win situations could only be avoided by a wholesale verificationist thinning-down of ordinary psychology, to a point where not much more than intentions to bodily movement could be attributed. So, if we ever want to be able to say, as we do, that a piece of behaviour manifests a particular emotion but that it could have manifested something else, just as the emotion could have been manifested in other, diametrically opposed ways, then we have to accept enough slack and subtlety in our general 'principles of reasoning' about other minds to warrant psychoanalytic interpretative procedures in full.

To elaborate the point, consider Othello's situation with regard to Desdemona, or Golaud's with regard to Mélisande. Each is tormented by the thought that what he knows of his lover's behaviour is *no less compatible* with the hypothesis of infidelity than that of fidelity. The vicious predicament of jealousy is possible only because people are taken to love either truly or falsely, an often evidence-transcendent supposition. Just as jealousy is not to be escaped from by denying the distinction of true from false love, the psychoanalyst's epistemological situation is not to be dissolved by denying the phenomenon of unconscious motivation.

A remaining objection might be, that Freud has no right to base interpretations on anything as ethereal as a 'way of reading patient's faces'. But once again the objection risks proving too much. If such quasi-perceptual forms of access to other minds are disallowed, the bulk of significant human intercourse will be epistemologically eroded to the point of extinction. Consider Henry James' narrator's declaration: 'I liked immensely the motion with which, in reply to this, she put it behind her: her gesture expressed so distinctly her vision of her own lesson.' James helps to remind us how limitlessly rich the content of our quasi-perceptual access to one another's minds can be, for an appropriately sensitive observer.

There are two points to be extracted. First, it would be impossible to attribute motives of the complexity that we do attribute ordinarily, without granting ourselves more epistemological access than a systematic theoretical reconstruction of our evidential procedures could validate. Psychoanalytic interpretation, which no doubt brings out the vulnerability to scepticism of all our intersubjective knowledge claims, should not be made a sacrificial victim of our general tendency to search irritably after systematic foundations for knowledge claims.

Second, knowledge of other minds presupposes appropriate experiential sensitivity. That of the psychoanalyst is special in two ways: it is *individualised*, in being built up over the course of a long and profound acquaintance with a particular person; and it is *informed*, in that the psychoanalyst is distinguished by having undergone an extensive conceptual and clinical training.[110] It nevertheless remains of a kind with the sensitivity which sustained interpersonal acquaintance ordinarily creates.

The general conclusion is that the epistemology of psychoanalytic claims preserves, whilst intensifying, features of the epistemology of ordinary psychology. Popper's objection is therefore either misplaced, or it jeopardises all our claims to knowledge of one another's minds.

(2) Grünbaum has made much of the charge of illicit suggestion, and so-called 'contamination of data', in psychoanalytic interpretation.[111] The main points to be made in response are the following.

First, there are equipollent means of guarding against the increased danger of suggestibility in psychoanalysis, and counter-balancing reasons for trusting its results. The suggestibility objection represents the analyst's contribution as nothing but a barrier to objectivity. But this is to forget that minds have constitutive connections with possibilities of interpretation: to a large and ineliminable extent, a mind grasps itself with reference to the possibility of its being interpreted by others,[112] and this establishes a necessary connection between minds and intersubjective interrogative procedures. For which reason, we are entitled, prima facie, to privilege rather than devalue the epistemological role of the analyst. The analyst in any case employs a variety of procedures, derived from those employed in ordinary interrogation, to sift out the effects of suggestion.[113]

Because the problem of suggestibility in the psychoanalytic context is a problem in human intercourse as such, the suggestibility charge, as it appears in Grünbaum, amounts only to a heightened scepticism about the possibility of discriminating correctly between those features of others' minds that precede, and those that result from, interrogation; if Grünbaum were right that the psychoanalyst's power of suggestion directly invalidates clinical data, it would never be possible for one person to claim justifiably to have assisted another to obtain a better view of her motivation – an unacceptable implication.

Second, suggestibility is not an autonomous objection. Suggestibility would only provide a deeper problem for psychoanalytic than ordinary psychology if there were *independent* reason for doubting psychoanalytic theory, or if its basis lay ultimately in the analysand's self-ascription of psychoanalytic states. The last is incorrect; as argued in 8.4, psychoanalytic theory is based on explanation.

(3) What is to be said about the disagreement and factionalism that exist in the psychoanalytic movement? First, it can not be overstressed that in myriad other contexts of human understanding – including morality, aesthetic judgement, and social, political and economic explanation – massive disagreement is tolerated without

abandoning realism: we do not in general take widespread disagreement in areas of human understanding to signify the unreality of the object-domain. Second, the development of psychoanalysis does in fact display a fair amount of convergence, and analysts of different schools are in fact able to discern levels of agreement between their superficially incompatible clinical interpretations.[114] Third, non-convergence has an explanation, fully compatible with the theory's claims to truth: access to clinical data requires conceptual training, and consequently commitment to a particular metapsychology, making the 'trans-factional' perspective which would be necessary to bring about convergence very hard to attain in practice.

This does not mean, of course, that all non-convergence can be written off by regarding competing theories as mere 'notational variants' of one another. Even if orthodox-Freudian, Kleinian, Jungian and Lacanian clinical interpretations were always perfectly isomorphic with one another, fundamental disagreements between the schools remain, in so far as each takes a radically different stand on *the nature of the mind*: each metapsychology gives the mind a different conceptual characterisation, regarding its relation to language, the body, collective and spiritual reality and so on. To this extent, psychoanalytic factional disagreements are *conceptual*, and require philosophical attention. This enquiry has sought to give conceptual reasons for favouring Kleinian metapsychology: it is supported by the same kinds of reasons that support the general strategy of psychoanalytic explanation.

(4) To turn now to a different complaint, Grünbaum's main objection is that Freud's interpretative methods, such as free association, do not warrant an inference to unconscious causation. This is because, according to Grünbaum, mere 'thematic affinity' – on which, he believes, psychoanalytic claims depend fundamentally – is not in general, in psychological contexts, sufficient for adducing a causal relationship: according to Grünbaum, further, inductive justification is needed for causation.[115]

The same sort of response as to Popper is again appropriate. We know, for example, that if a thought is freely associated with a parapraxis, and investigation reveals a connection of content, charged with affect, between them, then a wish is disclosed, because it is *generally true* that psychological proximity, and affectively charged connections of content, signify causal influence. Reasoning of this kind draws on a priori considerations concerning mental order: the alternative is to view the mind as an atomised jumble of ideas, which would contradict its identification *as* a mind. That is why thematic coherence in psychoanalytic interpretation licences causal conclusions.[116]

If psychoanalysis is, as urged in 8.4, a legitimate and necessary extension of commonsense psychology, this shows why psychoanalysts are not enthusiastic about extra-clinical testing: they do not see the point of such an exercise. The insistence of psychoanalysts, following Freud, on the evidential primacy and exclusivity of clinical material reflects their grasp, implicit or explicit, of their activity as continuous with ordinary psychology. Their attitude is not different in kind from that which we would have if challenged to *prove*, by inductive means, that there *really is* such a phenomenon as human anger.

James Hopkins puts the objection to Grünbaum as follows:

> Grünbaum's use of neo-Baconian canons prompts an objection. In commonsense psychological practice we already establish causal connections (in particular concerning the role of motives) interpretively, in ways that are autonomous, cogent, and prior to such canons. So it seems wrong to hold generally that cogency in a psychology of motive must satisfy them; indeed, for motives, it is unclear how such canons could be used, or how inductive methods could replicate commonsense interpretation [...] psychoanalytic theory may also be cogent, but related to inductive methods no more closely than commonsense psychology itself.[117]

Ultimately, the epistemology of psychoanalytic interpretation resembles somewhat an attempt to piece together a whole picture, on the basis of fragments, half-glimpses and second-hand descriptions. These limitations do not mean that psychoanalytic enquiry is concerned, to any degree less than ordinary psychology, with matters of *fact*. What is important here is to avoid confusing the arguable epistemic fragility of psychoanalytic claims, their looser relation to criteria, which may indeed indicate a difference of degree of epistemic security from the attributions of ordinary psychology, with a *qualitative* difference. Just such a confusion seems to underlie most epistemologically orientated critiques of psychoanalysis. The onus is on the critic of psychoanalytic explanation to demonstrate that its epistemology differs in kind from that of ordinary psychology; to show this would require a more intimate engagement with psychoanalysis than its critics have frequently accorded it.

Appendices

I A TAXONOMY OF METAPSYCHOLOGIES

What are the major metapsychological alternatives to Kleinian theory? Here I will give a brief, philosophically motivated enumeration of the basic kinds of metapsychology that have been proposed. Metapsychologies sort themselves chiefly in terms of two issues: the relation of the clinical to the theoretical components in psychoanalytic thought, and the relation of psychoanalytic theory to the physical sciences. The possibilities may be grouped as follows:

(1) The first group is comprised of metapsychologies undertaking reconstructions, to varying degrees reductive, of psychoanalytic theory in terms of concepts and methods of the *physical sciences*. See Maze, *The meaning of behaviour*, ch. 6; Gill and Pribram, *Freud's 'Project' re-assessed*; and the writings of Emmanuel Peterfreund and David Rapaport. Also included are attempts to subsume psychoanalytic theory under cognitive psychology (see 2.11 n56).

(2) *Anti-metapsychological* positions overlap in some respects with those just described. Here the characteristic strategy is to separate the metapsychological from the clinical components in Freud's writings, condemn the former and salvage the latter. See the papers in Gill and Holzman eds., *Psychology versus metapsychology*. Gill, for example, argues that the job of metapsychology is properly done by biological and neurological theory, and that metapsychology, considered as a higher-order abstraction from clinical psychology, consists only of 'pseudo explanations'. Rubinstein sees clinical hypotheses as requiring metapsychological support, on the grounds that clinical theory, in its 'simple' form, consists only of 'unproven' presupposition or 'dogma', and, in its 'extended' form 'poses a problem but offers no solution'. Rubinstein therefore suggests that a reformulation of psychoanalytic metapsychology based on neurophysiology, and

employing a depersonalised causal language, is needed, and has yet to be produced.

Schafer's *A new language for psychoanalysis* is frequently cited as a philosophical authority for anti-metapsychological positions.

(3) The third group attempts to reconstruct psychoanalytic theory in terms of concepts of *language and communication*. It includes (a) Lacan (see Appendix III); (b) hermeneutic theories (see 5.10 n60); and (c) other writings connecting the unconscious to linguistic concepts, such as Descombes, *L'inconscient malgré lui*; Laing, *The self and others*; and Timparano, *The Freudian slip*, esp. ch. 10.

(4) Existential psychoanalysis is an example of a metapsychology which recasts psychoanalytic theory in terms of essentially *philosophical concepts*, which are taken to be psychologically explanatory. See Sartre, *Being and nothingness*, pt IV, ch. 2, and pp. 568–9; Binswanger, *Being-in-the-world*; Boss, *Psychoanalysis and Daseinanalysis*, esp. pt II; and Jaspers, *General psychopathology*, esp. pt IV.

Arguably, Jung too should be assigned to this category, as ultimately tending to subordinate psychoanalytic concepts to theological or semi-philosophical concepts, drawn from the context of cultural anthropology.

(5) Another group of positions holds that psychoanalytic theory must be extended sooner or later into *social, political or historical* studies: see Frosh, *The politics of psychoanalysis*; Kovel, *The radical spirit*; and the writings of Herbert Marcuse, Wilhelm Reich, and Erich Fromm, which link psychoanalysis with Marxist theory.

(6) The remaining group comprises all the metapsychologies that seek a *purely psychological* foundation for psychoanalytic thought. It includes, of course, Kleinian theory; the post-Kleinian work of Donald Winnicott and Wilfred Bion; and other forms of neo-Freudian theory, such as ego-psychology (see 7.1 n16), and object-relations theory (see 7.1 n26).

Works surveying the different metapsychologies include Brown, *Freud and the post-Freudians*; and Eagle, *Recent developments in psychoanalysis*.

II KLEINIAN METAPSYCHOLOGY AND ITS CRITICS

Edward Glover's 'An examination of the Klein system of child psychology' is a lengthy, detailed and highly polemical attack on Klein and the Klein Group. It was written in response to the Controversial Series of Discussions – concerned with the differences between Klein and Anna Freud – held at the British Psycho-Analytical Society in 1943–4. Glover's case is hard to summarise (see pp. 15–16 of the 'Examination'), but some central points can none the less be identified, and I will try to indicate how a Kleinian might respond to them. The interest of Glover's piece is that it focuses on the main alleged weakness of Kleinian theory.

Glover concedes that Kleinian theory legitimately identifies a gap in classical Freudian theory at the level of pre-Oedipal life. He furthermore admits the cogency of the basic concept of phantasy, and the existence of some 'true generalisations' in Kleinian theory. Glover's chief complaints are that Kleinian theory is either (i) theoretically confused and/or non-Freudian, or (ii) dependent on clinical suppositions which are either unproven, or presuppose some contentious bit of theory.

With regard to (i): Glover alleges in very general terms that the concept of phantasy is over-employed (pp. 19–25). His arguments largely re-analyse into distinct elements concepts that Klein explicitly intends as synthetic in relation to their Freudian precursors; or, he points out that Kleinian theory presupposes forms of psychological organisation that would not be available to it on other theories (such as Glover's own). His complaint that phantasy is over-extended by Klein fails to show any fault in its theoretical motivation. Because Glover does not come to grips with the claim that Kleinian theory represents a continuous development, which has simplifying and unifying power, of Freud's central theoretical impulses, his general charge that Klein parts company from Freud lacks force.

Glover's case must be seen as resting on (ii), his clinical disagreement. To some extent, of course, this places it outside the scope of an enquiry into the philosophy of psychoanalysis. Still, there is a problem with Glover's contentions at this level, in that – rather than offering clinical reports that contradict Kleinian interpretations – his claims tend to presuppose that there *could not be* observations that would give application to Kleinian concepts; that Kleinian thought is, as it were, *intrinsically* 'hypothetical' and unverifiable (as Popper alleges with regard to Freud: see 8.5). But to establish this would require, at the very least, an argument showing a difference between Klein's and Freud's concepts regarding their susceptibility to being fitted out with criteria, and none such is provided by Glover. In the absence of a clinical differential between Freud and Klein, parity of argument would entail a wholesale rejection of psycho-analytic theory in all its forms, as a confused deviation from ordinary psychology. Glover does not want this conclusion, but his attack on Klein gives him no reason to resist it.

Glover works out his charge of illicit theoretical presupposition with reference to only one Kleinian tenet, the assumption of a primitive ego, which conflicts with Glover's own theory of ego-nuclei. On this issue – which must be settled on its own terms (see 7.6 n100) – it should however be noted that Glover's own theory is in the same position as Klein's on the score of theoretical presupposition. That Glover is au fond unconfident as to the very application of psychoanalytic concepts may be seen from his Preface and Introduction to *The birth of the ego*, and it may be conjectured that his dissatisfaction was diverted from Freud to Klein. The spirit of Glover's critique is captured in the following statement: 'It avails nothing to extend theoretical postulates beyond their legitimate scope, to extenuate them, as it were, with the help of axioms that are not self-evident truths' (ibid., pp. 65–6).

It is fair to conclude that Glover's 'Examination' ought only to persuade someone who is either in possession of clinical observations inimical to Kleinian theory, or independently persuaded of the superiority of an alternative metapsychology.

Glover's criticisms may be compared with those of others. Guntrip (in *Personality structure and human interaction*) objects to Kleinian theory on account of the importance it attaches to the inner, and its use of the death-instinct, as perpetuating Freud's 'outmoded' 'psycho-biology'. Guntrip considers Glover's criticisms unjustified on clinical grounds, and generally misplaced, except in so far as they manifest antipathy to the death-instinct (ibid., pp. 234–6). Contrast Winnicott's favourable perspective on Klein in 'A personal view of the Kleinian contribution'.

III LACAN ON KLEIN

In the course of a discussion of Klein's child analysis of Dick, Lacan complains that Klein lacks a 'theory of the imaginary' (*Seminar* I, p. 82). This is of course true, in that Klein does not give an explicit philosophical account of what it is for something to be imaginary (which suggests that Lacan is, characteristically, placing inappropriately philosophical demands on psychoanalytic theory: see pp. 202–6). But Lacan's more specific charge is that Kleinian attributions of phantasy can not sustain themselves outside of Lacan's own theory of the orders of the symbolic and the imaginary, which stems from his general theory of the mind's relation to language.

Leaving aside the details of Lacan's theory, it may be noted that, for Lacan's objection to be good, a demonstration that the attribution of phantasy is somehow a function of linguistic activity would be needed. The difficulty that confronts any such argument – for anyone, like Klein, with a realistic view of phantastic content – is that it will prove too much, by showing that there is no 'content' to phantasy except that which is *created* by the subject's interaction with the mind of the psychoanalyst-interpreter. And this is indeed a consequence that Lacan is prepared to accept: '*the unconscious is the discourse of the other.* Here is a case where it is absolutely apparent. There is nothing remotely like an unconscious in the subject. It is Melanie Klein's discourse which brutally grafts the primary symbolisations of the Oedipal situation on to the initial ego-related [*moïque*] inertia of the child. Melanie Klein always does that with her subjects, more or less implicitly, more or less arbitrarily' (ibid., p. 85). So it seems that Lacan is in the end realistic only about Freud's metapsychological discourse, or selected parts of it, and only in so far as it is rendered in his own terms; and that first-order clinical interpretations do not qualify for him as true or false.

The argument underlying Lacan's objection to Klein appears to be something like the following. On the basis of independently given considerations about (a) the nature of linguistic meaning, as conventional and constituted solely by internal differentiation, and (b) the nature of subjectivity, as forever embroiled in paradoxes of self-reference, it is thought by Lacan that the subject's production of linguistic meaning creates an aspect to the subject which is inaccessible to it. This occurs in such a way that the 'bar' of the distinction signifier/signified coincides with that of *Cs./Ucs.* But the question is, why should such an 'unconscious' – effectively a shadow cast over the speaker by his use of language – be identified with the dynamic unconscious, rather than just identified with a sub-set of the elements of *Pcs.*? And, even if it were shown that this inaccessible aspect does have a connection with motivation – constituting as Lacan says a *manque* in the subject, that it must strive to compensate for – its connection with *Freudian* interpretation remains mysterious. The Lacanian 'unconscious' therefore borders on being a variation of the existentialists', Hegel-inspired search for a metaphysical origin for human desire (see Butler, *Subjects of desire*, pp. 186–204, on Lacan and Hegel). Thus disengaged from genuinely psychoanalytic themes, the next question is whether or not Lacan's emphasis on language gives his theory any edge over other metaphysical accounts of human motivation, such as Sartre's (described in 1.7). For one to think so, would require one to be impressed by Lacan's underlying theory of language (for which see 'The agency of the letter in the unconscious', sec. 1). See Wollheim's criticisms in 'The cabinet of Dr Lacan'; and *Freud*, pp. xxxviii-xl.

Notes

INTRODUCTION

1 In ordinary thought, however, madness and irrationality blur into one another: see 4.3 n9.
2 This means leaving akrasia – the form of irrationality most discussed in analytical philosophy – rather to one side; a proper treatment of akrasia would have led in different philosophical directions from those pursued here.
3 Suggested by Ricœur, *Freud and philosophy*, p. 375. These should be understood in a fully realistic sense, i.e. as those conditions required for irrationality to be real; as distinct from conditions for the attribution of irrationality, which would imply that irrationality is a function of attribution (see 8.3 on Davidson).
4 O'Shaughnessy, *The will* 1, p. 23.
5 Indeed, it follows from the way things have been set up that, if it does take special methods, perhaps ones involving quantification, to show that we are being 'irrational', then what is being demonstrated is not an irrational phenomenon in the sense with which this enquiry is concerned. Even if such faults – at the level of competence – did exist, they would ex hypothesi not be such as to bring subjects into contradiction with themselves, and so would not fall under the definition of irrational phenomena.

ORDINARY IRRATIONALITY

1 I will use the term *ordinary psychology* to refer to what is also called 'folk' or 'commonsense' psychology. Other key terms are *intentional psychology* – explanation in terms of the content of mental states – and *propositional psychology* – explanation in terms of propositional attitudes. I will use *propositional attitude* to refer to mental items that can be combined so as to form reasons for action, and their correlates, i.e. principally to beliefs, desires and intentions (the rationale for this arguably rather narrow use will emerge later, and nothing important for the argument hangs on it). Propositional attitudes combine to form what I will call the *propositional network*. Because it attributes reasons for action, propositional psychology is also *rational psychology*. Intentional psychology need not be propositional or rational (psychoanalytic explanation is intentional but, I

250

will argue, not propositional or rational psychology). Ordinary psychology is not the same as propositional psychology: much of what it attributes (e.g. sensations, habits, competences) does not consist of propositional attitudes.

2 A view which lends itself readily to an eliminativist extrapolation: it is claimed that irrationality shows a lack of integrity in ordinary psychology sufficient to cast doubt on its reality. As someone sharing Dennett's general outlook will be likely to argue, on an analogy with the 'irredeemable incoherency' which Dennett claims to find in the concept of pain: see *Brainstorms*, p. 228. I return to Dennett in 4.10 and 8.4.

3 This does not exhaust the forms of irrationality: 4.3 will introduce psychoanalytic grades of irrationality, which are propositionally opaque.

4 See Elster, *Ulysses and the sirens*, pp. 36ff.; and Parfit, *Reasons and persons*, sec. 5.

5 Contrast Sartre, who implies that the 'metastability' of self-deception (*Being and nothingness*, p. 49) is necessarily a result of intention, on the grounds that the 'unity' of self-deception must be 'recovered by a more profound synthetic intention leading from one level to the other and unifying them' (ibid., p. 473); whereas I take it that, although there is confusion *in* self-deceptive intent, it is not intended *that it be* confused.

6 An organism preparing for combat with another may put itself into a state which misrepresents its own power, and so avoid registering its own fear or debilitation. I am grateful to Andrew Pomiankowsky for this information.

7 *Anna Karenina*, p. 143. The choice of illustrative material presents nigh insoluble problems, since any selection can be accused of prejudicing the argument. Literary material is at least less likely to be specious than improvised or anecdotal case-descriptions.

8 *The longest journey*, pp. 149–50.

9 See Freud's definition of wishful thinking, (1915b) 287 / 74–5. Suggesting that self-deception may be simplified in the direction of wishful thinking, see Pears, 'The paradoxes of self-deception'; and Mele, *Irrationality*, ch. 10.

10 Optimally, the self-deceiver's particular choice of rationalisation – its striking cleverness – supplies evidence for this, but such conclusiveness is not necessary for each attribution of strong self-deception: once the existence of the phenomenon is established, other, weaker criteria may suffice. Analogously in explaining rational action: we confidently attribute practical reasoning even when the best evidence, namely an avowal of intention, is not to hand.

11 The argument here is analogous to Davidson's, regarding the attribution of belief, in *Inquiries into truth and interpretation*, chs. 9–11. See also Wittgenstein, *Remarks on colour*, sec. 297–8.

12 See Hopkins, 'Introduction: philosophy and psychoanalysis', p. xxviii n21; and Wollheim, *The thread of life*, pp. 171–3.

13 That this way of viewing the evidence for attributions of belief can not in general be correct is testified by the fact that, if we accepted it,

attributions of insincerity and a multitude of other basic psychological complexities would become unavailable.

14 See Price, 'Half-belief'.

15 Davidson himself does not take such a view: see *Inquiries into truth and interpretation*, pp. 153, 168.

16 See Wollheim, *The thread of life*, pp. 170–3.

17 See O'Shaughnessy, *The will* I, pp. 21–8.

18 Which would seem sufficient for strong self-deceivers to be held just as responsible for their condition and its consequences as agents ordinarily are for their actions. This does not mean, however, that conditions which do not rest on intention are necessarily ones for which the agent can not be held responsible: see n37 below, and 6.7 n68.

19 This suggestion is due to James Hopkins.

20 See Peacocke, *Thoughts*, p. 63; and Searle, *Intentionality*, pp. 6–7.

21 This suggestion is due to James Hopkins.

22 See White, *Attention*, ch. 4.

23 We *might* then choose to redefine strong self-deception, dropping the reference to belief, saying that it involves an intention to promote the *thought* that p in order to prevent the *realisation* that q.

24 *Remembrance of things past* 2, p. 784.

25 Ibid., I, p. 1010.

26 Proust's selves define a psychological sense in which persons may not be 'wholly present' at a point in time – they may be wholly absorbed in one aspect of their personality. There is no pressure to translate this observation into Parfit's picture of persons as composed of 'successor selves' (see *Reasons and persons*, pt III, esp. p. 305).

27 Attributing self-deceptive intent involves, of course, a mass of counterfactual suppositions, but this, again, is common to all attributions of intention.

28 See 4.3 n9.

29 The line between such empirical denials, and denials based on conceptual claims, is of course extremely thin.

30 An idea which will be expanded in 3.2.

31 Nothing hangs on the analysis of strong self-deception here, which is contentious, for the later account of psychoanalysis.

32 This perspective on irrationality is suggested by Sartre, *Sketch for a theory of the emotions*, pp. 62–5.

33 Which does not mean that the Assumption of Alternatives applies to all forms of irrationality: in 4.6, psychoanalytic grades of irrationality will be described as ones to which the Assumption hardly applies.

34 There is no space here to make a 'certain degree' more precise, but a vague contrast will do for my purposes.

35 This issue will be returned to in 8.4.

36 See *Essays on actions and events*, ch. 2.

37 For which reason it is not quite as clear in akrasia as it is in strong self-deception that the agent's responsibility is of the normal, unqualified strength.

38 Aristotle compares the akrates to one who is asleep, drunk, in the grip of emotion, or paralysed: see *Nicomachean ethics*, 1147a11–19 and 1102a14–26.

39 See Peters, 'Emotions and the category of passivity'.

40 Nor does the perspective suggested here nullify or exclude other contributions to the explanation of akrasia: see Pears, *Motivated irrationality*, pp. 173ff.

41 Note that, to elucidate bad faith, Sartre does not strictly require this extravagance – it will do for persons to *experience* themselves and the world in such terms.

42 See Baldwin, 'The original choice in Sartre and Kant'.

43 *Being and nothingness*, p. 56.

44 Ibid., pp. 59–60.

45 Metaphysical motivational stories such as Sartre's may consequently seem to have the advantage over empirically constructed stories, such as psychoanalytic theory's, that they never risk *running out* of explanation; whereas empirical theories may well have to adduce contingent constitutional factors at the end of the day. But of course the explanatory totalitarianism of metaphysical stories may equally be a reason for viewing them with suspicion.

46 See *Phenomenology of spirit*, sec. 78–84, 166–75.

47 See *The birth of tragedy*, esp. sec. 7. Nietzsche's vision of the Greeks is substantially borne out by Dodds' account, in *The Greeks and the irrational*, of the Homeric concept of *ate*, a direct injection, originating in supernatural agency, of irrationality into the mind of the individual.

48 'On the essence of truth', pp. 135–7.

49 See *Phenomenology of perception*, pp. 168–9, 377–83.

50 See 7.6, esp. n105. Speculatively, one might trace these metaphysics of irrationality back to Kant's bifurcation of human personality into phenomenal and noumenal aspects: Kant was arguably the first to insist on, not human duality (a much older thought), but the impossibility of fully coherent self-representation.

51 In much modern American drama, self-blinding is portrayed as an undertaking with a truly heroic dimension (e.g. Larry, in O'Neill's *The iceman cometh*).

PERSONS IN PARTS

1 See Lacan, *Seminar* 1, p. 24; Schafer, *A new language for psychoanalysis*, ch. 5; and Scruton, *Sexual desire*, pp. 197–8.

2 This form of partition receives support from (although it does not strictly require) rejection of the Principle of the Possibility of Contradictory Belief. Christopher Janaway has drawn my attention to Plato's distinction of the parts of the soul on the basis of conflict of motivation, in *Republic*, IV, 435.

3 'Was't Hamlet wrong'd Laertes? Never Hamlet. / If Hamlet from himself be ta'en away, / And when he's not himself does wrong Laertes, / Then Hamlet does it not. / Who does it then? His madness.'

4 See also Champlin's account of the fallacious assumption that self-contradicting entities must be compounds, in *Reflexive dilemmas*, pp. 56–8.

5 (1915e) 169 / 170–1. See also (1925d) 32 / 215; and (1933a) 70 / 102.

6 (1915e) 170 / 171.

7 On Janet's concept of '*désagrégation*', see Hilgard, *Divided consciousness*. See also 3.2 n10 on hypnoid states; and 7.1 n9.

8 Multiple personality is discussed later in 2.6 and 3.8.

9 (1915e) 170 / 172. See also (1925d) 32 / 215.

10 See MacIntyre, *The unconscious*, pp. 44–5. Further suggesting Freud's adherence to Second Mind modelling, see (1916–17) 215–16 / 253.

11 Which goes well beyond the aspectual sense of part involved in Sartre's account of the subject in bad faith as having a 'double property' (*Being and nothingness*, p. 57).

12 *Being and nothingness*, pp. 50–1.

13 Ibid., pp. 53–4.

14 At least, it will be suggested in 3.8, none that exceed those of ordinary psychology.

15 Ibid., pp. 51–3. Here Sartre uses bad faith to refer to what has been called strong self-deception (incorrectly, for it was said in 1.7 that they are not the same).

16 (1955a) 260.

17 (1914d) 16 / 73. See also (1933a) 68 / 100.

18 (1933a) 68 / 100.

19 (1926d) 157–60 / 316–20.

20 (1926d) 157 / 316. See also (1940a) 178–9 / 412–13.

21 Whether this is in fact so will be considered in chapter 4.

22 *Being and nothingness*, pp. 53–4.

23 I follow the argument in *Being and nothingness*, pp. 50–4. See also Volosinov, *Freudianism*, p. 70.

24 This is an inaccurate statement of Freud's concept of the ego, but it makes no difference to the argument.

25 Freud (1926d) writes: 'the ego is an organisation and the id is not' (97 / 249). See also (1933a) 73–5 / 105–7.

26 See (1900a) 143–4, 308 / 225–6, 419; (1916–17) 140–1, 174 / 173–4, 208–9; and (1933a) 13–16 / 42–5.

27 The superego is not treated by Sartre, but the omission is unimportant, since it could only be a successful candidate for C by taking over the relevant descriptions of the censor: i.e. it would have to be unconscious yet distinct from *Ucs.*, and more than merely a source of judgement.

28 Sartre also expresses this inconsistency by saying that 'the unconscious is one moment another consciousness, and the next moment other than consciousness' ('The itinerary of a thought', p. 38).

29 See O'Shaughnessy's example of similarly gratuitous homuncularism in *The will* 1, p. 113.

30 Note that the argument against partition does not turn on an objection to postulating causal relations between persons and the elements which compose them, since in cases of internal conflict we say that persons

resist, cede to, and are weaker or stronger than their desires. Such forms of description are fully intelligible, and do not confuse the personal with the sub-personal.

31 It is what Sartre calls an 'autonomous consciousness in bad faith': see the passage quoted on pp. 43–4.

32 The following analogy may help. Suppose there is a character in a detective novel who knows the identity of the murderer and everything which passes in the minds of the detective and other characters, and is able with this information to shape the plot: such a figure would be in the position of the *author*, of whom we would be unable to resist viewing them as a representation.

33 *The three faces of Eve.*

34 Whether there are other, indirect evidential links between multiple personality cases and the postulation of Second Minds is considered in 3.8.

35 The point about causal genesis can also be stated in terms of C's *desires*. Since persons are not identical with their mental parts, and a reason for a person is not necessarily a reason for a mental part of theirs, an account is owed for why the person's motivation should carry over to C.

36 See Dennett, *Brainstorms*, chs. 7 and 11; and Fodor, *The modularity of mind*, and *Psychosemantics*, pp. 23ff.

37 *An essay concerning human understanding*, II, ch. 21, 17. See also Plato, *Republic*, IV, 435.

38 *The modularity of mind*, p. 25.

39 *Representations*, p. 63.

40 Ibid., pp. 65–7.

41 Dennett's approach is the same: see *Brainstorms*, pp. 12, 122–4. On homuncularism, see *Brainstorms*, pp. 59, 86–9, 102.

42 Depending on one's view of metaphor.

43 'Freud's anatomies of the self', pp. 253–7.

44 See Wilkes, 'Anthropomorphism and analogy in psychology'.

45 *The language of thought*, pp. 75–7, 198.

46 'The boundaries of inner space', 453. Dennett agrees with Nagel that sub-personal and personal psychologies do not match in such a way as to permit a reduction, and reacts by denying reference to the personal: see *Content and consciousness*, pp. 90–6; and *Brainstorms*, pp. 102–5, 219. Stich argues for a similar conclusion in *From folk psychology to cognitive science*.

47 'The boundaries of inner space', 457.

48 *The language of thought*, pp. 52–3.

49 See *Representations*, ch. 5.

50 See *The language of thought*, p. 52 and n19.

51 Ibid. Similarly, see Taylor, 'Cognitive psychology', esp. p. 91. This conclusion runs contrary to Fodor's intention, which is to 'vindicate' ordinary psychology: see *Psychosemantics*, ch. 1; and 8.4.

52 The option canvassed by Churchland, in 'Eliminative materialism and the propositional attitudes'; and, more tentatively, Stich, in *From folk psychology to cognitive science*, pp. 228–46.

53 See McDowell, 'Functionalism and anomalous monism', p. 397 and n29; and Taylor, 'Cognitive psychology'.

54 The circularity which is evident at this point is, it should be noted, no argument against the definition: personhood is not being set up as an explanatory concept; and we are not attempting to define the concept 'externally', i.e. for the use of anybody who is not, already, an instance of a person.

55 *The modularity of mind*, pp. 126–9.

56 See Erdelyi, *Psychoanalysis*; and Wegman, *Psychoanalysis and cognitive psychology*.

57 Note that these remarks do not rule it out that isomorphisms may be found between personal and sub-personal psychologies – once each has been independently completed and legitimated.

58 Festinger, for example, in *A theory of cognitive dissonance*, makes a disposition to 'reduce dissonance' the base-line in the explanation of irrationality, and claims it to be 'itself a motivating factor' (see pp. 276–9). Pears agrees that an autonomous structure of 'perversion of reason' underlies both conscious and (at least some) psychoanalytic unconscious processes ('Motivated irrationality, Freudian theory and cognitive dissonance', pp. 280–8). However, the areas of behaviour with respect to which this vague disposition can be made definite are extremely remote from psychoanalytic and other irrational explananda, so that when it is carried over to these contexts, it seems to have been equated with some very general (and scarcely explanatory) disposition already available in ordinary psychology, e.g. 'to avoid thinking of oneself as irrational'. Dissonance-reduction contrasts with the specific dispositions – e.g. to defence against anxiety – which psychoanalytic theory attributes.

PERSONS AND SUB-SYSTEMS

1 'Paradoxes of irrationality', p. 298. I will discuss this formula in 3.7.

2 Ibid., p. 304.

3 Ibid., pp. 290–1.

4 I will use 'sub-system' initially to refer to mental parts in the theories of both Davidson and Pears, and refine my terminology later.

5 Ibid., p. 303.

6 Ibid., p. 304.

7 Plato, *Republic*, 604b: 'when a man is drawn in two opposite directions, to and from the same object, this, as we affirm, necessarily implies two distinct principles in him'.

8 As will be explained below, these are identical with the Proustian 'cohesive groupings of mental states' referred to in 1.3.

9 See Hopkins, 'Mental states, natural kinds and psychophysical laws', 228–35.

10 Freud concurs in viewing mental distance as fundamental to explanation

and by no means metaphorical: his early explanation of hysteria in terms of dissociated 'hypnoid states' clearly exploits the concept, as does his much later retention of 'isolation' (disconnection of ideas as manifested in failures to associate) as a distinct mechanism of defence. See (1895d) esp. 11–17 / 62–9; Hilgard, *Divided consciousness*; and, on isolation, (1926d) 120–2 / 275–8. On these, and all other psychoanalytic concepts, see the relevant entries in Laplanche and Pontalis, *The language of psychoanalysis*.

11 This suggestion is due to James Hopkins. See Mackie, 'Multiple personality', pp. 4–6; and Heil, 'Minds divided', 580–1. Explanation in terms of characterised compartments is well illustrated by Meltzer's observation: 'intelligence as a personality attribute can be partitioned and distributed, often very unequally, amongst the parts of the self' (*Sexual states of mind*, p. 91).

12 See Morton, *Frames of mind*, ch. 6, on character and ordinary psychology; and 'Freudian commonsense', on character and psychoanalytic theory.

13 Illustrating this conception, see Wollheim's description of the selves of Bradley's moral psychology, in 'The good self and the bad self', pp. 163–4.

14 *Motivated irrationality*, p. 69.

15 See 'Reply to Annette Baier', p. 136.

16 Reflecting a general difference of outlook: Pears wishes to demonstrate the independence of psychological explanation from strong assumptions of rationality (see *Motivated irrationality*, pp. 3, 257). Pears (ibid., chs. 9–10) rejects the 'backward' and 'forward' connections that Davidson upholds in the form of the 'Medea' and 'Plato' principles ('Paradoxes of irrationality', pp. 294–5).

17 Pears sometimes calls it a 'wish', but it is clear that he has nothing Freudian in mind.

18 *Motivated irrationality*, p. 71.

19 Ibid.

20 Pears notes and discusses his differences with Davidson in *Motivated irrationality*, pp. 94–7; and 'Reply', pp. 135–6.

21 Pears views the malformation of belief by desire as asymmetrical with the inertness of the cautionary belief, in *not* requiring any special explanation, because he takes the process of belief-malformation itself to be either plain wishful thinking or a 'perversion of reason' (see 2.11 n58).

22 Mele, in *Irrationality*, pp. 80–4, considers how it would apply to a case of akrasia.

23 *Motivated irrationality*, p. 70.

24 The functional criterion is then well-named: this difficulty exemplifies the general danger of triviality in functionalist causal-role reductions of the mental. Sub-systems suit frameworks which minimise the metaphysical commitments of ordinary psychology: see 3.8 and 8.3.

25 *Motivated irrationality*, p. 86.

26 'Goals and strategies of self-deception', p. 71.

27 *Motivated irrationality*, p. 87. See also 'Reply', pp. 136–7; and 'Goals and strategies', pp. 74–5.

28 The gap between a sub-system selected by Pears' negative criterion, and one selected by his positive criterion, is thereby narrowed considerably, if not eliminated: when the causal role of Pears' sub-systems is rationalised by reasons for action, as much will be entered into a sub-system that fails to intervene rationally as into one that intervenes irrationally.

29 As already indicated in 3.1, the two conceptions do not correspond exactly to what can be found in the writings of Davidson and Pears respectively, since Davidson's conception encompasses more than is included in what I have called characterised compartments. Davidson's ambiguity on this score is not an oversight: his attributionism drains the choice of conceptions of metaphysical significance (see 8.3).

30 See Mele, *Irrationality*, p. 147.

31 Just as Davidson's event-causationist analyses of action are not meant to falsify identifications of persons as agents (see *Essays on actions and events*, ch. 4).

32 Note that this condition is consistent with S-statements' being *ultimately* reducible to P-statements. Davidson describes the goal of sub-systemic theory weakly, as the provision of 'conceptual aids to the coherent description of genuine irrationalities' ('Deception and division', p. 92). The option of claiming heuristic value for sub-systems, but no reality, is taken – for a different set of reasons from those considered in this chapter – by de Sousa, in 'Rational homunculi'. See also Heil, 'Minds divided', 575.

33 See Davidson, *Essays on actions and events*, ch. 14.

34 In the Kantian sense that Nagel gives the term, as a means for deriving reasons for action from judgements (*The possibility of altruism*, ch. 6). Numerically distinct motivational structures, in this sense, within a person, would do nothing to explain irrationality: why should the reasons derived by one motivational structure diverge from those derived by another, when both are one person's?

35 This recapitulates Sartre's point that the required relations between mental parts cannot just be mechanical: 'the censor must choose' (*Being and nothingness*, p. 52).

36 An analogy with social theory may help to highlight the contrast: characterised compartments correspond to a weak view of social entities as supervening on individuals, Pears' sub-systems to a collectivist, Durkheimian view of social entities as explanatorily autonomous.

37 'Goals and strategies', p. 74.

38 See ibid., pp. 73–4; and 'The paradoxes of self-deception', pp. 88–90.

39 *Motivated irrationality*, p. 92.

40 There are echoes of Freud's ego and id in Pears' idea that O is S's environment, the crucial difference being that the id is not rational. The objection here is not to the concept of differently orientated mental

systems, but to Pears' right to use it in this context: sub-systems must be fully rationalised; any residual incoherence in their attitudes means that no gain in explanation has been made.

41 *Motivated irrationality*, pp. 92–3.

42 'Goals and strategies', p. 74 (the full story is to be found in pp. 71–4). See also 'The paradoxes of self-deception', p. 85. Davidson refers to the issue of sub-systems' genesis in 'Paradoxes of irrationality', pp. 300–1.

43 Note that akrasia does not help to provide a point of entry for sub-systemic theory, for, as 1.6 implied, although it involves failure of self-control (see Mele, *Irrationality*, chs. 4–5), its propositional structure does not require a distinction between 'controlling' and 'controlled' selves.

44 This possibility was indicated to me by David Papineau. Here it is not the existence of individual sub-systems which is envisaged as causally prior to propositional explanation (an idea discussed earlier in the context of cognitive-psychology, 2.11), but a general mechanism of creation of sub-systems. The present proposal at least circumvents the objection of analyticity.

45 Psychoanalytic mechanisms, such as repression, and its few arguably innatist elements (see 6.3 n7), will be seen to have by contrast carefully worked out and independent rationales, deriving from within ordinary psychology.

46 Pucetti makes this inference in considering commissurotomy ('Brain bisection and personal identity'). Nagel outlines the issues in 'Brain bisection and the unity of consciousness'. There are parallels between the argument in this section and competing views of commissurotomy .

47 A further point: if the interpersonal analogy held, breaks between sub-systems would be clean, and marked by relations to different propositions. But what we invariably end up having to say of an individual's mental fractures is that the propositions she believes are separated from one another *in some respects but not others*. This delicate way of describing mental distance does not square with the interpersonal model.

48 In agreement with Heil, 'Minds divided'; and Mele, *Irrationality*, pp. 80–4 and ch. 10.

49 For which reasons it is consistent to require sub-systems to be fully rationalised, and yet allow unrationalised elements (such as the blurring of intention, and loss of control, in self-deception) to explain irrationality in the context of ordinary psychology.

50 What follows applies equally to Pears' modification of Davidson's formula (see 3.3).

51 That the concept of mental distance is primitive and can not be analysed at the level of personal psychology does not of course mean that information about particular instances of mental distance can not be provided.

52 *Meditations*, p. 59. Similarly, Reid, 'Of identity', p. 109.

53 See Strawson, *Freedom and belief*, Appendix E.

54 See Elster, Introduction to *The multiple self*.

55 This isolates the fundamental respect in which self-deception is paradoxical: in the name of guarding personal unity, its violation is undertaken.

56 Which allows us to see that philosophical theories of irrationality may symptomatise their object.

57 The issue of how the sub-system's possession of rational capacities is to be squared with its lack of (self-)consciousness has not been taken up here, because it seems so indeterminate. See Pears, *Motivated irrationality*, pp. 98–100; and Elster, *The multiple self*, p. 22.

58 See Nagel, 'The boundaries of inner space', 454–5; and Nietzsche, *Beyond good and evil*, sec. 19.

59 See Strawson, *Individuals*, pp. 95–7.

60 Pears himself expresses uncertainty on this score in 'Goals and strategies', p. 73.

61 See Mackie, 'Multiple personality'; Wilkes, *Real persons*, ch. 4; and (with regard to commissurotomy) Nagel, 'Brain bisection', pp. 163–4. That belief in personal unity is due to the projection or 'overvaluation' of consciousness is widely supposed: see ibid., pp. 163–4; Pears, *Motivated irrationality*, p. 82; and Lacan, *Seminar 2*, ch. 4.

62 What follows applies equally to post-commissurotomy syndrome.

63 Expressions can be unidirectional signs: something can be an expression and sign of a condition C without also having the capacity to signify not-C.

64 On this issue see Haight, *Self-deception*, chs. 3–4; Pears, *Motivated irrationality*, p. 99; and James, *The principles of psychology* 1, ch. 8.

65 See Evelyn White's self-description in *The three faces of Eve*, pp. 227–8.

66 See *A treatise of human nature* 1, IV, 6; and Parfit, *Reasons and persons*, p. 251.

67 See Leibniz, *New essays on human understanding*, II, ch. 27; Wiggins, 'The person as object of science, as subject of experience, and as locus of value'; and Wollheim, 'On persons and their lives', pp. 318–20.

68 See McGinn's proposal in *Mental content*, pp. 209–11; and O'Shaughnessy, *The will* 1, pp. li–lii. Perhaps it should be said that whereas persons are substances, minds have the kind of identity-conditions appropriate to 'systems' (see ibid., p. xix).

UNCONSCIOUS MOTIVES AND FREUDIAN CONCEPTS

1 This chapter, like chapter 2, is concerned with Freud's earlier writings, chiefly the 1915 metapsychological papers. Freud's later theories will be discussed in 7.1.

2 Laplanche and Leclaire, 'The unconscious', p. 129.

3 This may be put by saying that the phenomenologist's layer of implicit meaning does not comprehend the unconscious proper. On the relation of psychoanalysis to phenomenology, see Ricœur, *Freud and philosophy*, pp. 390–418.

4 Among Freud's earliest psychoanalytic conceptualisations is the characterisation of the hysteric as one who lies also to herself. The following

exchange occurs between Freud and Frau Emmy von N.: '"Don't you know?" "No." "Why not?" "Because I *mayn't*! (She pronounced these words violently and angrily.)', (1895d) 61 / 118. Many writers are quick to identify unconscious motivation and self-deception, if only implicitly. Hartmann writes: 'a great part of psychoanalysis can be described as a theory of self-deceptions' (*Ego psychology and the problem of adaptation*, p. 64). Freud does not employ the concept of self-deception, although he confronts the concept of contradictory belief in (1909d) 196 n1 / 77 n1; (1916–17) 101 / 130; and (1895d) 117 n1 / 180 n1.

5 Or, arguably, into those of Sartre's own existential psychoanalysis: see Appendix I, (4).

6 An example of such, suggested to me by James Hopkins, is Jane Austen's Emma. At the end of the novel the heroine, in what is described explicitly as a realisation of self-deception, appreciates that her actions have been motivated by love for Knightley, but the deeper features of her motivation (her exaggerated attachment to her father) which have contributed to her self-ignorance are never brought to awareness.

7 The relevant notion of interpretation is independent from Davidson's claim that all psychological attribution is interpretative.

8 See (1909d) and (1955a).

9 Neurosis doubtless does count as madness in loose, popular usage. For the purposes of this enquiry, however, madness is regarded as a failure of mental order and competence so radical that, from the point of view of ordinary psychology, no psychological explanation can be proposed for it; it is distinguished from irrationality by not even having enough psychological structure to allow for the identification of self-contradiction. This (perhaps somewhat stipulative) definition, which is intended to simplify the issues without distorting them, allows one to remain agnostic regarding the possibility of explaining madness psychologically. It leaves open the possibility that ordinary psychology may get an explanatory grip on madness via its own psychoanalytic extension: irrationality, as an intermediary phenomenon, may allow the development of a theory of the mind subsequently applicable to madness. See Freud's explanations of psychosis, (1915e) pt VII; and (1911c).

10 In this chapter I follow without querying Freud's interpretation of the Ratman, since it is the workings of Freudian concepts that I want to exhibit here. See Hopkins, 'Introduction', pp. xxxi-xxxvi.

11 (1909d) 167 / 48.

12 (1909d) 205–6 / 85–6; the sexualised consequences of the beating are explained in 206 n1 / 86 n2.

13 (1909d) 217 / 97.

14 (1909d) 166 / 47. See also (1955a) 283–4. The phenomenon of transference (in its negative form) is exemplified here: see (1916–17) Lecture 27.

15 (1909d) 232 / 112. See also (1895d) 92–5 / 151–6.

16 (1909d) 198–9 / 79.

17 (1909d) 184 / 64.

18 (1909d) 217–18 / 97–8.

19 (1909d) 245–6 / 124–5. See also (1912–13) 89–90 / 147–8.

20 (1909d) 180 / 60.

21 (1909d) 180–1 / 60–1.

22 This distinction is meant to be understood as *de re*. It is suggested by Wollheim's use of it in a different context ('Seeing-as, seeing-in, and pictorial representation', pp. 210–11).

23 See Davidson, *Essays on actions and events*, p. 285.

24 See Greenspan, 'A case of mixed feelings'.

25 This last requirement, it will be seen in 6.3, is in the Ratman's case in a deep sense unfulfilled.

26 (1916–17) 433 / 484.

27 Or choice; there being no reliably recognisable differences between these terms in the present context.

28 See Wollheim, 'Thought and passion', 19–21.

29 See Wollheim, *The thread of life*, pp. 173–85.

30 Contrast Sartre: 'the inferiority complex is a free and global project of myself as inferior' (*Being and nothingness*, p. 459).

31 (1905e) 81–5 / 118–22.

32 Freud's use of the term in the expression 'choice of neurosis' in (1913i) is clearly pleonastic; see Wollheim, *Freud*, p. 36.

33 (1895d) 7 / 58. See also (1937d) 267–8.

34 See for example (1901b) ch. 1.

35 Freud refers to 'a kind of intellectual acceptance of the repressed, while at the same time what is essential to the repression persists', (1925h) 236 / 438.

36 E.g. Dora's experience of Herr K's sexual assault: see (1905e) 27–8 / 58–9 . See 7.1 n38.

37 Freud also talks of emotions – such as the Ratman's hatred – as repressed: Freud's solution to the problem of repressed emotion is discussed further in 8.2.

38 See 'Suppression' in Laplanche and Pontalis, *The Language of psychoanalysis*. Freud sometimes conceives repression broadly (as in (1915d) 147 / 147), but he distinguishes it from mere non-attention, and in (1915e) 173, 192 esp. n1 / 175, 196 esp. n2, he distinguishes repression from censorship between *Cs.* and *Pcs.*

39 The details of the theory of repression are mostly in the metapsychological papers (1915d) and (1915e). See Madison, *Freud's concept of repression and defence*; Wollheim, *Freud*, ch. 6; and Forrester, *Language and the origins of psychoanalysis*, ch. 2.

40 In Pears' terms (see 3.3), they are unable to form an effective cautionary belief.

41 My condition requires some slight (but harmless) qualification in view of Freud's early suggestion that an intentional act may *initiate* repression: see Laplanche and Pontalis, *The language of psychoanalysis*, pp. 392–3.

42 (1915e) 177 / 179.

43 (1915e) pt III. See Wollheim, *Freud*, pp. 162–3; and 8.2.

44 See (1915e) pt VII, and Appendix C; (1917d); and (1923b) 19–21 / 357–9. See Wollheim, *Freud*, pp. 168–72; and Forrester, *Language and the origins of psychoanalysis*, pp. 27–9.

45 (1926d) 125–6, 160–8 / 280–1, 320–9.

46 (1915d) 146 / 145.

47 See (1895d) 121–3 / 186–8.

48 (1950a) 255.

49 (1915e) 173–4 / 176. See n56 below. On the concept of topography, see (1915e) pt II.

50 (1923b) 15 / 353: 'we obtain our concept of the unconscious from the theory of repression'.

51 I owe this point to Richard Wollheim.

52 (1916–17) 436 / 488.

53 Psychoanalytic theory's heavy involvement in questions of mental individuation illustrates its commitment to psychological realism. See Wollheim, *The thread of life*, ch. 2; and Morton, 'Freudian common-sense', pp. 66ff.

54 The notion wanted here, of two ideas of one object in a single mind, is consequently stronger – because their degree of divergence is far greater – than that, in 1.3, of two representations of a single object.

55 Proust, *Remembrance of things past* I, p. 441.

56 That the theory's inelegance is partly due to a strain of Second Mind conceptualisation in Freud's thinking is suggested by its embroilment with the problem of 'double registration': the choice between the 'topographical' hypothesis (of different ideas in different loci), and the ultimately preferred 'functional' hypothesis (which says that there is one idea which alters locus). Such a choice is necessitated by sub-systemic conceptualisation. See (1915e) 175, 180 / 177, 183; Davidson, 'Paradoxes of irrationality', p. 300 n6; and Pears, 'Goals and strategies', p. 73. The issues here are extremely complex: see Laplanche and Leclaire, 'The unconscious', pp. 132–3; and Wollheim, *Freud*, pp. 167–72.

57 On this notion, see Wollheim, 'On persons and their lives'; and *The thread of life*, ch. 5.

58 However, see Proust, *Remembrance of things past* 3, pp. 1105–7: again Proust seems to stand mid-way between ordinary and psychoanalytic conception.

59 Which does not, in any sense, rule out causal and representational characterisations of present experience: the theory here is independent of any particular theory of perception or memory.

60 And of unconscious phenomenology; see 8.2.

61 (1915e) 187 / 191. The achronological conception of the unconscious prepares the ground for the Kleinian concept of an inner world; by treating the unconscious as distinct from memory, it need not be seen as just an inexplicably distorted imaginative elaboration of one's stock of memories.

62 Contrast Merleau-Ponty, *Phenomenology of perception*, p. 413; and Meltzer, *The Kleinian development* I, p. 98.

63 As Pears notes in *Motivated irrationality*, pp. 70ff.

64 The important issue left over from that discussion is how it is possible for a mental state to be unconscious at all, considered in 8.1.

65 (1909d) 181 / 61.

66 (1915e) 168 / 169–70.

67 See for example Cheney, 'The intentionality of desire and the intentions of people'.

68 *A theory of human action*, p. 122.

69 As in Davidson's partial reconstruction of Freudian theory: see 'Paradoxes of irrationality', p. 291. Dilman's view seems to be that psychoanalytic explanation does not rupture at any point with ordinary psychology: see *Freud and the mind*.

70 See (1912g) 260–2 / 50–3; and (1933a) 70–1 / 102–3 on *descriptive* versus *dynamic* unconsciousness. The class of dynamic unconscious states includes psychoanalytic, and some non-psychoanalytic, states (e.g. self-deceptive intent); each class is independent of the other.

71 See Cioffi, 'Wishes, symptoms and actions'. Volosinov considers it an incoherence that Freudianism '*preserves fully intact in the unconscious the specific differences and logical distinction of all these [conscious] elements*' (*Freudianism*, p. 70).

72 See Mischel, 'Concerning rational behaviour and psychoanalytic explanation', 328.

73 This is how the Ratman will have to be understood if additional axioms about maximising satisfaction are added to ordinary psychology, which may be argued to be committed to them implicitly: see Elster ed., *Rational choice*, Introduction.

74 This strategy is symmetrical with Lévi-Bruhl's (equally questionable) anthropological explanations. The problems of psychoanalytic understanding are in many respects comparable to those facing anthropology, magic and ritual taking the place of symptoms.

75 See Dennett, *Brainstorms*, pp. 10–12, 285, and 'Making sense of ourselves', pp. 64–7; and Wilkes, *Real people*, p. 161. Dennett's specific argument is that, once a breakdown has occurred, all too many intentional stories can be suggested to fill in the hiatus – a slip in arithmetic can be accounted for in a thousand and one ways – all of which are arbitrary and incomplete.

76 Undoubtedly, Freud always conceived psychoanalytic theory as congruent with a scientific world-view ((1933a) 181 / 219), and continued after the 'Project' to entertain some loose idea of its unification with physical science ((1914c) 78 / 71; and (1920g) 60 / 333–4). But there can be no significant difference for Freud between the physiological remediability of psychoanalytic and ordinary psychology (lest his inference to the existence of the unconscious be undermined). For pellucid statements of the autonomy of psychology, see (1900a) 536 / 684; and (1915e) 168 / 169. Freud regarded psychological concepts as no less real than physiological concepts: see (1923b) 60 / 334. Contrast Appendix I, (1).

77 Unless, of course, one is *already*, like Dennett, an instrumentalist about intentionality.

78 This strategy may be seen as converting what is a *problem* for sub-systemic theory – the 'residual irrational attitudes' required for sub-systemic explanation (see 3.7) – into the materials for a solution.

79 In detail in *The thread of life*.

80 See (1920g) pts V–VI; further elaborated in (1923b) pt IV.

81 See (1905b) 135–6, 167–8 / 45–6, 82–3; and (1915c) 125–9 / 122–6. See Laplanche and Leclaire, 'The unconscious', pp. 140–4; and Thomson, *Needs*, pp. 65–6. The idea of such a kind of state occurs in Plato, *Republic*, IV, 437.

82 These criteria are suggested by Thomson, in *Needs*, p. 61. Motivational states may be regarded as the psychological components of needs.

83 Contrast Morton, *Frames of mind*, ch. 5.

84 Talk of motivational states has often been viewed with suspicion, and they are whole-heartedly rejected in 'anti-metapsychological' psychoanalytic theory; see Appendix I, (2). The crucial points are however that the psychoanalytic (unlike behaviourist) use of the notion retains intentional states among the ways of individuating motivational states, and that they are, although dispositional, at least 'multi-track' dispositions. See Maze, *The meaning of behaviour*, ch. 6; and Ricœur, *Freedom and nature*, pp. 93–9. The concept of a motivational state is straightforwardly dependent upon a picture of persons as subject to biological need; consequently, Sartre disparages the notion of libido (*Being and nothingness*, p. 571; echoed by Scruton in *Sexual desire*, pp. 202–5).

85 Ambiguity threatens at this point: Are these 'desire-like' states desires or not? We need to distinguish the *species* 'desires as ordinarily conceived', from the *genus* of which these propositional attitudes are only the most familiar, paradigm instances (no opportunity to make this distinction arises outside the psychoanalytic context). The states basic to psychoanalytic explanation are desires in the second and not in the first sense. Henceforth, context will show which sense is meant.

86 I return to this notion in 7.2. Some of the literature regarding 'neurotic rationality' – an issue intimately connected with the general controversy regarding reasons and causes (see 5.10) – is surveyed in Shope, 'The significance of Freud for modern philosophy of mind'. See for example Alexander, 'Rational behaviour and psychoanalytic explanation'; and Mischel, 'Concerning rational behaviour and psychoanalytic explanation'.

87 It is frequently assumed – without argument – that the explanation of human action, if it is not to be behaviourist or otherwise at odds with ordinary psychology, must be *exclusively* in terms of reasons for action; see for example Taylor, *The explanation of behaviour*, esp. pp. 59–68.

88 This accords with Freud's own very broad use of the terms purpose, sense and intention: see (1916–17) 40 / 66.

89 See *Brainstorms*, ch. 1.
90 See (1950a) 295.
91 The need to conceive persons as having a consistent metaphysical texture is well expressed by Sartre: see *Being and nothingness*, pp. 441–2. It also motivates Freud's insistence that the gaps in ordinary psychology be filled with psychological rather than organic elements: see (1915e) 168 / 169.
92 See Wollheim, *Freud*, pp. 61–3.

WISH

1 See (1950a) 317–21; and (1916–17) Lecture 14.
2 See (1900a) ch. 3.
3 Phantasy, a level of mind permanently dissociated from action, provides a third, *standing* source of wish, whose continual generation of wish is independent from circumstance; see 6.2.
4 See (1950a) 317–21; and (1917d).
5 Such a 'safety-valve' arrangement is consistent with evolutionary pressures: it prevents the organism from incurring damage through excessive frustration.
6 See Wollheim, *The thread of life*, pp. 42–5. Contrast Wittgenstein, *Lectures and conversations*, p. 50.
7 See (1916–17) 175 / 209; (1900a) 542ff. / 692ff.; and (1917d) 228 / 235–6.
8 See (1950a) 318.
9 See (1950a) 325.
10 (1900a) 118–19 / 196. The dream of Irma's injection is in (1900a) ch. 2; on which, see Hopkins, 'Epistemology and depth psychology', pp. 42ff. On the dream-work, see (1900a) ch. 6; (1916–17) pt II; and (1933a) 17–22 / 46–51.
11 See 7.3.
12 See (1900a) 560–1 / 713–14.
13 This point will be amplified in 7.3.
14 See (1917d) 230–1 / 238–40.
15 By contrast with repression, where it individuates more finely.
16 See (1895d) 263 / 346; and (1900a) 292–3 / 398–400.
17 See O'Shaughnessy, *The will* 2, pp. 230–2.
18 Suggested by James Hopkins. It is designed for purposes of contrast with wish-fulfilment. See Hopkins, 'Introduction', pp. xxvi-xxvii, for the conception of wish-fulfilment at the core of this chapter: 'We can think of [wish-fulfilling] imagining as like breathing, which follows a natural course in adjustment to need'; and Wollheim, *The thread of life*, pp. 90–1.
19 See the 'psychological cycle' of need described by Wollheim in 'Needs, desires and moral turpitude'.
20 (1900a) 118–19 / 196: 'The dream represented a particular state of affairs as I should have wished it to be. *Thus its content was the fulfilment of a wish and its motive was a wish.*' See also (1917d) 230 / 238.

21 It is because the difference of structure is not appreciated, and wishes are equated with propositional desires, that some critics hold that Freud fails to distinguish the representation *of* the fulfilment of a wish, from something's *being* the fulfilment of a wish: see Shope, 'The psychoanalytic theories of wish-fulfilment and meaning'; and Wittgenstein, *Lectures and conversations*, p. 47.

22 Reflexive forms of description are used elsewhere in characterising mental states: phenomenal states are self-presenting, and memory experiences represent themselves as past-directed: see Wollheim, 'The bodily ego', pp. 126–9; Searle, *Intentionality*; and Pears, 'Motivated irrationality', pp. 275–6.

23 Although, of course, the two may be linked, in that an individual or event figuring in a consciously wished-for state of affairs may become the object of a psychoanalytic wish, and vice versa.

24 I owe this point of clarification to Richard Wollheim. See Hopkins, 'Epistemology and depth psychology', pp. 44–8, on ordinary and psychoanalytic concepts of wish.

25 See Balmuth, 'Psychoanalytic explanation', 232–3. Freud partially qualifies the thesis of fulfilment in (1900a) 160–2, 579–83 / 245–6, 736–40; and (1923c) 118.

26 In (1895d) 9–1 / 150–2, Freud distinguishes 'expression of the emotions' from hysterical symptoms, whose explanation requires the more powerful hypothesis of recollection.

27 For this concept, see Searle, *Intentionality*, ch. 1.

28 The insufficiency of this condition alone to explain how gratification results is in line with Freud's abandonment of 'hypnoid states': see (1905e) 27 n1 / 57 n2.

29 See Wollheim's full account in 'Wish-fulfilment'. On the Omnipotence Belief, see (1909d) 233–5 / 113–14; and (1912–13) 85–92 / 143–50.

30 See *The thread of life*, pp. 142–4, on the 'archaic theory of the mind'.

31 Which is Sartre's view: see *The psychology of imagination*, ch. 4.

32 The second approach avoids difficulties that may be associated with attempting to relocate what may seem to be a sophisticated kind of mental state back in psychological development: what ordinary psychology knows of imagination may make unconscious imagining seem problematic.

33 On the fundamental structures of the imagination see Wollheim, *On art and the mind*, ch. 3; and *The thread of life*, ch. 4.

34 See (1900a) *passim*; and (1916–17) 138–40 / 170–3.

35 For this we need suppose only a very early point of evolution in the psychic apparatus, before the Reality Principle impinges. See 4.6 on the kind of conflict involved.

36 On displacement, see (1900a) ch. 6, sec. B; and (1916–17) 173–5 / 208–9. On condensation, see (1900a) ch. 6, sec. A; and (1916–17) 171–3 / 205–8. On primary and secondary process, see (1950a) 324–7; (1900a) ch. 7, sec. E; and (1915e) pt V.

37 See (1916–17) 345 / 389–90.

38 *Sketch for a theory of the emotions*, pp. 50–4; similarly, Wittgenstein, *Lectures and conversations*, p. 47.

39 *Being and nothingness*, p. 53.

40 Ibid., pp. 53 and 458–60.

41 Habermas writes: 'Psychoanalytic interpretation is concerned with those connections of symbols in which a subject deceives itself about itself' (*Knowledge and human interests*, p. 218).

42 The difficulties for psychoanalysis indicated by Sartre again make room for an alternative, sceptical response: see Cioffi, 'Wishes, symptoms and actions'.

43 The psychoanalytic model will however be redrawn, with additional complexities, in 7.3.

44 Without reducing symbolisation to the provision of merely *compensatory* sensuous pleasure.

45 See Morton, *Frames of mind*, pp. 138–9.

46 See the Ratman's 'Dick' association in (1909d) 188–9 / 68–9. Freud speculated continually about the conditions for association: see for example (1901b) 6 / 42–3. See Forrester, *Language and the origins of psychoanalysis*, esp. ch. 3; and Jaspers, *General psychopathology*, ch. 4.

47 See Forrester, *Language and the origins of psychoanalysis*, pp. 127–9: Jones distinguishes metaphor, a preconscious process, from symbolism, an unconscious process, in 'The theory of symbolism'.

48 See Wollheim, *Art and its objects*, sec. 18.

49 Contrast Wittgenstein's puzzling assertion that the grounds of symbolism may always be taken for granted, and require no special explanation, in *Lectures and conversations*, pp. 43–4. Phenomenology's role in psycho-analytic explanation is discussed in 8.2.

50 See (1900a) 193–8 / 282–7.

51 (1916–17) 231 / 270.

52 Appreciation of this point invalidates several of Wittgenstein's objections to psychoanalytic interpretation.

53 There is however one more important thing to be said on this topic, held over for 7.3.

54 See Jung, *Two essays on analytical psychology*, pp. 286–7; and Forrester, *Language and the origins of psychoanalysis*, pp. 102–10. My remarks here do not of course do justice to the complexity of Jung's views, and mean only that a preference for Jung's theory over Freud's would require independent, extra-psychological motivation (which Jung considers to be provided by, among other things, trans-cultural uniformities).

55 See Forrester, *Language and the origins of psychoanalysis*, pp. 111–22. The picture is to some extent complicated by Freud's admission of innate symbolism: see (1916–17) Lecture 10. The important point is that the role of pre-established symbols is auxiliary: Freud never allows the explanation of an individual's symbolism to rest on the existence of merely pre-established meanings.

56 (1900a) 349 / 465. See Forrester, *Language and the origins of psychoanalysis*, pp. 72–3.

57 (1916–17) 154 / 187.
58 See for example Toulmin, Flew, and Peters, in MacDonald ed., *Philosophy and analysis*.
59 See *Sketch for a theory of the emotions*, pp. 53–4.
60. See Habermas, *Knowledge and human interests*, chs. 9–11; and Ricœur, *Freud and philosophy*.
61 See Davidson, *Essays on actions and events*, ch. 1; Hopkins, 'Introduction'; and O'Shaughnessy, *The will* 1, p. lii.
62 Should it turn out that such reconstruction is impossible, that will just be an invitation to think that Davidsonian compatibilism is true after all.
63 The role of laws in psychoanalytic theory is discussed in 8.4.

PHANTASY AND KLEINIAN EXPLANATION

1 (1911b) 222 / 39.
2 (1911b) 225 / 42.
3 The distinction of fantasy from phantasy, like that of ordinary and psychoanalytic wish, is a matter of different modes of explanation: it is not just a distinction between conscious and unconscious, or occurrent and dispositional, mental states.
4 Which, it should be noted, is not the same as saying that they alone provide sufficient grounds for the *existence* of phantasy; these lie in the general considerations about explanation given above.
5 'The nature and function of phantasy', p. 81. Whether infantile phantasy is best described as conscious or unconscious is unclear: see (1918b) 104–5 / 346. Wollheim, like Isaacs, introduces the concept of phantasy independently from wish-fulfilment: see *The thread of life*, pp. 97–101; and *Freud*, pp. xxix-xxxvi.
6 See p. 181.
7 A third view is that the power to phantasise is innate. This need not contradict Isaacs' account, which does after all assume a pre-experiential disposition to represent instincts. The fundamental Kleinian structures of phantasy (see 6.3) are also candidates for being innate, although Klein does in fact offer an a posteriori account of their formation. That the dynamic unconscious rests at some points on an innate basis should not be excluded; whether it needs to be assumed is a complex question.

  Stronger innateness claims have been made regarding the content of phantasy, such as that concepts like that of a feeding breast compose a 'phylogenetic heritage'. This elaborates a strand in Freud's thought: see (1939a) 100–2 / 345–8; (1940a) 166–7 / 399; Jones, *Sigmund Freud* 3, ch. 10; and Forrester, *Language and the origins of psychoanalysis*, pp. 18–22. This is one of the very few respects in which Freudian theory goes beyond folk biology; generally it is independent of specific scientific biological hypotheses (although it of course remains open to being informed from such quarters). See Wollheim, 'Was Freud a crypto-biologist?'
8 Isaacs, 'The nature and function of phantasy', p. 79.
9 These concepts are treated more fully in 7.1.

10 Narrative appears in psychoanalysis at the levels of universal mental development, the analysand's personal history, and the progress of therapy. It is neither a merely heuristic device, nor evidence that psychoanalysis just constructs personally satisfying fictions, nor a sign of psychoanalysis' non-scientificity: narrative structures the mind which is the theory's object. A conjecture as to why this should be: narratives are transformations of instinctual patterns (see Burkert, *Structure and history in Greek mythology and ritual*, chs. 1–2). See Wollheim, *The thread of life*, pp. 150–3, 209; and Habermas, *Knowledge and human interests*, pp. 263–4.

11 I follow the outlines of Hanna Segal's exposition in *Introduction to the work of Melanie Klein*; *Klein*; and 'Phantasy'. See also Wollheim, *The thread of life*, esp. pp. 92–101, 19–29, 142–61 (to which this chapter is heavily indebted). On phantasy, and all other Kleinian concepts, see the relevant entries in Hinshelwood, *A dictionary of Kleinian thought*.

12 See Wollheim, *The thread of life*, pp. 120–5; and Heimann, 'Certain functions of introjection and projection in early infancy'.

13 See Klein, 'Some theoretical conclusions regarding the emotional life of the infant', pp. 78–9.

14 See Wollheim, *The thread of life*, pp. 154, 270–4; Meltzer et al., *Studies in extended metapsychology*, ch. 5; Grotstein, *Splitting and projective identification*; and Sandler ed., *Projection, identification, projective identification*.

15 See Klein, 'Envy and gratitude', p. 180.

16 See (1926d) 163–4 / 322–4; and (1936c) 235–7. Phantasy is the 'vehicle' of defence: see Wollheim, *The thread of life*, p. 122.

17 This diachronic account might be recast in synchronic terms: see Wollheim, *Freud*, p. 60.

18 See Klein, 'A contribution to the psychogenesis of manic-depressive states', and 'Notes on some schizoid mechanisms'; Segal, *Klein*, chs. 7–10; Hopkins, 'Synthesis in the imagination'; and Grotstein, *Splitting and projective identification*.

19 See Hopkins, 'Introduction', pp. xxxi–xxxvi.

20 'Envy and gratitude', p. 181.

21 Ibid., p. 180. See also ibid., pp. 179–83; and 'On the theory of anxiety and guilt', pp. 28–33.

22 Here, as elsewhere, Klein's phantastic structures seem to underpin Freud's attributions of pleasure as a motive (see e.g. 'A study of envy and gratitude', p. 215).

23 'Envy and gratitude', p. 183.

24 See Wollheim, *The thread of life*, pp. 206–10.

25 'Envy and gratitude', pp. 20–26.

26 Ibid., pp. 220–1. See also pp. 184, 216.

27 'Envy and gratitude', p. 188.

28 'Envy and gratitude', pp. 221–30.

29 This is closely connected with the Kleinian conception of sublimation: see 6.8.

30 'Envy and gratitude', p. 196.

31 See Wollheim, 'The good self and the bad self', p. 166.
32 'The function of dreams', p. 586. The Kleinian view is generally of dream as a manifestation of phantasy.
33 Segal, *Introduction to the work of Melanie Klein*, p. 16.
34 (1927e). See also (1905b) 165 / 79; (1924e); and (1940e).
35 See (1908e) 148–9 / 134–5. I owe this point to James Hopkins.
36 In the loose sense, in 4.11, of a connection of content. See Hopkins, 'Epistemology and depth psychology', pp. 50ff.
37 Suggested by Jim Hopkins.
38 Although phantasy may take an occurrent form, it does not thereby coincide with fantasy: fantasy can not be analysed into 'awareness of phantasy', since not all fantasies draw off phantasy, and those that do may in fact *mis*represent its content.
39 This argument is in line with, but does not require anything as strong as, Davidson's attributionism (see 8.3).
40 See Campbell, 'Conceptual structure'; and Davies, 'Tacit knowledge and sub-doxastic states', pp. 146–8.
41 Note, to avoid misunderstanding, that this sense of aboutness has nothing to do with the issues of internalism versus externalism, or of intrinsic versus derivative content.
42 *The varieties of reference*, sec. 6.3.
43 Ibid., pp. 122–5, 226–7; Peacocke, *Sense and content*, pp. 6–7; and McGinn, *Mental content*, p. 62. See also Hopkins, 'Synthesis in the imagination', pp. 155–6.
44 'Beliefs and sub-doxastic states'.
45 See Block ed., *Imagery*, Introduction.
46 See O'Shaughnessy, *The will* 1, pp. 222–3; and 2, pp. 64–6.
47 See Davies, 'Perceptual content and local supervenience', 22–4.
48 See Searle, *Intentionality*, ch. 5.
49 'Affective unconscious and cognitive unconscious'.
50 See p. 189.
51 (1915e) 186–7 / 190–1. The pictorial analogy accords with Freud's account of the unconscious as composed of thing-presentations. See Wollheim on 'iconic' mental states in *The thread of life*, ch. 3.
52 See 7.2 n41.
53 (1933a) 68–9 / 100–1; and (1914d) 16 / 73. The Ratman's resistance is detailed in (1955a) *passim*.
54 The theme of emancipation from passion through cognition is of course Spinoza's: see *Ethics*, pt IV.
55 See (1937c) 227–30; and Hopkins, 'Epistemology and depth psychology', p. 54.
56 See (1914g) 155–6; and (1926d) 159–60 / 38–19. See also Klein, 'Envy and gratitude', pp. 231–2.
57 See (1936a) 243–6 / 452–5.
58 See (1914g) 150–3; (1916d) 31–12 / 294–5; (1916–17) 454–5 / 507–8.
59 See 7.1; (1916–17) Lecture 28; and p. 185.
60 See Meltzer, *The psycho-analytical process*, ch. 5.

61 Discussed in 8.2.

62 The argument need not assume this to be the best analysis of pictorial representation; see Wollheim, 'Seeing-as, seeing-in, and pictorial representation'.

63 In Pears' terms (in 3.3), the absence of a power to form cautionary beliefs is constitutive of the unconscious.

64 See Wollheim, *On art and the mind*, ch. 13.

65 By Wollheim.

66 See Meltzer, *The psycho-analytical process*, Appendix F.

67 See (1909d) 233–5 / 13–14; and (1912–13) 85–90 / 143–9.

68 By no means, of course, does what follows begin to do justice to the perplexing question of how psychoanalytic causes impinge on human freedom and responsibility. This would require a lengthy treatment. To grasp the depth of the problem, consider the following paradox: discovering an action to be unconsciously motivated shows it to have been *desired*, and hence *increases* the propriety of holding responsibility-attributing attitudes such as blame towards the agent; at the same time, unconscious motives are much of a kind with the sorts of causes that ordinarily *exculpate* agents, and hence *undermine* the propriety of responsibility-attributing attitudes. (So it may be that the psychoanalytic perspective, like those referred to in 1.7, is tragic: it sees people as required to take responsibility for conflicts that are *forced* upon them.) What is needed is a view of freedom that can rationalise the exculpating role of at least some unconscious causes, but which does not have the consequence that no human action is free. See (1900a) 69–21 / 781–3; and (1925i) 131–4.

69 See Jaspers, *General psychopathology*, pp. 133–4.

70 See 'Free will and the concept of a person'.

71 See Wollheim, 'Needs, desires and moral turpitude', pp. 178–9; and pp. 215–16.

72 See p. 181 on constitutive concepts of the mind.

73 'The importance of symbol-formation in the development of the ego', pp. 224–5. See also 'The psychoanalytic play-technique'; and *Narrative of a child analysis*.

74 'Notes on symbol-formation'. Segal's view of sublimation as a *kind* of symbolisation differs from Freud, who regarded them as alternatives. See (1914c) 94–5 / 88–9; (1916–17) 345–6, 375–7 / 389–91, 423–4; and Jones, 'The theory of symbolism', pp. 126, 135–6, 141.

75 'Notes on symbol-formation', pp. 55–7. The account does not imply that sublimation can only occur as a result of psychoanalysis, or requires the explicit self-application of psychoanalytic concepts.

76 See 'Motivated irrationality', pp. 278–9. The table-cloth ritual is described in (1916–17) 261–4 / 300–3 (a second case that might be taken to suggest that belief is desired is described in Lecture 16). Another excellent example of acting-out is the 'pathological ceremonial' that a girl enacts every night, described in (1916–17) 264–9 / 303–9. It 'tormented her parents'. The two 'most important stipulations' were

that the 'pillow at the top end of the bed must not touch the wooden back of the bedstead', and that the eiderdown 'had to be shaken before being laid on the bed so that its bottom end became very thick'; after which 'she never failed to even out this accumulation of feathers'. The ceremony's 'central meaning' is as follows: the girl's mother is represented by the pillow, and her father by the bedstead, their separation signifying prevention of sexual intercourse; a correlative wish, of undoing pregnancy, is expressed by the girl's smoothing down of the eiderdown.

77 And, presumably, for Pears psychoanalytic theory must also employ the notion of a sub-system, located in *Pcs.* and aiming at the desired belief; it would be formed out of a wish in the main system, comprehending *Ucs.*, the rest of *Pcs.*, and *Cs.*

78 (1916–17) 263 / 302. On acting-out, see (1914g) 150–4; Wollheim, *Freud*, pp. 134–5, and *The thread of life*, pp. 155–8.

79 See (1916–17) 262 / 301.

80 In acting-out, an intentional doing is brought under two descriptions, each characterising it intrinsically. Their combination is not a coincidence: acting-out is *realised in* intentional action.

81 See Schafer, *A new language for psychoanalysis*, ch. 7.

82 See O'Shaughnessy on phantasy and striving as natural expressions of desire, in *The will* 2, p. 296.

83 It helps here to recognise that psychoanalytic theory regards the capacity for pleasure as more primitive than the phenomenon of desire; which allows that specific forms of that capacity may *explain* desires, a possibility explored in Freud's theory of zones (see (1905b) pt I). The concept of repetition-compulsion also lurks in this area; see (1920g). It is unclear whether repetition-compulsion is a further basic motivational determinant.

84 This shows why sexuality should have a central place in psychoanalytic explanation: the phenomenological homogeneity between sexual pleasure and pleasure in expressing phantasy 'sexualises' the latter, as well as reinforcing the propensity of sexuality to serve as a vehicle of phantasy.

85 See O'Shaughnessy, *The will* 2, pp. 337–8.

86 (1920g) 20 / 290.

METAPSYCHOLOGY AND PSYCHOANALYTIC PERSONALITY

1 (1915e) 181 / 184.

2 See Arlow and Brenner, *Psychoanalytic concepts of the structural theory.*

3 See (1933a) 59–68 / 90–100; Klein, 'Early stages of the Oedipus complex'; and Wollheim, *The thread of life*, pp. 200ff.

4 See (1933a) 68–9 / 100–1. (By now it is clear that it would be a mistake to take this to mean that the ego is self-deceived.)

5 See (1923b) pt II; and (1940a).

6 See (1925d) 32 / 216.
7 See Wollheim, *Freud*, pp. 174–5. Nor does this picture change when Freud moves on to the structural theory.
8 See O'Shaughnessy, 'The id and the thinking process'.
9 This shows the difference between the unconscious and conceptualisation in (Janet's) terms of a 'dissociated' part of the mind: the unconscious is more metaphysically conservative.
10 (1926d) 159–60 / 318–20.
11 See p. 145.
12 See (1940a) 203–4 / 439–40; and (1927e) 153–4 / 352–3.
13 See (1926d) 119–22 / 274–8; (1936a) 243–6 / 451–5; and Wollheim, *The thread of life*, pp. 269–71.
14 See (1950a) 322–4; (1917d) 233 / 241; (1950a) 255; (1923b) 25 / 363–4; (1940e) 275 / 461; (1940a) 150–1 / 382; (1926d) 93 / 244; (1933a) 68 / 100; (1923b) 29 / 368; (1915c) 134–6 / 132–4; (1914c) 75 / 67; (1917e) 247–8 / 256; and Wollheim, *Freud*, ch. 6.
15 See *The ego and the mechanisms of defence*.
16 See Hartmann, *Ego psychology and the problem of adaptation*; and Kris, *Selected papers*. At times ego-psychology seems to accord the ego a properly sub-personal character.
17 *Introduction to the work of Melanie Klein*, pp. 20–1.
18 *The language of psychoanalysis*, p. 131.
19 See *On art and the mind*, pp. 36–7, 44–5; and 'The bodily ego', p. 137 n11. Wollheim's analogy indicates that the ontological status of internal objects is in part a general problem; it suggests that, whereas internal objects such as the bad breast exist in the way that characters in novels do, the ego may be thought of as a character that 'doubles' as a representation of its author.
20 Echoing Freud's idea of a residue of 'historical truth' in delusion, (1939a) 130 n1 / 379 n1.
21 It follows that what is in question when the ego 'represents itself' is not the full-blooded reflexivity of a *person*'s self-consciousness.
22 *Freud*, p. 203. See also *On art and the mind*, ch. 2.
23 See ibid., pp. 52–3.
24 See Wollheim, *The thread of life*, pp. 120–9; *On art and the mind*, pp. 43–5; and 'The good self and the bad self'.
25 Or, they require such further thoughts for their explanation: see the more complex model described in n83 below.
26 It follows, as a conceptual matter, that Klein's is a form of what is called object-relations theory: see 'The origins of transference', p. 53, and 'Notes on some schizoid mechanisms', pp. 3–4; and Greenberg and Mitchell, *Object relations in psychoanalytic theory*. It is widely assumed that the thesis of object-relations contradicts Freud's theory of drives and instincts (see Fairbairn, *Psychoanalytic studies of the personality*). But it is unclear that explanation in terms of something's being a vehicle of a drive precludes, rather than underpins, explanations in terms of

interpersonal relations, and that 'interest in objects' is intelligible as an autonomous motive; and consequently uncertain that the concept of object-relations marks a deep contrast of metapsychologies separating Freud and Klein.

27 Consequently the contrast of psychoanalytic and propositional mental processes can not be reduced to two ways of thinking about the same world, their divergence being due to a difference of 'logic': see n41 below.

28 *The thread of life*, p. 125.

29 *Studies in extended metapsychology*, p. 102. See also *The Kleinian development* 3, p. 69.

30 Rosenblatt and Sandler, 'The concept of the representational world'; see Wollheim, 'The bodily ego', pp. 135–6.

31 A distinguishing mark of the content of experience as opposed to that of belief: see Peacocke, *Sense and content*, pp. 5–6.

32 See p. 47.

33 See (1915e) pt VI.

34 See 'Our adult world and its roots in infancy'.

35 See Meltzer, *Sexual states of mind*, pp. 91–2.

36 See Meltzer, *Sexual states of mind*.

37 See James, *The principles of psychology*, pp. 229–37.

38 See Klein, 'Some theoretical conclusions regarding the emotional life of the infant', pp. 86–7; Segal, 'Phantasy', pp. 43–4; and Isaacs, 'The nature and function of phantasy', pp. 89ff. This claim depends on the sanction of clinical material: it must be shown that the memory-akin data that first provoked Freud's theory of repression can be reinterpreted in terms of phantasy. The notion that the reality of events such as physical abuse in childhood directly 'refutes' psychoanalytic theory's stress on phantasy assumes, incredibly, that mental disorder derives, exclusively and without significant psychological mediation, from external causes. See Wollheim, *Freud*, pp. xxiii–xxiv; Freud's grasp of the complexity of the relation of reality and phantasy is shown in (1916–17) 370 / 417–18.

39 See Sartre, *Being and nothingness*, p. 132. The 'paradox' is described by Freud, (1940e) 275–6 / 461–2.

40 See Sartre, *Being and nothingness*, p. 473. Freud describes one aspect of the ego in similar terms, (1926d) 98 / 250.

41 A decisive reason for not understanding psychoanalytic causation in terms of an 'alternative logic', as does Alexander in 'The logic of emotions and its dynamic background', is that there is no room for a subjective representation of such processes as *valid*. See Wollheim, *The thread of life*, p. 129.

42 See ibid., p. 47; 3.8 n61; and Sartre, *Being and nothingness*, p. 166.

43 This discussion shows how likely it is that psychoanalytic theory is committed to a realistic, representational theory of the mind: see 8.3.

44 *Sigmund Freud* 2, p. 350.

45 Sartre expresses this point in terms of a 'magic unity': see p. 47.
46 This does not of course mean that psychoanalytic explanation is a form of functional explanation (one might be misled into thinking this on account of the fact that neither makes direct reference to intentions). See O'Shaughnessy, *The will* 2, pp. 315–16.
47 This being, roughly, Schafer's strategy in *A new language for psychoanalysis*.
48 See Wollheim, *The thread of life*, pp. 59–61.
49 See 3.5 n34.
50 See O'Shaughnessy, *The will* 1, pp. xlv–xlvii, 7–8, 16–20, 82–3.
51 *The will* 2, ch. 10.
52 See Ricœur, *Freud and philosophy*, bk II, pt I.
53 See Klein, 'Envy and gratitude', p. 180 n1.
54 Also, the Bodily Ego: see pp. 215–16.
55 E.g. Strawson, *The bounds of sense*, pp. 272–3.
56 This response would fail if pre-propositional content were conceived here as it is in classical empiricism; but, as defined here, it differs in not being designed to provide immediate, purely sensory objects of knowledge.
57 The argument does not make instrumentality *necessary* for rationality: it is left open that there is a class of 'rational symbolic' action.
58 See also the Ratman's examples in 4.4.
59 See Cioffi, 'Wishes, symptoms and actions', 100–3. (Readers who are happy with the non-strategic thesis could skip this section.)
60 (1916–17) 459–60 / 513–14.
61 (1905e) 46 / 79.
62 (1909b) 25 / 188.
63 (1916–17) 267 / 307: see 6.9 n76.
64 (1918b) 74–80 / 311–17.
65 (1901b) 167–8 / 220–1; see also 170 / 224.
66 (1900a) 414–18 / 540–5.
67 (1900a) 321–2 / 433–4; and (1933a) 13–14 / 42–3. See also (1900a) ch. 7, sec. A.
68 (1923c) 113–17. See also (1911e) 92 and 96.
69 (1905e) 42–6, esp. 43 n1 / 75–9, esp. 75 n1; (1916–17) 382–5 / 429–33; and (1926d) 98–100 / 250–3.
70 (1916–17) 383–4 / 431. See also (1937c) 237–8.
71 (1918b) 113 / 356.
72 (1901b) 169 / 223.
73 Similarly, see (1901b) 208–10 / 266–8.
74 See (1900a) 541 / 690–1; (1915e) 173, 188–9 / 175, 192–3; (1923b) 20–1 / 358–60; and (1925d) 32 / 215.
75 E.g. (1901b) 175–6, 191, 211 / 230, 247, 269.
76 (1900a) 418 / 545. See also (1900a) 445 / 576–7; and (1923c) 111.
77 In (1916–17) 140 / 173 Freud says that censorship is a 'dynamic relation', not a 'little manikin'.
78 See 8.5 n113.
79 Strategic readings can not of course be debarred on purely logical

grounds: but picturing anxiety as a *tool* is as perverse as conceiving laughter as not primarily expressive but as a method for creating conviviality.

80 (1905c) ch. 6.

81 This is a lucid commonsensical idea: a brilliant remark may express a stupid impulse.

82 See (1909d) 190 / 70; and Wollheim, *The thread of life*, p. 156.

83 Note that a more detailed discussion might show the need for more complex, three-level modelling, which would also distinguish *phantastic representations* from *thoughts* about the internal objects phantastically represented; these would be related somewhat in the way that a picture and a viewer's experience of it are related. See Wollheim, *On art and the mind*, p. 43; and *The thread of life*, p. 127.

84 See Meltzer et al., *Studies in extended metapsychology*, p. 21.

85 The same goes for psychoanalytic theory's distinction of causal levels, which extends ordinary psychology's distinction of 'primary' (sufficient) and 'secondary' (insufficient) motives.

86 Might sub-systems be added on at this late stage, linking phantasy-parts with propositional attitudes? This would be mistaken, for two reasons. First, the relation of phantastic influence leaves nothing for sub-systems to *do*, as intermediaries; second, there is nothing in phantasy to explain *how* sub-systemic entities could emerge.

87 (1924b) 152–3 / 217. See also (1940e); and (1940a) 202–4 / 438–40.

88 These conclusions are endorsed by Meltzer et al., *Studies in extended metapsychology*, ch. 8.

89 (1901b) 170–3 / 224–7.

90 See Scruton, *The aesthetics of architecture*, pp. 143–50.

91 The omnipresence of phantasy does not therefore 'pathologise the normal'.

92 Whether psychoanalytic theories of religion and morality – e.g. (1912–13); (1939a); and (1930a) – are truly reductionist is a complex question, for it is far from clear that, taken by themselves, they impinge on the rationality of beliefs. See Wollheim, *The thread of life*, ch. 7; and 'The good self and the bad self'.

93 See 'Our adult world and its roots in infancy'. The precise extent of unconscious motivation's contribution may be something that we can not know.

94 *Being and nothingness*, pp. 50–1.

95 See (1925i) 133. The concept of ownership calls, of course, for philosophical elucidation; in particular, regarding its relation to the logical concept of ascription (employed in 3.8).

96 *Ecrits*, pp. 164–6. Sartre and Lacan agree that psychoanalytic theory means a radical revision of commonsense, because both conceive ordinary psychology as Cartesian. They differ over the consequences: Sartre infers its rejection; Lacan thinks that the 'decentring of the subject' is psychoanalysis' outstanding achievement.

97 E.g. Ricœur, *Freud and philosophy*, pt III, ch. 2; and Lacan.
98 E.g. Winnicott, *Playing and reality*, ch. 4.
99 See 6.6 n56.
100 See Glover, *The birth of the ego*; and Winnicott, 'Ego integration in child development'.
101 *Contingency, irony and solidarity*, p. 10.
102 Ibid., ch. 2.
103 This occurs because the 'I' mode of self-presentation comes to be elided with a descriptive mode of self-presentation.
104 See Wollheim, 'Memory, experiential memory, and personal identity', pp. 189–91.
105 In these terms, Lacan's 'decentred subject' is not a psychoanalytic concept: it is due to the concepts under which human beings fall *qua language-users* being *unaufgehoben*, and has more to do with Hegel's notion of alienation than psychological non-integration or conflict.
106 A mistake that some accounts of the self as 'socially constructed' arguably repeat.

CONSCIOUSNESS, THEORY AND EPISTEMOLOGY

1 See James, *The principles of psychology*, pp. 163, 175.
2 As Freud asserts: see his discussions of unconscious mentality in (1912g); (1915e) pt I; (1923b) pt I; (1925d) 31–2 / 214–5; (1925e) 216–17 / 266–8; and (1940b). See Wollheim, *Freud*, ch. 6. The unconscious is *broader* than the repressed: see (1907a) 48 / 72–3; (1915e) 166 / 167; (1923b) 18 / 356; (1939a) 95–6 / 340–1; and Wollheim, *Freud*, p. 163. That Freud allowed for non-accidentally inaccessible mentality is shown by (1940a) 163 / 394–5. Also relevant are Leibnizian explananda: see *New essays on human understanding*, pp. 53–6, 164–6; (1940b) 283–4; and Laplanche and Pontalis, 'Subconscious', in *The language of psychoanalysis*.
3 Freud describes the 'equation' 'of what is conscious with what is mental' as 'either a *petitio principii*' or 'a matter of convention', (1915e) 167 / 169; see also (1912g) 260 / 50. Nevertheless, (1940b) 283 shows that Freud thought of it as in some sense the natural view.
4 See Wollheim, *The thread of life*, pp. 45–8.
5 Which renders Freud's statement that 'mental processes are in themselves unconscious', (1915e) 171 / 172. In systemic terms: not all mental states belong to *Cs*.
6 See Sartre, *Being and nothingness*, pp. xxvii–xxxi.
7 A consequence that Sartre accepts: ibid., pp. xxxviii–xliii.
8 Note that the motivation for phenomenalism is standardly unrelated to *explanation*.
9 See *An essay concerning human understanding*, I, ch. 4, 20. Freud's early interpretations in the *Studies on hysteria* do in fact tend to meet this condition.
10 See MacIntyre, *The unconscious*, pp. 29–30.

11 This view may be seen as applying to the mental some of the considerations that Evans applies, in 'Things without the mind', to the external world.

12 See Ricœur, *Freud and philosophy*, pp. 422ff.

13 'Consciousness of self and knowledge of self', p. 140; see also *Being and nothingness*, p. xxx. Some of Freud's remarks might be taken to suggest the view attacked by Sartre: (1895d) 300 / 388; (1900a) 593, 615 / 751, 776; (1915e) 171, 192–3 / 172, 196–7; (1925d) 31 / 214; and (1939a) 96 / 340.

14 See (1900a) 616–17 / 777–8.

15 See Hopkins, 'Introduction', p. xxviii.

16 (1940a) 157 / 388.

17 (1950a) 360–1.

18 (1900a) 612–21 / 773–83. See also (1940a) ch. 4; and Wollheim, *Freud*, p. 171.

19 See 4.7 n44.

20 E.g. (1950a) 307–12; (1920g) pt IV; and (1925a).

21 This is the objection of those philosophers referred to by Freud as granting unconscious 'psychoid', but not mental, states: see (1923b) 15 / 353; (1925d) 32 / 215; and Scruton, *Sexual desire*, p. 198. The objection has as its converse, a line of criticism of Freud's concept of the unconscious as *overly Cartesian* (see Gellner, *The psychoanalytic movement*, pp. 99–100); but since psychoanalytic theory is no more exaggeratedly Cartesian than ordinary psychology, this line of thought terminates in eliminativism.

22 See 8.3.

23 See James, *The principles of psychology*, ch. 6.

24 See (1940b) 286.

25 See O'Shaughnessy, 'Mental structure and self-consciousness'.

26 Contrast Sartre, *Being and nothingness*, pp. 600–14.

27 See p. 181.

28 Furthermore, psychoanalytic explanation is committed to viewing phenomenological properties as directly efficacious, and not as playing their role (as certain functionalist analyses of qualia propose) through the negotiation of belief.

29 (1895d) 71 n1 / 129 n1.

30 See Meltzer, *The Kleinian development* 3, p. 65.

31 *The Kleinian development* 1, pp. 80–1. See also Bion, *Elements of psychoanalysis*, chs. 11–14.

32 See Meltzer et al., *Studies in extended metapsychology*, esp. chs. 2 and 15; and Meltzer, *Sexual states of mind*, p. 103.

33 Which is why realism about unconscious pain is to be preferred to an account according to which unconscious thoughts only acquire phenomenological properties in the course of being consciously represented, as in the manifest content of dream.

34 'The bodily ego', pp. 129–30. See also Wollheim, *The thread of life*, pp.

144–7, and *On art and the mind*, pp. 42–3; (1923b) 26 / 364; O'Shaugnessy, *The will* 1, pp. 231–4; and Meltzer et al., *Studies in extended metapsychology*, ch. 5.

35 See Wollheim, *The thread of life*, p. 144.

36 This is obviously relevant to the elucidation of repression.

37 A finer issue surrounds the idea of mental pain: Is it *genuine*, or only 'ersatz', sensationless pain (as when I dream that I am 'in terrible pain', without having any inclination to wake up)?

38 A line of thought that will lead one to think that psychoanalytic theory requires a functionalist analysis of qualia; see 8.3 on theoreticality.

39 See Lockwood, *Mind, brain and the quantum*, pp. 161–7.

40 Wittgenstein, *Philosophical investigations*, 302.

41 (1915e) 177 / 179.

42 See p. 103.

43 Indeed, Freud speaks elsewhere of the unconscious as a locale of unpleasure and satisfaction: see p. 172.

44 See Meltzer et al., *Studies in extended metapsychology*, ch. 15.

45 See Meltzer on anxiety, *Sexual states of mind*, p. 103.

46 See McGinn, *Mental content*, pp. 59–63 ; and Peacocke, *Sense and content*, ch. 4.

47 See Wollheim, *The thread of life*, pp. 168–70.

48 In psychoanalysis, 'I can know myself only through the mediation of the other' (Sartre, *Being and nothingness*, p. 51).

49 Quasi-manifestability does not contradict the non-accidental inaccessibility of psychoanalytic states: these come to be manifested *accidentally* through psychoanalysis.

50 As noted in 3.8, sub-systemic theory does not capture the phenomenology of irrationality: either sub-systemic theory has no phenomenological implications, or those it has lack realisations.

51 See Evans, 'Things without the mind'; and McGinn, *Mental content*, p. 120 n1.

52 This formulation ignores, of course, the complexity of the issues, but a blunt formulation will suffice here.

53 See Dilman, 'Is the unconscious a theoretical construct?'

54 *Being and nothingness*, p. 51.

55 See Alston, 'Psychoanalytic theories'. On this view, Freud's statement that mentality is in itself unconscious (n5 above) asserts the mental's theoreticality$_i$. Other statements of Freud's may also seem to suggest this: (1925e) 217 / 267–8; and (1940a) 158–9 / 389–90.

56 See Smythe, 'Unconscious desires and the meaning of "desire"'.

57 See ibid., 420; and Shope, 'Dispositional treatment of psychoanalytic motivation terms', 208. Although the theoretical$_i$ view of psychoanalytic states is naturally associated with, and tends to imply the Cartesian view of mentality, it does not strictly require it.

58 See Volosinov, *Freudianism*, p. 73.

59 It is, however, not argued that psychoanalytic states could not be

reconstrued in theoretical$_1$ terms, since functional redescriptions can be provided for most things. The measure of the theoretical$_1$ view's success consists, however, not in its translational capacity, but its power to *motivate* psychological hypotheses of an acceptable kind.

60 See *Inquiries into truth and interpretation*, ch. 11.

61 'Paradoxes of irrationality', p. 292.

62 See Wittgenstein, *Lectures and conversations*, p. 45.

63 Davidson acknowledges the problem in 'Paradoxes of irrationality', p. 289.

64 See ibid., p. 299. Note that non-rational causes can not be arrived at by 'abstraction' from rational causes: subtracting rationality properly leaves nothing at all, for Davidson. Saying that phantasies may be considered *as if* they were reasons, and actions as reasonable in the light of them, saves the Principle of Charity in name, but empties it of content.

65 Davidson is in fact prepared to *end* with a 'paradox of irrationality, from which no theory can entirely escape' (ibid., p. 303). His idealism about mental content licences this, just as it rationalises his equivocation (noted in 3.1) regarding sub-systems' resemblance to agents: both issues can, in Davidson's own terms, be downplayed legitimately.

66 Ibid., p. 303.

67 These comments apply equally to Habermas' reduction of the unconscious to that which is excluded from public communication; Habermas shares Davidson's rationalistic view of the mind.

68 See 4.10.

69 See Fodor, *Representations*, pp. 107–23. See Barnes, *On interpretation*, chs. 2–3, for a purely epistemic conception of interpretation.

70 See *Essays on actions and events*, pp. 35–6.

71 Or, more broadly, to the genus 'psycho-physical substance'.

72 See Wollheim, *The thread of life*, pp. 170–3, 185–7.

73 (1900a) 613 / 773.

74 (1925d) 32 / 215.

75 (1915e) 166 / 168.

76 They provide the explananda of cognitive psychology.

77 As in 1.4, their recognition may be compared with aspect-perception, and their non-recognition with aspect-blindness.

78 Indeed, the logic of explanation requires the tie between explanation and explananda not to be analytic.

79 And, even if neurophysiology did come to impinge on psychoanalytic explanation, our first preference should surely be for a double-aspect or dialectical theory of mental and physical co-causation; see (1910i) 217–18 / 113–14. Note that non-psychological remedies do not entail non-psychological causes; and that organic causes may easily be necessary for psychoanalytic explananda without being sufficient.

80 Their view is that ordinary psychology is too shaky an edifice to allow of being extended; see Gellner, *The psychoanalytic movement*, pp. 99–100.

81 See Wollheim, *Freud*, pp. xxvii–xxxviii.

82 It is as well to remember that ordinary belief and desire too can be made to look like extravagant extrapolations from overt physical behaviour.

83 Contrast Wittgenstein, *Lectures and conversations*, pp. 42, 49.

84 It is not suggested that these explananda (which, again, can not be logically 'proved') would alone suffice to generate psychoanalytic theory.

85 See 4.10 on Dennett; Churchland, 'Eliminative materialism', 73–4; and Stich, *From folk psychology to cognitive science*, pp. 98–101. Contrast Fodor, *Representations*, pp. 105–9; and *Psychosemantics*, pp. 4–6.

86 See McGinn, *Mental content*, pp. 123–7, esp. n9 and n14.

87 E.g. (1908b).

88 See 5.7–5.9.

89 See Wollheim, *The thread of life*, p. 186.

90 Contrast Davidson's view that there is nothing between bare behaviour and propositional attitudes.

91 It may be left open whether this derives from infantile experience, or is present innately in a conceptual form.

92 See n110 below.

93 (1915e) 169 / 170.

94 See Wollheim, *Freud*, p. xxxvii.

95 (1937c), which separates psychoanalysis' therapeutic value from its epistemology; see also (1926e) 252–4 / 356–9; and Hopkins, 'Epistemology and depth psychology', pp. 50–4.

96 *Conjectures and refutations*, p. 37 (restated by Gellner in *The psychoanalytic movement*, ch. 9).

97 *Conjectures and refutations*, pp. 37–8.

98 *The foundations of psychoanalysis*, ch. 1; and 'Is Freudian psychoanalytic theory pseudo-scientific?'

99 (1915f).

100 (1933a) 28–30 / 57–9.

101 See Hobson and Squires, in Clark and Wright eds., *Mind, psychoanalysis and science*.

102 See n95 above.

103 (1908b); see n106 below.

104 (1909d) 206, n1 / 86, n2. See also Glymour, 'Freud, Kepler and the clinical evidence', pp. 23–98; and (1913i) 318–19 / 135–6.

105 (1906a).

106 See Eysenck and Wilson eds., *The experimental study of Freudian theories*; and Kline, *Fact and fantasy in Freudian theory*.

107 *Conjectures and refutations*, pp. 34–5; see also p. 38 n3. It may be wondered how discriminating this complaint can be made, for it is equally true that ordinary psychology is logically capable of at least *pretending* to explain, after a fashion, everything in its domain.

108 (1937d) 257; see n113 below.

109 (1895d) 79 / 138.

110 On the role of counter-transference, where affective states caused in the

analyst are viewed as indices of the analysand's phantasies, see Meltzer, *Sexual states of mind*, pp. 6–10; and *The Kleinian development* 3, p. 14. This form of the psychoanalyst's access to the unconscious is the inter-subjective analogue of quasi-manifestation.

111 *The foundations of psychoanalysis*, ch. 2.

112 One need not be an attributionist to hold this.

113 Freud deals with the charge of suggestibility, and discusses the criteria for correct interpretation, in (1916–17) 446–56 / 498–509; (1923c) 114–17; and (1937d).

114 I owe this point to James Hopkins.

115 See *The foundations of psychoanalysis*, p. 55. It is then natural to think that only extra-clinical considerations can be decisive: see ibid., ch. 9.

116 And why there may be some truth in the idea that undergoing psychoanalysis is necessary for accepting its claims: only through close-up exposure to the fine-grain of psychoanalytic interpretation can its thematic force be fully appreciated.

117 'Epistemology and depth psychology', p. 37.

Works of Freud cited

References are given to the *Standard edition of the complete psychological works of Sigmund Freud*, 24 vols., trans. under the general editorship of James Strachey, in collaboration with Anna Freud, assisted by Alix Strachey and Alan Tyson (London, 1953–74); and, when appropriate, to the *Pelican Freud library*, 15 vols., trans. James Strachey, ed. Angela Richards (Harmondsworth, 1973–86).

References are given in the notes by date, followed by page number (first to the *Standard edition*; second, when appropriate, to the *Pelican Freud library*); title and volume number (again, first the *Standard edition*, second the *Pelican Freud library*) are given below.

(1895d)   *Studies on hysteria* [1893–95] (with Josef Breuer) 2 / 3
(1900a)   *The interpretation of dreams* 4–5 / 4
(1901b)   *The psychopathology of everyday life* 6 / 5
(1905b)   *Three essays on the theory of sexuality* 7 / 7
(1905c)   *Jokes and their relation to the unconscious* 8 / 6
(1905e)   'Fragments of an analysis of a case of hysteria' ('Dora') [1901] 7 / 8
(1906a)   'My views on the part played by sexuality in the aetiology of the neuroses' [1905] 7 / 10
(1907a)   *Delusions and dreams in Jensen's 'Gradiva'* [1906] 9 / 14
(1908b)   'Character and anal eroticism' 9
(1908e)   'Creative writers and day-dreaming' [1907] 9 / 14
(1909b)   'Analysis of a phobia in a five-year-old boy' ('Little Hans') 10 / 8
(1909d)   'Notes upon a case of obsessional neurosis' ('The Ratman') 10 / 9
(1910i)   'The psychoanalytic view of psychogenic disturbance of vision' 11 / 10
(1911b)   'Formulations on the two principles of mental functioning' 12 / 11
(1911c)   'Psychoanalytic notes on an autobiographical account of a case of paranoia (dementia paranoides)' 12 / 9
(1911e)   'The handling of dream-interpretation in psychoanalysis' 12
(1912g)   'A note on the unconscious in psychoanalysis' 12 / 11
(1912–13) *Totem and taboo* [1912–13] 13 / 13
(1913i)   'The disposition to obsessional neurosis' 12 / 10

(1914c)   'On narcissism: an introduction' 14 / 11
(1914d)   'On the history of the psychoanalytic movement' 14 / 15
(1914g)   'Remembering, repeating and working-through (Further recommendations on the technique of psychoanalysis II)' 12
(1915b)   'Thoughts for the times on war and death' 14 / 12
(1915c)   'Instincts and their vicissitudes' 14 / 11
(1915d)   'Repression' 14 / 11
(1915e)   'The unconscious' 14 / 11
(1915f)   'A case of paranoia running counter to the psychoanalytic theory of the disease' 14 / 10
(1916d)   'Some character-types met with in psychoanalytic work' 14 / 14
(1916–17)   *Introductory lectures on psychoanalysis* [1915–17] 15–16 / 1
(1917d)   'A metapsychological supplement to the theory of dreams' [1915] 14 / 11
(1917e)   'Mourning and melancholia' [1915] 14 / 11
(1918b)   'From the history of an infantile neurosis' ('The Wolfman') [1914] 17 / 9
(1920g)   *Beyond the pleasure principle* 18 / 11
(1923b)   *The ego and the id* 19 / 11
(1923c)   'Remarks on the theory and practice of dream-interpretation' [1922] 19
(1924b)   'Neurosis and psychosis' [1923] 19 / 10
(1924e)   'The loss of reality in neurosis and psychosis' 19 / 10
(1925a)   'A note upon the "mystic writing-pad"' [1924] 19 / 11
(1925d)   *An autobiographical study* [1924] 20 / 15
(1925e)   'The resistances to psychoanalysis' [1924] 19 / 15
(1925h)   'Negation' 19 / 11
(1925i)   'Some additional notes on dream-interpretation as a whole' 19
(1926d)   *Inhibitions, symptoms and anxiety* [1925] 20 / 10
(1926e)   *The question of lay-analysis* 20 / 15
(1927e)   'Fetishism' 21 / 7
(1930a)   *Civilization and its discontents* [1929] 21 / 12
(1933a)   *New introductory lectures on psychoanalysis* [1932] 22 / 2
(1936a)   'A disturbance of memory on the Acropolis' 22 / 11
(1937c)   'Analysis terminable and interminable' 23
(1937d)   'Constructions in analysis' 23
(1939a)   *Moses and monotheism: three essays* [1937–39] 23 / 13
(1940a)   *An outline of psychoanalysis* [1938] 23 / 15
(1940b)   'Some elementary lessons in psychoanalysis' [1938] 23
(1940e)   'Splitting of the ego in the process of defence' [1938] 23 / 11
(1950a)   *The origins of psychoanalysis* [1887–1902] (including 'Extracts from the Fließ papers' [1892–1899] and 'Project for a scientific psychology' [1895]) 1
(1955a)   'Original record of the case' (Addendum to 'The Ratman') [1907–8] 10

Bibliography

See also the Select Bibliography in Wollheim and Hopkins eds., *Philosophical essays on Freud*, on philosophically orientated secondary literature; and, on all aspects of Freud, Peter Gay's comprehensive Bibliographical Essay in *Freud: a life for our time* (London, 1988).

Alexander, Franz, 'The logic of emotions and its dynamic background', *International Journal of Psychoanalysis* 16, 1935

Alexander, Peter, 'Rational behaviour and psychoanalytic explanation', in Wollheim ed., *Freud*

Alston, William, 'Psychoanalytic theories, logical status of', in P. Edwards ed., *Encyclopedia of philosophy* 6 (New York, 1967)

Aristotle, *Nicomachean ethics* (as *Ethics*), trans. J. Thomson, ed. Hugh Tredennick and Jonathan Barnes (Harmondsworth, 1983)

Arlow, J., and Charles Brenner, *Psychoanalytic concepts of the structural theory* (New York, 1964)

Baldwin, Thomas, 'The original choice in Sartre and Kant', *Proceedings of the Aristotelian Society* 80, 1979–80

Balmuth, J., 'Psychoanalytic explanation', *Mind* 74, 1965

Barnes, Annette, *On interpretation: a critical analysis* (Oxford, 1988)

Binswanger, Ludwig, *Being-in-the-world: selected papers of Ludwig Binswanger*, trans. Jacob Needleman (London, 1975)

Bion, Wilfred, *Elements of psychoanalysis* (London, 1984)

Block, Ned, ed., *Imagery* (Cambridge, Mass., 1981)

Boss, Medard, *Psychoanalysis and Daseinanalysis*, trans. Ludwig Lefebvre (New York, 1963)

Brown, J., *Freud and the post-Freudians* (Harmondsworth, 1961)

Burkert, Walter, *Structure and history in Greek mythology and ritual* (Berkeley, 1979)

Butler, Judith, *Subjects of desire: Hegelian reflections in twentieth-century France* (New York, 1987)

Campbell, John, 'Conceptual structure', in Charles Travis ed., *Meaning and interpretation* (Oxford, 1986)

Champlin, T., *Reflexive dilemmas* (London, 1988)

Cheney, James, 'The intentionality of desire and the intentions of people', *Mind* 87, 1978

286

Churchland, Paul, 'Eliminative materialism and the propositional attitudes', *Journal of Philosophy* 78, 1981

Cioffi, Frank, 'Wishes, symptoms and actions', *Proceedings of the Aristotelian Society Supplementary Volume* 48, 1974

Clark, Peter, and Crispin Wright, eds., *Mind, psychoanalysis and science* (Oxford, 1988)

Cleckley, Hervey, and Corbett Thigpen, *The three faces of Eve* (London, 1957)

Davidson, Donald, 'Deception and division', in Elster ed., *The multiple self Essays on actions and events* (Oxford, 1980)

Inquiries into truth and interpretation (Oxford, 1984)

'Paradoxes of irrationality', in Wollheim and Hopkins eds., *Philosophical essays on Freud*

Davies, Martin, 'Perceptual content and local supervenience', *Proceedings of the Aristotelian Society* 92, 1992

'Tacit knowledge and sub-doxastic states', in Alexander George ed., *Reflections on Chomsky* (Oxford, 1989)

Dennett, Daniel, *Brainstorms* (Brighton, 1978)

Content and consciousness (London, 1969)

'Making sense of ourselves', in J. Biro and Robert Shahan eds., *Mind, brain and function* (Brighton, 1982)

Descartes, René, *Meditations on first philosophy*, in *The philosophical writings of Descartes* 2, trans. John Cottingham, Robert Stoothof and Dugald Murdoch (Cambridge, 1984)

Descombes, Vincent, *L'inconscient malgré lui* (Paris, 1977)

Dilman, Ilham, *Freud and the mind* (Oxford, 1984)

'Is the unconscious a theoretical construct?', *Monist* 56, 1972

Dodds, E., *The Greeks and the irrational* (Berkeley, 1951)

Eagle, Morris, *Recent developments in psychoanalysis: a critical evaluation* (Cambridge, Mass., 1984)

Elster, Jon, *Ulysses and the sirens: studies in rationality and irrationality* (Cambridge, 1979)

Elster, Jon, ed., *The multiple self* (Cambridge, 1985)

Rational choice (Oxford, 1986)

Erdelyi, Matthew, *Psychoanalysis: Freud's cognitive psychology* (New York, 1984)

Evans, Gareth, 'Things without the mind', in Zak van Straaten ed., *Philosophical subjects: essays presented to P.F. Strawson* (Oxford, 1980)

The varieties of reference, ed. John McDowell (Oxford, 1982)

Eysenck, Hans, and Glenn Wilson, eds., *The experimental study of Freudian theories* (London, 1973)

Fairbairn, W., *Psychoanalytic studies of the personality* (London, 1952)

Festinger, Leon, *A theory of cognitive dissonance* (London, 1962)

Fodor, Jerry, *The language of thought* (Hassocks, 1976)

The modularity of mind (Cambridge, Mass., 1983)

Psychosemantics: the problem of meaning in the philosophy of mind (Cambridge, Mass., 1987)

Representations: philosophical essays on the foundations of cognitive science (Brighton, 1981)

Forrester, John, *Language and the origins of psychoanalysis* (London, 1980)

Forster, E. M., *The longest journey* (Harmondsworth, 1989)

Frankfurt, Harry, 'Free will and the concept of a person', in Rorty ed., *The identities of persons*

Frosh, Stephen, *The politics of psychoanalysis: an introduction to Freudian and post-Freudian theory* (London, 1987)

Gellner, Ernest, *The psychoanalytic movement: or the coming of unreason* (London, 1985)

Gill, Merton, and Philip Holzman, eds., *Psychology versus metapsychology: psychoanalytic essays in memory of George S. Klein* (New York, 1976)

Gill, Merton, and Karl Pribram, *Freud's 'Project' re-assessed* (London, 1976)

Glover, Edward, *The birth of the ego: a nuclear hypothesis* (London, 1968)
'An examination of the Klein system of child psychology', *The Psychoanalytic Study of the Child* 1, 1945

Glymour, Clark, 'Freud, Kepler and the clinical evidence', in Wollheim and Hopkins eds., *Philosophical essays on Freud*

Goldman, Alvin, *A theory of human action* (Princeton, 1970)

Greenberg, Jay, and Stephen Mitchell, *Object relations in psychoanalytic theory* (Cambridge, Mass., 1983)

Greenspan, Patricia, 'A case of mixed feelings: ambivalence and the logic of emotion', in Rorty ed., *Explaining emotions*

Grotstein, James, *Splitting and projective identification* (New York, 1981)

Grünbaum, Adolf, *The foundations of psychoanalysis: a philosophical critique* (Berkeley, 1984)
'Is Freudian psychoanalytic theory pseudo-scientific by Karl Popper's criterion of demarcation?', *American Philosophical Quarterly* 16, 1979

Guntrip, Henry, *Personality structure and human interaction: the developing synthesis of psychodynamic theory* (London, 1961)

Habermas, Jürgen, *Knowledge and human interests*, trans. Jeremy J. Shapiro (Boston, 1971)

Haight, M., *A study of self-deception* (Brighton, 1980)

Hartmann, Heinz, *Ego psychology and the problem of adaptation* (New York, 1975)

Hegel, G. W. F., *Phenomenology of spirit*, trans. A. Miller (Oxford, 1977)

Heidegger, Martin, 'On the essence of truth', in *Basic writings from 'Being and time' (1927) to 'The task of thinking' (1964)*, ed. David Krell (New York, 1977)

Heil, John, 'Minds divided', *Mind* 98, 1989

Heimann, Paula, 'Certain functions of introjection and projection in early infancy', in Riviere ed., *Developments in psychoanalysis*

Hilgard, Ernest, *Divided consciousness: multiple controls in human thought and action* (New York, 1977)

Hinshelwood, R., *A dictionary of Kleinian thought* (London, 1991)

Hopkins, James, 'Epistemology and depth psychology: critical notes on *The foundations of psychoanalysis*', in Clark and Wright eds., *Mind, psychoanalysis and science*

'Introduction: philosophy and psychoanalysis', in Wollheim and Hopkins eds., *Philosophical essays on Freud*

'Mental states, natural kinds and psychophysical laws', *Proceedings of the Aristotelian Society Supplementary Volume* 52, 1978

'Synthesis in the imagination: psychoanalysis, infantile experience and the concept of an object', in James Russell ed., *Philosophical perspectives on developmental psychology* (Oxford, 1987)

Hume, David, *A treatise of human nature* 1–2, ed. D. Macnabb (London, 1962 and 1972)

Isaacs, Susan, 'The nature and function of phantasy', in Riviere ed., *Developments in psychoanalysis*

James, William, *The principles of psychology* (New York, 1980)

Jaspers, Karl, *General psychopathology*, trans. J. Hoenig and M. Hamilton (Chicago, 1963)

Jones, Ernest, *Sigmund Freud: life and work* 1–3 (London, 1953–7)

'The theory of symbolism', in *Papers on psychoanalysis*, 5th edn (London, 1950)

Jung, Carl, *Two essays on analytical psychology*, *Collected works* 7, trans. F. Hull (London, 1953)

Klein, Melanie, 'A contribution to the psychogenesis of manic-depressive states', in *Love, guilt and reparation*

'Early stages of the Oedipus conflict', in *Love, guilt and reparation*

'Envy and gratitude', in *Envy and gratitude*

Envy and gratitude and other works 1946–1963, *The writings of Melanie Klein* 3, ed. Roger Money-Kyrle (London, 1975)

'The importance of symbol-formation in the development of the ego', in *Love, guilt and reparation*

Love, guilt and reparation and other works 1921–1945, *The writings of Melanie Klein* 1, ed. Roger Money-Kyrle (London, 1975)

Narrative of a child analysis, *The writings of Melanie Klein* 4, ed. Roger Money-Kyrle (London, 1975)

'Notes on some schizoid mechanisms', in *Envy and gratitude*

'The origins of transference', in *Envy and gratitude*

'On the theory of anxiety and guilt', in *Envy and gratitude*

'Our adult world and its roots in infancy', in *Envy and gratitude*

'The psychoanalytic play technique: its history and significance', in *Envy and gratitude*

'Some theoretical conclusions regarding the emotional life of the infant', in *Envy and gratitude*

'A study of envy and gratitude', in *The selected Melanie Klein*, ed. Juliet Mitchell (Harmondsworth, 1986)

Kline, Paul, *Fact and fantasy in Freudian theory* (London, 1972)

Kovel, Joel, *The radical spirit: essays on psychoanalysis and society* (London, 1988)

Kris, Ernst, *Selected papers of Ernst Kris*, ed. Lottie Newman (New Haven, 1975)

Lacan, Jacques, 'The agency of the letter in the unconscious or reason since Freud', in *Ecrits*

Ecrits, trans. Alan Sheridan (London, 1977)

The seminar of Jacques Lacan 1: *Freud's papers on technique* 1953-1954, trans. and notes by John Forrester (Cambridge, 1987)

The seminar of Jacques Lacan 2: *the ego in Freud's technique and in the theory of psychoanalysis* 1954–1955, trans. Sylvana Tomaselli, notes by John Forrester (Cambridge, 1987)

Laing, Ronald, *Self and others* (Harmondsworth, 1971)

Laplanche, Jean, and Serge Leclaire, 'The unconscious: a psychoanalytic study', *Yale French Studies* 48, 1972

Laplanche, Jean, and J.-B. Pontalis, 'Fantasy and the origins of sexuality', *International Journal of Psychoanalysis*, 49, 1968

The language of psychoanalysis, trans. Donald Nicholson-Smith (London, 1983)

Leibniz, G. W., *New essays on human understanding*, trans. Peter Remnant and Jonathan Bennett (Cambridge, 1981)

LePore, Ernest, and Brian McLaughlin, eds., *Actions and events: perspectives on the philosophy of Donald Davidson* (Oxford, 1985)

Locke, John, *An essay concerning human understanding*, ed. Peter Nidditch (Oxford, 1985)

Lockwood, Michael, *Mind, brain and the quantum: the compound 'I'* (Oxford, 1989)

MacDonald, Margaret, ed., *Philosophy and analysis* (Oxford, 1954)

McDowell, John, 'Functionalism and anomalous monism', in LePore and McLaughlin eds., *Actions and events*

McGinn, Colin, *Mental content* (Oxford, 1989)

MacIntyre, Alasdair, *The unconscious: a conceptual analysis* (London, 1958)

Mackie, John, 'Multiple personality', in *Persons and values: selected papers* 2 (Oxford, 1985)

Madison, P., *Freud's concept of repression and defence* (Minneapolis, 1961)

Maze, J., *The meaning of behaviour* (London, 1983)

Mele, Alfred, *Irrationality: an essay on akrasia, self-deception and self-control* (Oxford, 1987)

Meltzer, Donald, *The Kleinian development* 1–3 (Perthshire, 1979)

The psycho-analytical process (Perthshire, 1967)

Sexual states of mind (Perthshire, 1979)

Meltzer, Donald, et al., *Studies in extended metapsychology: clinical applications of Bion's ideas* (Perthshire, 1986)

Merleau-Ponty, Maurice, *Phenomenology of perception*, trans. Colin Smith (London, 1962)

Mischel, Theodore, 'Concerning rational behaviour and psychoanalytic explanation', in Wollheim ed., *Freud*

Morton, Adam, *Frames of mind: constraints on the common-sense conception of the mental* (Oxford, 1980)
  'Freudian commonsense', in Wollheim and Hopkins eds., *Philosophical essays on Freud*
Nagel, Thomas, 'Brain bisection and the unity of consciousness', in *Mortal questions* (Cambridge, 1979)
  'The boundaries of inner space', *Journal of Philosophy* 66, 1969
  The possibility of altruism (Princeton, 1961)
Nietzsche, Friedrich, *Beyond good and evil*, trans. Walter Kaufmann (New York, 1966)
  The birth of tragedy, trans. Walter Kaufmann (New York, 1967)
O'Shaughnessy, Brian, 'The id and the thinking process', in Wollheim and Hopkins eds., *Philosophical essays on Freud*
  'Mental structure and self-consciousness', *Inquiry* 15, 1972
  The will: a dual aspect theory 1–2 (Cambridge, 1980)
Parfit, Derek, *Reasons and persons* (Oxford, 1984)
Peacocke, Christopher, *Sense and content: experience, thought and their relations* (Oxford, 1983)
Pears, David, 'Goals and strategies of self-deception', in Elster ed., *The multiple self*
  Motivated irrationality (Oxford, 1984)
  'Motivated irrationality, Freudian theory and cognitive dissonance', in Wollheim and Hopkins eds., *Philosophical essays on Freud*
  'The paradoxes of self-deception', in *Questions in the philosophy of mind* (London, 1975)
  'Reply to Annette Baier: rhyme and reason', in LePore and McLaughlin eds., *Actions and events*
Peters, R., 'Emotions and the category of passivity', *Proceedings of the Aristotelian Society* 62, 1961–2
Piaget, Jean, 'Affective unconscious and cognitive unconscious', *Journal of the Psychoanalytic Association* 21, 1973
Plato, *The republic*, trans. Benjamin Jowett (London, 1970)
Popper, Karl, *Conjectures and refutations: the growth of scientific knowledge* (London, 1963)
Price, H., 'Half-belief', *Proceedings of the Aristotelian Society Supplementary Volume* 38, 1964
Proust, Marcel, *Remembrance of things past* 1–3, trans. C. Scott Moncrieff and Terence Kilmartin (Harmondsworth, 1983)
Pucetti, Roland, 'Brain bisection and personal identity', *British Journal for the Philosophy of Science* 24, 1973
Reid, Thomas, 'Of identity', in Rorty ed., *The identities of persons*
Ricœur, Paul, *Freedom and nature: the voluntary and the involuntary* (Evanston, 1966)
  Freud and philosophy: an essay on interpretation, trans. David Savage (New Haven, 1970)
Riviere, Joan, ed., *Developments in psychoanalysis* (London, 1962)
Rorty, Amélie, ed., *Explaining emotions* (Berkeley, 1980)

The identities of persons (Berkeley, 1976)

Rorty, Richard, *Contingency, irony and solidarity* (Cambridge, 1989)

Rosenblatt, Bernard, and Joseph Sandler, 'The concept of the representational world', *Psychoanalytic Study of the Child* 17, 1963

Sandler, Joseph, ed., *Projection, identification, projective identification* (London, 1988)

Sartre, Jean-Paul, *Being and nothingness: an essay on phenomenological ontology*, trans. Hazel Barnes (London, 1958)

'Consciousness of self and knowledge of self', in Nathaniel Laurence and Daniel O'Connor eds., *Readings in phenomenological psychology* (Englewood Cliffs, 1967)

'The itinerary of a thought', in *Between existentialism and Marxism*, trans. John Matthews (London, 1974)

The psychology of imagination, trans. Bernard Frechtman (London, 1972)

Sketch for a theory of the emotions, trans. Philip Mairet (London, 1971)

Schafer, Roy, *A new language for psychoanalysis* (New Haven, 1976)

Scruton, Roger, *The aesthetics of architecture* (London, 1979)

Sexual desire: a philosophical investigation (London, 1986)

Searle, John, *Intentionality: an essay in the philosophy of mind* (Cambridge, 1983)

Segal, Hanna, 'The function of dreams', in James Grotstein ed., *Do I dare disturb the universe? A memorial to Wilfred R. Bion* (London, 1983)

Introduction to the work of Melanie Klein (London, 1973)

Klein (Brighton, 1979)

'Notes on symbol-formation', in *The work of Hanna Segal*

'Phantasy and other mental processes', in *The work of Hanna Segal*

The work of Hanna Segal: a Kleinian approach to clinical practice (New York, 1981)

Shope, Robert, 'Dispositional treatment of psychoanalytic motivation terms', *Journal of Philosophy* 67, 1970

'The psychoanalytic theories of wish-fulfilment and meaning', *Inquiry* 10, 1967

'The significance of Freud for modern philosophy of mind', in Gutton Fløistad ed., *Contemporary philosophy: a new survey* 4: *philosophy of mind* (Netherlands, 1983)

Smythe, Thomas, 'Unconscious desires and the meaning of "desire"', *Monist* 56, 1972

de Sousa, Ronald, 'Rational homunculi', in Rorty ed., *The identities of persons*

Spinoza, Benedict, *Ethics* (New York, 1949)

Stich, Stephen, 'Beliefs and subdoxastic states', *Philosophy of Science* 45, 1978

From folk psychology to cognitive science: the case against belief (Cambridge, Mass., 1984)

Strawson, Galen, *Freedom and belief* (Clarendon, 1986)

Strawson, Peter, *The bounds of sense: an essay on Kant's 'Critique of pure reason'* (London, 1966)

Individuals: an essay in descriptive metaphysics (London, 1959)

Taylor, Charles, 'Cognitive psychology', in *Human agency and language*: *philosophical papers* 1 (Cambridge, 1985)

The explanation of behaviour (London, 1964)

Thalberg, Irving, 'Freud's anatomies of the self', in Wollheim and Hopkins eds., *Philosophical essays on Freud*

Thomson, Garrett, *Needs* (London, 1987)

Timparano, Sebastiano, *The Freudian slip*: *psychoanalysis and textual criticism*, trans. Kate Soper (London, 1985)

Tolstoy, Leo, *Anna Karenina*, trans. Rosemary Edmonds (Harmondsworth, 1978)

Volosinov, Valentin, *Freudianism*: *a Marxist critique*, trans. and ed. I. Titunik (New York, 1976)

Wegman, Cornelius, *Psychoanalysis and cognitive psychology*: *formalization of Freud's earliest theory* (London, 1985)

White, Alan, *Attention* (Oxford, 1964)

Wiggins, David, 'The person as object of science, as subject of experience, and as locus of value', in Anthony Peacocke and Grant Gillett eds., *Persons and personality*: *a contemporary inquiry* (Oxford, 1987)

Wilkes, Kathleen, 'Anthropomorphism and analogy in psychology', *Philosophical Quarterly* 25, 1975

Real people: *personal identity without thought experiments* (Oxford, 1988)

Winnicott, Donald, 'Ego integration in child development', in *The maturational processes*

The maturational processes and the facilitating environment: *studies in the theory of emotional development* (London, 1965)

'A personal view of the Kleinian system', in *The maturational processes*

Playing and reality (Harmondsworth, 1980)

Wittgenstein, Ludwig, *Lectures and conversations on aesthetics, psychology and religious belief*, ed. Cyril Barrett (Oxford, 1978)

Philosophical investigations, trans. Elizabeth Anscombe (Oxford, 1976)

Remarks on colour, ed. Elizabeth Anscombe, trans. Linda McAlister and Margaret Schättle (Oxford, 1978)

Wollheim, Richard, *Art and its objects*, 2nd edn (Cambridge, 1980)

'The bodily ego', in Wollheim and Hopkins eds., *Philosophical essays on Freud*

'The cabinet of Dr Lacan', *The New York Review of Books*, 28 January 1979

Freud, 2nd edn (Glasgow, 1991)

'The good self and the bad self: the moral psychology of British idealism and the English school of psychoanalysis', in Anthony Kenny ed., *Rationalism, empiricism and idealism* (Oxford, 1986)

'Memory, experiential memory, and personal identity', in G. MacDonald ed., *Perception and identity* (Ithaca, New York, 1979)

'Needs, desires and moral turpitude', in R. Peters ed., *Nature and conduct* (London, 1975)

On art and the mind (London, 1973)

'On persons and their lives', in Rorty ed., *Explaining emotions*

'Seeing-as, seeing-in, and pictorial representation', in *Art and its objects*
'Thought and passion', *Proceedings of the Aristotelian Society* 68, 1967–8
The thread of life (Cambridge, 1984)
'Was Freud a crypto-biologist?', *The New York Review of Books*, 8 November 1979
'Wish-fulfilment', in Ross Harrison ed., *Rational action* (Cambridge, 1979)
Wollheim, Richard, ed., *Freud: a collection of critical essays* (New York, 1974); reprinted as *Philosophers on Freud: new evaluations* (New York, 1977)
Wollheim, Richard, and James Hopkins, eds., *Philosophical essays on Freud* (Cambridge, 1982)

Index